Ken Eldred's *God Is at Work* is a remarka[ble] Body of Christ. It is nothing short of a com[plete] a *calling* but also as a *Kingdom change agent*. Th[ose] ho sense God's call to a business career as well as for those w[ho] [are] [seekin]g who desire greater insight into the major focus of the majority of those who make up their congregations. It is among the finest books of its kind that I have encountered in my 35 years pursuing my own business calling.

Edward G. Atsinger III
PRESIDENT AND CEO, SALEM COMMUNICATIONS CORPORATION
CAMARILLO, CALIFORNIA

This is more than a book. It is a *handbook*! Comprehensive, clear, compelling and carefully thought out, *God Is at Work* breaks new ground. "The opportunity is ripe for Kingdom business," and so is the timing for this expansive and valuable work.

John D. Beckett
CHAIRMAN, THE BECKETT COMPANIES, ELYRIA, OHIO
AUTHOR, *LOVING MONDAY: SUCCEEDING IN BUSINESS WITHOUT SELLING YOUR SOUL*

I am honored to be Ken's friend, local pastor and occasional hunting buddy. Ken is a global visionary; everything he does, whether business or church ministry, he does with the kingdom of God in mind. This powerful book is a must-read for people who see the "big picture."

Dick Bernal
FOUNDER AND SENIOR PASTOR, JUBILEE CHRISTIAN CENTER
SAN JOSE, CALIFORNIA

For years, my mission has been to encourage those who have found professional success recognize how their talents and training can further God's Kingdom. *God Is at Work* speaks squarely to that objective in a refreshing way—by showing how those in the marketplace can pursue Kingdom business. Ken Eldred lays out the biblical basis for business as ministry and offers practical examples to illustrate how that can be pursued anywhere in the world. I recommend this book to businesspeople seeking to use their abilities and passions for God's glory.

Bob Buford
FOUNDER, THE BUFORD FOUNDATION
FOUNDER, LEADERSHIP NETWORK
AUTHOR, *HALFTIME* AND *FINISHING WELL*

Ken Eldred has discovered secrets to prosperity in the kingdom of God, and he reveals them in a simple and practical way for each person to take hold and make those blessings become his or her own.

Cesar Castellanos
FOUNDER AND SENIOR PASTOR,
MISSION CHARISMATIC INTERNATIONAL AND G12

The title says it wonderfully: God is at work and is uniquely using Kingdom business to bring about spiritual, social and economic transformation in our world today. As Ken Eldred shows in this exciting book, artificial barriers between business and missions—between work and faith—are melting, and the Lord is using an unexpected tool—business—to reach the lost.

Christopher A. Crane

PRESIDENT AND CEO, OPPORTUNITY INTERNATIONAL

Ken Eldred has written one of the most profound books that I have read in years. The program outlined in *God Is at Work* has the potential to revolutionize the missionary work of the Church. Ken shows how it is possible to use business not simply to fund missions, but also to do missions and evangelism more effectively than either could ever be done with the current methods. Moving beyond theory to actual results, Ken demonstrates that business is already being used to extend the kingdom of God in extraordinary ways, even in third world countries. I heartily recommend this book to all Christian businessmen, pastors and church leaders.

Dr. Jack Deere

PASTOR AND AUTHOR, *SURPRISED BY THE VOICE OF GOD* AND *SURPRISED BY THE POWER OF THE SPIRIT*

So often the reaction to economic hardship in our country and abroad is an expectation that the government address the problem through financial aid. In *God Is at Work*, Ken Eldred has written a compelling case for private citizens becoming part of the solution through business. He is right: Economic and business development must go beyond simply providing financing. Indeed, the backbone of our own country's economic success has been the application of deeply held values and beliefs to business practices. I encourage every businessperson to read this book and get involved—for the sake of our country and the world's future.

Honorable J. Dennis Hastert

SPEAKER OF THE HOUSE OF REPRESENTATIVES

A meticulous study on God and business, *God Is at Work* provides both a theological and practical framework for understanding the potential of those in the marketplace to transform the world. This book offers helpful examples and ideas for Kingdom-minded businesspeople in all capacities and markets. As a venture capitalist, I found the practical discussion about Kingdom-focused investing particularly exciting. I have known Ken Eldred for years and can think of no person better suited to write this book. His integration of family life, business life and a passion for God has been a model for me and for others to follow.

Paul Kim

MANAGING PARTNER, PARAKLETOS@VENTURES

I have seen the incredible work of God transform Korea from the poorest nation on Earth in 1960 to the twelfth most developed country in the world today. *God Is at Work* pinpoints what has been the source of our economic success—the tremendous spiritual transformation of a large portion of our population—and shows that such spiritual transformation is the key to successful economic growth in other developing nations. Dr. Cho has always taught that those of us in the business world can advance the work of God through business development, but this book has put meat on that idea. I am so excited about the concept of Kingdom business that I have literally renamed my company to reflect its mission!

Soon Bae Kim

HEAD ELDER, YOIDO FULL GOSPEL CHURCH
SEOUL, KOREA

Ken Eldred has written the definitive work on the exciting business-as-missions movement. The movement comes alive through many examples and case studies explained by an accomplished, savvy businessman. But, whereas the participants of this movement may see only their little pieces, Ken has developed a systematic framework that explains how God will use their diverse activities to transform nations economically and spiritually. The book is scholarly in its carefully researched historical and biblical context, practical in its discussion of how to do Kingdom business, and inspirational in its call to action. I will use this book as the main text in my MBA course on Entrepreneurship and Economic Development.

John E. Mulford, Ph.D.

PROFESSOR AND FORMER DEAN, REGENT UNIVERSITY SCHOOL OF BUSINESS
DIRECTOR, CENTER FOR ENTREPRENEURSHIP AND ECONOMIC DEVELOPMENT

During 35 years as a venture capitalist, I have found that the most important factor in assessing a new business venture is the venture's team. Before doing business with an entrepreneur, we carefully consider his or her integrity, character and reputation. *God Is at Work* wonderfully demonstrates that what holds true for winning Silicon Valley start-ups also applies universally to business around the world: Values and culture are foundational to successful business ventures.

John Mumford

FOUNDING AND GENERAL MANAGING PARTNER,
CROSSPOINT VENTURE PARTNERS

All over the world today, God is using a new breed of missionary who has the same heart for service and the same passion to see the Kingdom expanded but is using business to do it. Ken Eldred is part of the leading edge of this Kingdom business movement that is sweeping the globe, bringing jobs, hope and new life in Christ to millions. The Church needs to recognize and embrace this fresh wave. Reading this book is a great way to start!

Luis Palau

PRESIDENT, PALAU ASSOCIATION

God is presenting a new paradigm for missions in the twenty-first century—that of Kingdom business. In *God Is at Work*, Ken Eldred takes us step-by-step through this paradigm and explores the role that we as Christians have in this new move of God. *God Is at Work* will challenge you to see the work of His kingdom in new and powerful ways.

Pat Robertson
FOUNDER AND CHAIRMAN, THE CHRISTIAN BROADCASTING NETWORK
HOST, *THE 700 CLUB*
AUTHOR, *BRING IT ON* AND *COURTING DISASTER*

In *God Is at Work*, Ken Eldred has captured a paradigm that is absolutely essential for the fulfillment of the Great Commission in our generation: how to use business to influence nations. Ken, a successful entrepreneur who has established successful Kingdom businesses in non-Christian nations, writes with the authority and insight of a seasoned practitioner. This book is a definite must for pulpit and marketplace ministers alike.

Ed Silvoso
PRESIDENT, HARVEST EVANGELISM, INC.
AUTHOR, *ANOINTED FOR BUSINESS*

Ken Eldred is a man focused on God's heart: missions. It's going to take major sources of capital to accomplish the task of worldwide evangelization, and Ken has a plan to make that happen. His life is accountable, and his track record is proven. May the Lord multiply Ken's plan and concept "a thousand times more" (Deut. 1:10, *NKJV*).

Larry Stockstill
SENIOR PASTOR, BETHANY WORLD PRAYER CENTER
BAKER, LOUISIANA

God Is at Work by Ken Eldred is by far the most comprehensive book to date on the subject of Kingdom business. Having founded numerous successful companies while constantly grappling with the issues of business versus ministry, Eldred has much to share. Everyone who is burdened with the Great Commission mandate should learn about Kingdom business as a strategy of choice for the twenty-first century.

Tetsunao Yamamori
INTERNATIONAL DIRECTOR, LAUSANNE COMMITTEE FOR
WORLD EVANGELIZATION

GOD IS AT WORK

KEN ELDRED

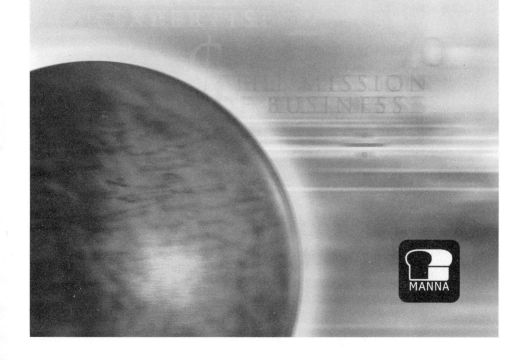

MANNA

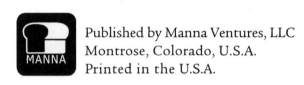

Published by Manna Ventures, LLC
Montrose, Colorado, U.S.A.
Printed in the U.S.A.

Publisher's Cataloging-in-Publication Data

Eldred, Kenneth A., 1943-
  God is at work / Ken Eldred.
    p. cm.
  Includes bibliographical references.
  ISBN 987-0-9840911-0-2 (paperback)
  1. Business—Religious aspects. 2. Entrepreneurship—Religious aspects. 3. Business
ethics. 4. Spiritual life. I. Title.
HF5388E43 2005
261.8'5—dc22   2009931387

1   2   3   4   5   6   7   8   9   10   /   14   13   12   11   10   09

Rights for publishing this book in other formats or languages are contracted by Manna
Ventures, LLC. For additional information, write to Manna Ventures, LLC, 236 South 3rd
Street, #330, Montrose, Colorado 81401.

DEDICATION

I dedicate this book to my wife, Roberta. She is an inspiration. She gladly and lovingly has provided her support to all I have felt called to do by God. She has encouraged me, challenged me, and sharpened me through the wisdom and gifts that the Lord has given her. She has freely shared and sacrificially used her many gifts—especially her gift of counseling—to advance the kingdom of God by helping me and so many others whom God has brought to her. She graciously accepted the long hours required of me to complete this work.

For your love and contributions, I am deeply indebted and thank you, Roberta, my love of more than thirty years.

CONTENTS

FOREWORD

I have witnessed firsthand the power of God to transform a nation's economic and moral-cultural state. When I started a church in Seoul, South Korea, in 1958, our country was recovering from a devastating war. Our small congregation of five believers met in an old U.S. military tent that had been donated to me. South Korea's Christian population was small and unimportant. But the following decades saw a massive move of the Holy Spirit, as millions started to follow Jesus. Lives were changed. Today, South Korea has twenty times as many Christians, and more than a third of the country's 50 million people call themselves evangelical Christians. Only the United States sends more missionaries abroad than our country does. Yes, Korea has seen a tremendous spiritual growth!

During the same period, our nation experienced tremendous economic growth as well. After the Korean War, ours was one of the poorest, if not the poorest, nations in the world. Indeed, per capita income was equivalent to only one U.S. dollar a week. Our economy was comparable to those of destitute nations in Africa and Asia. Today, South Korea has risen from the depths of Third-World status to boast a thriving economy that exports leading technology all over the globe. Our per-capita economic production is comparable to a number of nations in the European Union.

Those noting the changes in Korea might be tempted to believe that our country's spiritual and economic transformations over the past 50 years are unrelated, but I know that is not the case. The two are deeply linked as Christian faith and Christian values set the foundation for successful business. Without the power of the gospel changing the hearts and minds of our people, the country would not have witnessed the same economic blessing.

This is a book about kingdom business, the effort to promote Christian faith and commerce through profitable business. It recognizes and describes the fundamental connection between spiritual transformation and economic transformation that I have witnessed in Korea. By mobilizing its business people, the church has a unique opportunity to make an impact in developing nations seeking the same changes my country has experienced. While secular development efforts focus solely on economic objectives, kingdom business recognizes that successful commerce, which improves a nation, requires a biblical moral-cultural foundation. Christian business people can make a difference by bringing the life-changing gospel of Jesus, modeling integrity in the marketplace, and teaching biblical principles that lead to successful business.

Our church in Korea, Yoido Full Gospel Church, is now a mighty force of 700,000 praying Christians. More than 150 business professional fellowship organizations form the backbone of our cell group system, and some 50,000 businessmen are members of our businessmen's fellowship. My spirit rejoices at their desire to serve God and their fellow man in the marketplace. Unfortunately, many churches today have accepted the view that business is essentially secular, void of any spiritual value, and thus unworthy of a Christian's pursuit. I have been fighting this deception for decades. God calls some of His people to work in the business world just as He calls others to work in the church, and those who attempt to classify the former as a lesser calling are misguided. The marketplace is just as legitimate a venue for serving God and others as the church is. I commend Dr. Eldred for his affirmation of believers in business. As he notes, the businessperson's work itself can have spiritual value as it serves and meets the needs of others.

Indeed, Dr. Eldred's own personal journey is evidence that one's business pursuits can be a ministry of love and service to others. I have known him for many years and have seen confirmation of what the Holy Spirit impressed on me from the beginning—that He would bless Dr. Eldred and use him in a powerful way. I was honored to have him and his close friend Dr. Paul Kim, Executive Director of Church Growth International, become the only non-Korea-resident elders in our church. The ideas and concepts in this book have been the subject of many hours of conversation, and I am happy to see them presented here in a clear, compelling and exciting manner for the benefit of others.

Kingdom business is purpose-driven business. It is business pursued with a goal of achieving spiritual, economic and social transformation in individuals and nations. My own country serves as a testimony to the transformation that is possible when "God is at work," and I believe that kingdom business efforts can lead other developing nations out of dark spiritual and economic conditions. I pray that as you read this book, the Holy Spirit will quicken your heart and give you a vision to do great things for His kingdom.

DAVID YONGGI CHO
Yoido Full Gospel Church
Seoul, Korea

PREFACE AND ACKNOWLEDGMENTS

The Kingdom business framework presented in this book has its origins in a comprehensive research study conducted at Living Stones Foundation. We consulted with over 100 key experts and practitioners at both Christian and secular institutions. The people with whom we spoke are in academics and at foundations. They are business people in the field. They are involved with funding Kingdom business efforts of many different sizes. Some assist and make small loans to simple sole proprietorships, while others raise capital and manage large corporations in certain locations. We analyzed expert opinions, anecdotal evidence, and internal data from these sources. We also performed thorough research on published aggregate and average data on secular and Christian economic development efforts. Drawing on these sources, a framework for understanding and presenting Kingdom business started to emerge.

A number of business people, pastors and academics who are pioneers in the Kingdom business field convened in Lexington, Kentucky, in 2003 to launch a series of conferences that promote Kingdom business as a missions strategy. That gathering also served as a venue for settling on some terms, definitions and approaches of Kingdom business. In short, both the lexicon for talking about this field and the framework for understanding Kingdom business were strengthened and validated. This book has benefited greatly from the contribution of these experienced participants.

No book is ever written alone. Even the Bible was written by the Holy Spirit with the help of many faithful authors. While this book is hardly of biblical proportions, it could not have been done without the help of many. To properly recognize all of the contributions of others, I would run out of space.

First, I would like to thank the Lord through the Holy Spirit for directing this work—for His wisdom, direction and leadership. That is not to say this is free of errors. I take responsibility for all that is not right before Him as a failure of mine.

I would like to recognize Alex Brubaker, my assistant and staff support, without whom this book would certainly not have been written. While I take responsibility for all that we have written, he has dedicated many hours to the creation of this book by writing, researching, contributing ideas and organizing the content. He is a self-starter who always goes beyond my expectations.

Dr. David Yonggi Cho, my pastor and pastor of the largest church in the world, Yoido Full Gospel Church located in Seoul, Korea, has provided me with a great deal of inspiration through his teachings, both public and private, on faith, business and nation development. Dr. Paul Kim, a fellow elder, is also a business partner, associate and close friend who spent many hours with me discussing ideas and reviewing this material.

Many others helped by contributing content, ideas and corrections. Gregory Slayton, a good friend, performed some of the initial research on microenterprise development (MED), small and medium enterprises (SME) and overseas private equity (OPE). Ted Yamamori, International Director of the Lausanne Committee for World Evangelism, and John Warton, International Director of the Business Professional Network, provided counsel and review of the text and concepts. Tom Henriksen, Associate Director of the Hoover Institution at Stanford University, guided me toward research materials and made available the resources of the Hoover Institution. I would also like to acknowledge others who provided valuable input and advice, including John Mulford, Dean of the Business School at Regent University; Jack Deere, pastor and former Professor at Dallas Theological Seminary; Steve Rundle, Professor of Business at Biola University; Tom Sudyk at Evangelistic Commerce and EC Group International; Scott McFarlane at the EC Institute; and Jim Willenborg, a dear friend and long-time business partner who provided many helpful suggestions. Roberta Eldred, my wife, read the manuscript for errors. My son, Kary Eldred, added many points of clarification to the text. Finally, I want to thank my three grown children and their wives, Eric and Becky Eldred, Kary and Monica Eldred, and Justin and Rachel Eldred, for their constant encouragement and emotional support throughout this project.

With all of this support, you might wonder what I did. I showed up.

FOR MORE INFORMATION
PLEASE VISIT:
WWW.GODISATWORK.ORG

AUTHOR'S NOTE

In early 1848, gold was found during the construction of a new lumber mill on the American River in Coloma, California. It took two months for news to reach San Francisco, where it was greeted with skepticism. Several months later, a man waved a bottle of gold dust and shouted, "Gold! Gold from the American River!" and San Francisco caught gold fever. Crewmen abandoned ships in the harbor and went off in search of gold. Teachers left their classrooms to head for the golden hills. Within a month, the *California Star* newspaper reported that seaports, towns and ranches all over the state had "become suddenly drained of human beings."[1]

I believe the opportunity in Kingdom business is every bit as exciting as the Gold Rush! In many ways, I feel like one of the early pioneers in California's Gold Country, recounting exciting discoveries, telling of wonderful opportunities, and providing a map for others who wish to come. In particular, this book provides the following:

- Some foundational groundwork that addresses the language, definition, theology, historical perspective, structure and promise of Kingdom business
- Exciting examples of diverse Kingdom business ventures that are advancing the church all over the developing world
- A framework for understanding how Kingdom business is becoming a major missions thrust of the Church
- Guidance for Christians who are interested in participating in and supporting Kingdom business efforts worldwide
- A lexicon of terminology and a structure for Kingdom business in order to stimulate further thinking, research and discussion

Seizing the Opportunity

Businessmen and women are people of action. As entrepreneurs, they charge full speed ahead, seizing on business or ministry needs and objectives. Successful shoe salesman Dwight L. Moody became a great nineteenth-century evangelist, and hard-charging entrepreneur Bill Bright went on to found Campus Crusade for Christ. Sensing a specific spiritual need, these men used skills honed in the business world to establish successful ministries.

Today, a growing number of business people who are every bit as committed to the Great Commission (see Matt. 28:19-20) are taking a slightly different approach. Unlike Moody and Bright, they are opting to remain in the business arena. They are using commerce and business development themselves as vehicles for blessing a people and bringing the gospel of Jesus. The approaches are varied, as are the needs that are being met. Some sense the vision of enabling the poor to engage in small entrepreneurial ventures. Others are seeking to create jobs by assisting and growing small- and medium-size businesses. Yet others are involved in operating larger ventures that have the potential to influence entire cities and industries.

Clearly, Kingdom business is a major opportunity, and the key will be the response of the Church. We can fight it—or we can see the opportunity in it. Perhaps more than any other missions movement, effective Kingdom business requires support and involvement from a wide range of members of the Body of Christ. It is my prayer that as you read this book, you will consider how God might use your gifts, training and passion to advance His Kingdom through business.

"Those two pioneers of civilization—Christianity and commerce—
should ever be inseparable."
—DR. DAVID LIVINGSTONE (1857)

CHAPTER 1

SILICON VALLEY TO BOMBAY

It's Saturday morning in Bombay (Mumbai). A dozen people are huddled in a home to study about God and to pray. They're praying for their community, for God to move in a powerful way, and for their own witness to those with whom they're all in daily contact. But these folks are not neighbors or members of the same church, and they're not praying for those who live around them. In fact, some have traveled quite a distance to participate in this group. No, they're meeting to pray for their company, ET. They're praying that Christians at ET would be salt and light to those around them in the marketplace, to employees, colleagues, partners and customers.

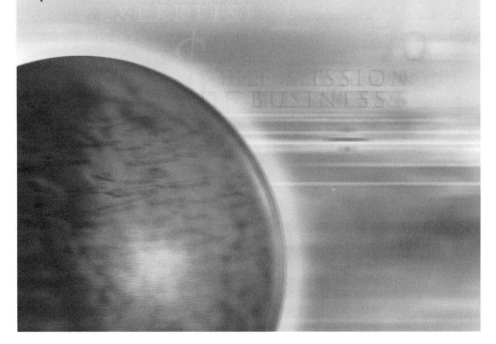

ET is a call center business in India with approximately one thousand employees—smart, college-educated professionals. It has grown at an astounding rate during the five years since its founding. The company's customers include major credit card issuers in the United States, and it has been recognized for its world-class level of service. On the surface, this might appear to be a typical, successful Indian company, but it's not. At ET, 60 percent of the employees call themselves Christians. How did that come about in a nation in which only two percent of the population identifies with the Christian faith? In short, it was the Spirit of God giving a vision for using business to further the gospel of Jesus.

I have had the privilege of participating in the ET business venture as a strategic advisor from its inception, both as a board member and as an investor. For years, my career consisted of starting and running companies, but I wasn't looking for another one, and I certainly wasn't looking for one in India! This opportunity found me. God's hand seemed to be in it. He showed me how my business skills could be used in a developing nation to meet economic and spiritual needs. Christians can face significant challenges to employment in India; God showed how they could be provided meaningful jobs with which to support their families and their local churches. They would have a venue for modeling biblical principles in the marketplace, for infusing the local business climate with the fragrance of Jesus, and for drawing people to Him.

Many others are also advancing the Church around the world through business. They are part of a massive sea change in the way the Church does missions. Christian business people are involved in a comprehensive ministry that creates jobs and profitable businesses, and strengthens the local church, enabling people to decide to follow Jesus. They're engaged in "Kingdom business."

Kingdom business is achieving economic and spiritual transformation around the globe and is welcomed even by developing nations that are traditionally closed to the gospel. Some have been called to help microentrepreneurs like Bintou, a widow in Mali, who sells goods out of her small shop. Others are assisting small- and medium-size enterprises and their owners, like David Berlancic who manages a stone-crushing quarry in Croatia. I discovered that my story is just one of many from

Christian business people who have been called to use their gifts in the worldwide missions effort, and each of them has a unique story of God's preparation and direction regarding Kingdom business opportunities.

What if I Missed It?

My story began on a noisy night in New York City thirty years ago. New York is the city that never sleeps—and neither could I. That day, my boss had called me into his office and, in a short conversation, had changed my life. No, it wasn't in the way you might have expected. In thirty minutes, I went from assisting him as an analyst to becoming manager of marketing services. I went from being an individual contributor to the head of a 350-person division with five managers reporting directly to me! I was floored.

As I lay in bed, I assessed the situation. Upon graduation from Stanford Business School, I had been ready to take on the world, armed with what I had learned. I felt as though I had come out of that institution like a proton comes out of a cyclotron, ready to blast through the business world with my understanding of the latest business tools. However, I found that the tools, while highly effective, did not help me explain or solve a number of tough issues.

Now I was a 27-year-old Stanford MBA, rapidly climbing the ladder at a major New York company. But where would it take me? What would I be in 30 years? I tried to chart my future career trajectory. At the end of all the perturbations and iterations, it all seemed somehow empty and purposeless. Mentally exhausted, a strange and frightening thought entered my mind: Is that all there is? What if I woke up at age 60 and realized that I had missed *it*? And I didn't even have a notion of what *it* was! But I knew that if I missed it now, only to discover it at age 60, I would never be able to recover those lost years. It was a scary thought; I never told anyone. But it nagged me for years and started me on a search for an answer. As I lay in bed, it never dawned on me that *it* was God.

A few years later I was married, had a son, and was living in California. My wife, Roberta, and I thought we owed our son the same opportunity to consider religion as we had been given, so he could come to his own decision about faith. A plan was hatched. Our first stop would be the local church I had attended as a child. Next would be the Catholic church where Roberta was raised, then the local Buddhist temple, the synagogue, and so on.

We never made it past the first church. As we went Sunday after Sunday, I began to wrestle with God. I knew I was hearing spiritual truth. I began to think seriously about the Lord, and I knew He wanted to enter into a relationship with me. My wrestling with God was not about following Jesus, it was about what I would do if I did take that step. By way of the Sunday sermons, I had come to the conclusion that any serious Christian could only serve God as a pastor; a true follower of Jesus would lay down his career and go into preaching.

I wanted to be a Christian, but I also wanted to be a businessman. My education, training, abilities and passion were in business. Could I really give those up to follow God? In the church parking lot after one Sunday morning service, I struggled with God over that choice. The Lord pointed me to Psalm 37:4, "Delight yourself in the Lord and He will give you the desires of your heart." My desires were for business, so I asked God to change my heart. That morning I decided to follow God, even if it meant I needed to become a pastor in a poor section of town.

My Ministry: Business

Sadly, I later discovered that even mature Christians often succumb to this line of thinking, concluding that they must change careers in order to serve God. They fail to see the opportunity for spiritual value of their work in the marketplace. The businessperson's ministry is to serve others through useful goods and helpful services and to infuse each personal interaction with the fragrance of Christ. That is his high calling from God, and it was *my* calling.

Business by the Book

God was giving me the desire of my heart. It would take years for me to fully understand the important concept that business was my ministry, but God started to teach me slowly. One Sunday, our pastor spoke on the topic of "weekend warriors." Was I one of those people who prayed and worshiped on Sunday and left all of that at home as I entered a different and unrelated world on Monday? After recognizing I fit the description of those "weekend warriors," I realized that my faith needed to impact my work. I needed to do my business by the Book. I needed to evaluate my actions in light of the biblical standards of integrity, morality and love.

So for many years, I faithfully took the Lord with me on my quest to serve Him in the business world. I used the Bible to carefully consider the morality of my actions. I wanted to please the Lord, and I could see the value of operating aboveboard. This was the first step of making my work my ministry, one I am sure many of you can identify with.

Partnering with God

Eventually, the Lord showed me that He wanted to be more than a moral standard or an example of loving concern for others in my business practice. He began to reveal that He wanted to *partner* with me in all that I was doing. Early on, I had seen God as the One who put me here and cared for me. I had seen Him as uniquely and significantly interested in the process of how I did my business. But ultimately, I thought He was uninterested in the *outcome* of my business, since that was not "spiritual." I didn't realize that this view sells God short. He is as interested in the outcome as He is in how we approach an issue.

Recently, a friend told me that when he prays, he asks only for strength and courage to do what is right in his business. That is fine as far as it goes, but God has and wants to give more. These prayers fall short of the potential in the relationship we have with God. I told him his prayer was fine but that it left God out of partnering with him in his business. He said, "I get it; I am only getting half of the equation. The other half in my business is God." I noted that his was a good analogy, except it is more like firing on one cylinder when we have available to us seven more.

Another friend expressed another common view of businessmen in the Church. "I never pray for specific outcomes," he said. "It is not right to bother God with these issues. I just pray that God's will be done in the situation." That is fine too, as far as it goes. But it fails to recognize that God wants to lead us and provide for us in every aspect of our lives as we follow His plans for us. We acknowledge that He *could* bring about specific outcomes, because we see Him do the miraculous when the doctors can't. However, since He does not always answer that type of prayer in the affirmative, we reckon it is better not to ask. Yet He is in the business of doing miracles to make up for where we fall short. King David spent a week on his face before God, asking Him to spare his child. God did not, but that never stopped David from asking.

The point here is that if we don't ask God specifically for answers to prayers, we cannot know when He has answered us specifically. That includes prayers for God to partner with us and affect miraculous business outcomes. In my case, He had wanted to help, but I had not been in the asking mode. The realization that God desired to partner with me—that He cared about business outcomes and wanted me to ask Him for specific results—deepened the sense of business as my ministry.

Business Success and the Bible

In the course of writing this book, God has taken me into a new area of awareness. I have understood for many years that God is interested in business and have noticed the correlation of biblical concepts with business realities. But only recently have I fully appreciated the depth to which the Bible is the foundation of all meaningful business concepts. Honesty, service, excellence, respect, commitment, value, trust, loyalty and quality are not only successful business practices, but are also biblical principles. They were biblical principles *first*. The credit is rarely given to Scripture, because so few recognize the genesis of the concepts. Thus, many of us have been taught the business principles without any reference to their biblical origin. I have come to appreciate that good business practices don't conflict with the Bible—they *are* the Bible.

When successful business people who operate on biblical principles are the subject of articles and book chapters, the writer is often incredulous that the individual succeeded despite the "albatross" of following God's laws. How could he or she possibly profit without cutting corners, engaging in dishonesty, and treating employees dispassionately?

I believe these individuals are not successful *despite* following biblical principles; they are successful *because* they follow biblical principles.

All meaningful business concepts have a biblical foundation. For example, nations of economic greatness display a very high level of trust in their moral, cultural and economic systems. Of course, trust is fundamental to our relationship with God, who is trustworthy. The rule of law, so fundamental to strong economies and stable societies, is also basic to the Bible. We are under a higher authority, and God's laws are immutable. Stability in government is fundamental to successful business. The biblical mandate to "do unto others as you would have them do unto you" is basic to the concept of good service. Ethics and morality are defined by a strong set of fundamental beliefs to which all adhere. And the Lord is the glue that holds it all together.

Because biblical principles lead to successful business, the marketplace affords us the opportunity to present God's truth in a uniquely relevant way. We just need to connect the dots between business and the Bible. In the process of teaching and demonstrating successful business practices, we can present the gospel by word and by deed. This opportunity to share the gospel through business exists at home and abroad, and it is what has prompted many missions-minded Christians to pursue Kingdom business.

Living Out the Calling

Before God had revealed any of these insights about how business was my ministry, He opened the door for me in business. I joined a small firm and went to work. I had committed to following God wherever that would lead me—even as a pastor in a poor area. But like Abraham, who was asked by God to offer his precious son as a sacrifice before the Lord provided another way, I was not required to carry out the sacrifice. He was more concerned with my demonstration of willingness. He was concerned with my heart, and the desire He gave me was to be a businessman.

I knew business opportunities were out there, but I struggled to see them at first. I felt like a hunter who could hear ducks all around him but couldn't identify a single one. So I asked God to open my eyes, to remove the veil. He did, and soon I saw business opportunities flash before me like ducks in a shooting gallery. I felt God's urge to start a business, so I conferred with a friend who said he had about a dozen ideas. We went through them one by one. At one point, I sensed God directing me toward a particular business concept. "Let's go back and discuss that one," I said.

We gave that idea a three-month review, developing a business plan and performing due diligence. It was the early 1970s, the era of minicomputers. Personal computers were still several years from entering the market, and only companies owned computers. The initial business concept focused on solving a problem faced by a significant number of those companies. Computer-support manufacturers focused heavily on large corporations and were set up to serve them. Orders for computer paper and other supplies were accepted only in bulk, and they took weeks to deliver. Their salespeople could not adequately serve the smaller companies or organizations that did not need a pallet of paper or a large box of printer ribbons, and it was not economically viable for computer accessory manufacturers to seek out and fulfill smaller orders. We believed there was an opportunity to provide cost-effective service to those customers whose average purchases totaled about $150. After considering several potential solutions, we finally decided that a mail-order catalog would be the best approach. While mail-order businesses of many different kinds have sprung up since then, it was actually quite a revolutionary concept at the time.

To properly serve customers, we needed to help them connect their minicomputers to peripherals such as printers. In those days, universal standards were far less common, and each manufacturer developed a unique design. Therefore, connecting products from the main minicomputer makers and the myriad of peripheral suppliers was a major problem. Unique connection design locked the customers of computer manufacturers into buying the manufacturer's peripheral products, often at a much higher price.

I discussed the business idea with a number of people, among them the president of Hewlett-Packard. He had been my father's protégé when my father was the number three person at Hewlett-Packard, behind Dave Packard and Bill Hewlett, the two founders. "That whole cable problem is a can of worms," Hewlett-Packard's president said, not optimistic that it could be solved. I took his comments as a challenge. My brilliant partner spent days studying manuals, coming up with ways to connect computers with peripherals manufactured by different companies. We were satisfied that we could offer helpful products by mail order that would serve a neglected segment of minicomputer owners and save companies hours developing their own solutions. With $5,000 of capital and a grocery bag full of connector parts, we founded Inmac.

God's Definition of Success

What is God's definition of success? He defines success differently than our culture does. As He demonstrated in sending His Son to reconcile man to Himself, He is focused on relationships. "Seek first his kingdom and his righteousness" (Matt. 6:33a). In God's economy, success means that my relationship with Him is good and growing. But, "If anyone does not provide for his relatives, and especially for his immediate family," God says, "he has denied the faith and is worse than an unbeliever" (1 Tim. 5:8). Therefore, in God's economy, success means that first I must have a relationship with God, and then second I must have a quality relationship with my wife and my children. Finally, if my company is prosperous, that's a bonus.

When I started Inmac, I had to decide what my personal involvement in the company would be. Because God was teaching me that He should be first, my wife and kids second, and the business third, I felt He wanted me to act out those priorities on a daily basis, not just pay lip service to them. As businesspeople are wont to do, I developed a plan. I counted the number of waking hours in the week and started with time devoted to God. How many hours a week would be needed to ensure that I was growing in knowledge of and intimacy with God? I repeated the exercise in order to set aside adequate time for my wife and kids. What remained in the week for work? Forty hours. That personal time commitment to the business would have to be sufficient, I concluded. Those forty hours would be intense, but God would be able to make it work.

That commitment was immediately put to the test when I met with venture capitalists, prospective investors in our fledgling company.

Those who fund start-ups expect the entrepreneurs to make a significant personal time commitment to the business. Venture capitalists want assurance that the founders will pour their lives into the venture, and they typically expect at least sixty or seventy hours a week, or more, from them. I knew what they expected and had to be honest with them upfront. As might be expected, my proposed forty-hour workweek did not go over particularly well. Venture capitalists would not invest in such a business, so we had to raise $50,000 from friends and family. But as a result of bootstrapping the start-up venture, we maintained a greater equity interest in the company. (In fact, Inmac never had more than $500,000 in paid-in-capital until the day it went public, and most of that came from the purchase of employee stock options.) Over the years I found that God repeatedly honored the commitment to prioritize Him and my family above the business.

Called to Inmac

Inmac was young and struggling, and I started to wonder whether this was indeed God's call for me. Everything we owned was in the business, including personal loan guarantees. I sensed His call to this business, but perhaps I was wrong. Did He want me to pursue some other venture or even become a pastor after all? Like Gideon, my wife, Roberta, and I agreed to set out a fleece before God. I needed a sign that was way out of the ordinary and unmistakably from Him. Sales were drifting downward from $2,300 to $2,200 to $2,100 per day. I was worried.

"You seem to be focused on the sales per day number," Roberta said. "What would be a sign that God is confirming your call to this business?"

"I don't know," I replied.

"Well, how about we take God's perfect number seven. Let's trust God for a $7,000 sales day," she suggested. "And just so you don't think it's a chance event, we're going to pray for three $7,000 days!" I did not want to be unspiritual, especially in front of my wife, so I agreed. But now I was really worried! How could God ever do anything like *that*?

We decided to pray about it for ten days. For five days, I was completely terrified about what might happen. But we continued on our knees every day. In the next couple of days, God gave me confidence that even if His answer was no, it would mean He had something better in store for us. On the eighth and ninth days of prayer, I had an increased sense that God was going to touch our fleece. And by the tenth day, a Sunday, Roberta and I both believed God would bless us with $7,000 in sales the following day.

On Monday morning, I announced to Nancy, our customer representative, that we were going to have $7,000 in orders that day. None of the employees knew about our prayer period, and during those ten days, sales had been trending further downward . . . $1,900 . . . $1,800. Nancy looked at me with extreme skepticism. Frankly, she probably doubted my sanity. I suspect other employees started preparing their résumés once word spread that the boss had gone mad. When the day started to look promising, Nancy came into my office to let me off the hook. She announced gleefully that we could possibly reach $5,000 in orders. "No," I said, "it's going to be $7,000." To her amazement, at the end of the day her final tally read just over $7,000. None of my employees at the time were walking with the Lord, and that certainly made an impression on them—not to mention on me!

The following Monday yielded the same result. And so did the next one. Then sales dropped right back down to their previous level, around $2,000 per day. But that didn't concern me, because God had demonstrated clearly that He cared about the venture, that He had His hand in it, and that He wanted me there. Since I knew I was where God wanted me, I also knew that I could trust Him to let me know when the time came for me to move on from Inmac; I promised I would be ready. But years later, I would still be able to point to three monuments to God on the sales graph.

Later I discovered a verse that spoke to my calling: "Each one should remain in the situation which he was in when God called him" (1 Cor. 7:20). He had affirmed my calling to that business.

Serve One Another in Love

The spiritual value of business is in serving one's fellow man. At Inmac, we did this by offering useful products and striving for superior service. Not only was serving others a biblical principle, but it also proved to be a competitive advantage. When we started selling computer products by direct mail, several large technology companies, including Digital Equipment Corporation (DEC) and Hewlett-Packard (HP), were looming. Would they immediately crush our fledgling business?

We were proud of our first catalog, and I sent a copy to HP's president with a note thanking him for his help. My partner happened to be in the president's office the day the catalog arrived, and he witnessed the reaction. The HP president took a look at the catalog and in one easy motion threw it in front of his division head. "If Eldred, a one-man operation, can build a catalog to care for our customers and the rest of the industry," he lambasted the executive, "why can't your entire division provide equally good support with a catalog of your own?"

Meanwhile, DEC had announced its own catalog of products similar to ours. Since together they represented two-thirds of the market, I was certain that we would have no future if HP and DEC both took care of their customers as we were intending to do. But I also knew that if we had two years before facing any real competition from these economic giants we would be well-enough established to survive. My wife suggested we pray to that effect, and right there we did.

When the DEC advertisement for its new catalog came out, I felt sick. I was fretting over it when my partner suggested that I call the toll-free number and ask to be sent a copy. I feared seeing it and hesitated to make the call. Finally, I got up the courage and dialed the number. As it turned out, the call was very revealing! The phone rang half a dozen times. I was starting to feel better. Our policy was to answer no later than the third ring, and we later changed the policy to answer on the first ring. Finally someone on the other end answered, "Hello?" My confidence was improving by the second. I asked for a copy of the catalog in the advertisement, and to my amazement she responded, "What catalog is that?" At first I thought I had the wrong number, but before I could apologize for misdialing, she said, "Just a minute. . . ." and without putting me on hold, she yelled to someone near her. "Hey, Mabel! Do you know anything about a DEC catalog?"

"Take his name and address," Mabel replied. "When it comes out we'll send him one." My fear that DEC was effectively serving its customers was completely gone. DEC would not pose a real threat early in our company history.

We decided to take the offensive with HP. We offered HP's Minicomputer Division a catalog for their customers, developed and managed by Inmac but branded with the HP name. Negotiations dragged on and on and finally led to nothing. At the end of the process, we had the two years without major competition, and we had established our position in the market. God had answered our prayer.

By Word and by Deed

A year after starting Inmac, I became concerned that it would adhere to biblical principles. "How can I make it a Christian company?" I asked a pastor.

In his wisdom, he replied that there is no such thing as a Christian company. "Only people are Christians," he stated. "But believers can use their businesses as opportunities to make Christ known." He was right. By word and by deed, we can make Christ known through our businesses.

Christ can be made known *by word* in many ways. We acknowledged and thanked God for His blessings in prayers at company banquets, lunches and meetings. After asking prospective employees what motivated them, I would then take the opportunity to share with them what motivates me. I also issued an open invitation for employees to come to me with concerns. Quite often, the concerns would be personal ones. After hearing each story and problem, I would ask if they would mind me praying for their concerns. Nobody ever objected to my offer. In fact, many offered heartfelt thanks, and I even witnessed tears from strong men who were deeply touched that someone cared enough to pray with them.

In Inmac's lobby, I placed spiritual and Bible tracts. An accompanying letter outlined my personal faith and how that affected the way people were treated and business was conducted at Inmac:

ABOUT THESE PAMPHLETS

These pamphlets represent the faith of the undersigned. When Inmac was started, I committed my work unto the Lord. This personal commitment has continued to grow over the years. His blessings have been bountiful to us at Inmac.

Faith is a very personal issue with a very personal God. God wants that all should come unto Him; but He does not force the relationship, although He could if He wished. He asks that each one make his own decision about Him, who His Son is, and what He did for us on the cross some 2,000 years ago. He has done a lot for me, and I give Him the glory for all He has done.

How does this strong, personal position benefit you as a vendor, employee, or visitor of Inmac?

1. *Every attempt will be made to treat you fairly.*
2. *In all ways we desire to be an ethical and aboveboard company.*
3. *Everyone will be treated with respect and consideration.*
4. *Personal faith is a privilege and a very private matter. Your privilege and privacy in this area are absolutely respected.*
5. *If for any reason you are not treated according to these principles, such treatment is not intentional and will be redressed.*

If anyone has any questions about these pamphlets or our policies, please feel free to pick up the house phone and call me at extension 5003.

Kenneth A. Eldred
CEO

One day, an outraged employee approached me to express her objection to the practice of displaying these tracts. She had been taking them from the lobby in protest, she informed me. A discussion ensued in which I explained the role of God in my own life and therefore in the management and direction of the company. Furthermore, I noted that she was free to ignore the tracts. But there was more to this encounter, and soon she revealed deep personal pain in her life. By the end of our conversation, she had prayed to become a follower of Jesus.

Christ can also be made known *by deed* in the way our business is conducted. Here is an example: In the early days of packaged software, the concept of single-use licensing was not ingrained. It was common to share software, even though the licenses granted the right of use only on a single computer. Inmac employees were no exception, as they were buying software and passing it around the office. God brought this to my attention, and when I asked our IT manager if this was going on, he said yes. I objected that the practice was wrong; it was stealing.

"Everybody does it," was the response.

"I don't care if everybody does it," I stated. "We need to do what is right before God." I commissioned him to figure out how pervasive the practice of software sharing was and how much it would cost to pay for all the software we were using illegally. Two weeks later, the IT manager came back with the figure: $250,000. That was far more than we could afford.

"God will provide the funds," I told him, "but we have to replace the illegal software with legitimately purchased copies." No more software would be shared. I'm not sure how God did it, but we made our numbers that year despite the money we spent on the software. (Maybe it was *because* of the money we spent on the software?) God taught everyone in the company a valuable lesson.

As Inmac grew significantly, I became concerned that I could no longer monitor its spiritual temperature. How could I make sure we were still operating according to biblical standards? I prayed about this, and God gave me this assurance. "Look, Ken," He said, "I know you have given me your business. If something is not right, I will bring it to your attention. If I do, then I want you to fix the problem. But if I don't, don't go looking for trouble." I had to trust that God would alert me to sin in the camp, as He had done with regard to the software.

Do Unto Others . . .

High-level service to the customer continued to be a hallmark of our company. We made sure that we were respecting our customers and their time. As a result, Inmac committed to shipping computer products the same day they were ordered. This level of service was unheard of in the industry, and even thought impossible by some within the company. But we achieved it, and customers loved it. Today, next-day service has become the industry standard.

The biblical tenet "do unto others as you would have them do unto you" is central to good service. A customer in England ordered a cabinet, paying the extra £30 to have the shelves assembled by our company. But it was shipped without the shelves installed, and we received an irate phone call. "I have been your customer for years," she rebuked us. "I had to spend £100 to hire someone to assemble the cabinet shelves that you should have installed! I will never do business with you again!" Our local manager apologized for the mistake and agreed to cover her costs, offering to refund not only the assembly fee but also the additional £100 she had spent remedying our error. She calmed down considerably.

The next day, the woman's office was abuzz over a bouquet of roses that had arrived for her. Who had sent these beautiful flowers? The attached note read, "I know the time and emotional cost you incurred as a result of our mistake goes well beyond any financial remedies. Please accept these as our gratitude for your years of business." She immediately picked up the phone and called our local manager, who had signed the card. "In all my years of working with vendors and partners, nobody has ever done anything so considerate and meaningful. Thank you," she said. "I will commit to buying from Inmac for as long as you're in business, and I will recommend you to everyone I know."

Inmac Growth and Sale

Over the years, I learned that business is part of a larger process, a walk with God through one's life. Inmac first struggled. Then it survived. Then it thrived. At every point along the journey, God had a new lesson to teach me, a new character trait to develop. The company went public in 1987. The day of the initial public offering on the New York Stock Exchange, God performed an outrageous miracle, the equivalent of making the sun stand still. (That event is described at the beginning of chapter 13.) The venture that was started with $5,000 and a bag of connector parts continued to grow into a company with 1,500 employees in 10 countries and annual revenues of $400 million.

The time came when I sensed God directing me away from the company, so I sold Inmac in 1996 to MicroWarehouse. The day of the merger, I met with the new chairman. "You're taking over a company that's been very important to me," I said. "I built it from scratch to around $400 million in revenues. I'm happy for you to have it, but I want to give you something more important." I wanted him to know that the company he was acquiring was the direct result of much prayer. I shared with him God's guidance over the years and my personal faith in Jesus.

After our half-hour meeting, he thanked me and proceeded to the office of our president. Looking a bit shell-shocked, he stammered, "Eldred just talked to me about Jesus. Is he serious?"

The president, also a Christian, smiled and replied, "Yes, he is." There was something far more valuable than Inmac that I wanted to pass along—and it was free!

The sale of Inmac was a major event in my life, not unlike seeing a child you've raised for more than twenty years marry and move on to start his own family. At the time I left Inmac, I also felt that God was calling me to leave all corporate boards on which I was sitting. It took a couple years to see how God's hand was at work and how He intended to bless that step of faith. Unbeknownst to me, while God was shutting one door, He was opening another.

The Birth of Ariba

While leading Inmac, I had a business idea that I thought held some promise. However, having developed the concept as an employee of Inmac, I felt it rightfully belonged to the company. Now, many would be tempted to rationalize away this legal point. It may be my idea, but how would the company be able to prove I conceived it while at Inmac? I only knew that God expected me to follow a higher standard of integrity. Simply put, doing otherwise would be stealing from the company. Therefore, when MicroWarehouse bought Inmac, I informed the new management about my business idea. It rightfully belonged to them. "Do you want it?" I asked.

"No, that really falls outside our business plan," was the response. "You're free to have it and pursue it if you like." Thus, with a clear conscience, I was able to explore the concept and ask for God's blessing on it. I had no idea how amazing His response to that act of obedience would be.

John Mumford is a Christian brother who has been a friend for decades. He was a cofounder of Inmac and the founding director of Crosspoint Venture Partners, a respected Silicon Valley venture capital firm. Together, we developed and molded my idea. The concept was fairly simple, though novel at the time. Many companies have a complex base of suppliers with whom communicating, coordinating, planning and ordering is paper-based, labor-intensive and inefficient. We could greatly simplify and improve that supply chain management process by using the Internet to facilitate procurement. With the additional help of some folks at Benchmark Capital Partners, we cofounded Ariba in 1996.

I was excited about this new venture, but what was I to do regarding God's leading to no longer sit on company boards? In the end, the answer was clear. "You and John Mumford are both accomplished businessmen and investors in this venture," Ariba's newly appointed CEO told me at a meeting. "However, we only have one board seat left. Because John represents a venture capital firm, I'm proposing we offer it to him. I hope there are no hard feelings." I have to admit I was disappointed in not being asked, but I had no hard feelings. I knew this was confirmation of God's direction.

Ariba grew, and by mid-1999, we decided to take it public. Our initial hopes were to price the public offering at $8 per share. But the stock market was hot, and as one of the first business-to-business Internet companies, Ariba was able to go public two months later at $23 per share. On opening day, it shot up and closed at $90 per share. The company we had founded three years earlier was now worth $6 billion! Unlike board members and managers, I had no official ties to the company. Therefore, I was not subject to a lockup period during which I was prohibited from selling my stock. I was unaware of the company's plans and results. It only made sense to diversify my investments. Over the course of the next year, Ariba reached a value of $40 billion, and I was able to divest at very attractive stock prices. Like many Internet companies, Ariba subsequently lost much of its value, but by providentially leading me away from a board position, God had enabled me to sell much of my investment during the most opportune time period.

Toward Kingdom Business

Around that time, God opened my eyes to the opportunity for business to transform individuals and nations around the globe. In early 1999, a long-time Indian friend approached me with a business start-up idea and asked for my help. The wrinkle: It was to be in India. His idea was to take advantage of the relatively low cost and high quality of labor available in India and the improvements in transpacific telecommunications to establish a call center that would serve customers in the United States. My previous ventures had been located in Silicon Valley, and I didn't particularly want to go through another start-up. But there was something about this opportunity. God gave me a vision for using this venture to advance His Kingdom. I agreed to help my friend under one condition—that he would give educated and capable young Christians in India the opportunity to work for him. "Absolutely!" he said, and ET was born.

Remembering God's leading to drop all board positions several years earlier, I was unsure how to respond when my friend subsequently asked me to serve on the board of his new company. I decided that prayer for guidance was the best course of action. One day, I was hosting a visiting missionary, chauffeuring him from place to place. In the process, I was introduced to the pastor of a local church, who said, "I have a word from God for you." I was startled, yet intrigued. "You're wrestling with a decision regarding a company," he continued. "God wants you to know He's in it, and He wants you to take the role. You're also involved with another company that will take off like a rocket." I was astounded. Yes, I was wrestling with a decision regarding ET, and I was also involved with Ariba, but was this really from God? When Ariba exceeded all expectations and took off like a rocket a couple months later, I knew God was directing me to a deeper involvement in ET. I agreed to join the board of directors.

A Vision for Kingdom Business

God gave me a vision for using my position of influence at ET to advance His Kingdom in India. Here's how it would work: We would be intentional about recruiting and hiring qualified Christians. The company would offer attractive wages to its employees. Christians at the company could be equipped and mentored in their faith. They would become salt and light to those with whom they would interact in the marketplace. They would also give to the local church, enabling it to free itself from dependence on Western funds. It was a vision to use a for-profit business to further the Church in India. It was a vision for Kingdom business.

Fiber-optic lines significantly increased the capacity and improved the quality of telecommunications between India and the United States. It was important that ET utilize this technology. The Prabhadevi Exchange in Bombay is the landing point for fiber-optic cables to the United States, so we decided to locate the company in Bombay, and God provided a building only 100 yards from the fiber-optic termination point. As it turns out, Bombay is one of the few cosmopolitan cities in India, and it has a relatively open religious attitude. The first 25 employees were Hindus, Muslims and Christians. By February 2001, ET had a 64-seat call center that featured leading-edge technology. Today, the company has grown to more than a thousand employees.

ET's call center staff is different from the workforce at other call center units. Almost all are university graduates, and a large majority of them have had formal computer training. True to his word, my friend started to recruit from local Christian schools. These talented Christians proved to be great employees, and the company no longer needs my encouragement to hire more. Several local Christian groups have even helped by prescreening candidates for the company. For hundreds of Indian Christians, ET has provided meaningful jobs in which they can use their gifts. Starting compensation is very generous by local standards, high enough to attract the best and brightest young people. At a salary of $350 to $400 per month, call center staff are able to contribute greatly to the local economy and can even afford to hire outside help, thus contributing even more to the economy and providing the opportunity to demonstrate the gospel to others.

There is an enormous opportunity to provide spiritual training and discipling for the hundreds of Christians at ET. Many have a faith that is more cultural than personal, and their understanding of Scripture is often limited. We watch their faith transform into an experience of following Jesus on a daily basis. The active faith of ET's hundreds of Christians can have a tremendous impact for the local church.

We have had the opportunity to introduce a Christian-based leadership development program within the company. PowerWalk, a Canadian organization that developed a Christian training course delivered primarily to churches, met with the top ET executives, many of whom are not Christians. Stating that it would remove explicit Christian language and Bible references though keep the Scripture excerpts and biblical concepts, PowerWalk offered a course for employees on a voluntary basis. It was designed to provide significant business and leadership training to ET's employees. While the management is Hindu, the company embraced the idea and expressed a desire to have the entire management group go through this Christian-based training course. PowerWalk's leadership training is fun and interactive and deals heavily with relationships. There was also opportunity to interact with participants in less formal settings outside the classroom and gauge their spiritual interest. Over a weeklong period, 80 or 90 people, a cross-section comprising about 10 percent of the company went through a training session. At the end of the week, it was agreed that this training should be offered to everyone in the company—including spouses.

The PowerWalk course is now a one-day component of the new-staff training program at the company, and a person who reports to the Chief of Human Resources has responsibility for maintaining and promoting it, with the support of a group of pastors. PowerWalk helped to establish a pastoral team of local men and women who are available for follow-on work that emerges from the ET effort. This team of Indian Christians is equipped to conduct in small-group settings an expanded course that includes topics such as marriage and stress management. The team is also available for counseling of ET staff and is committed to planting house churches in the area. "God is opening doors, and people are being challenged and exposed to the gospel," notes PowerWalk's Dan Sinclair.

A group of ET employees has committed to regular meetings in which they seek to develop their faith, following a ten-part curriculum on how to grow strong in the marketplace. They're also praying for the company and for the spiritual condition of those whom they encounter on a daily basis. When ET experienced an economic downturn that threatened the company, Christian employees got together to pray for their business. The company recovered, and many recognized the source of the turnaround.

Is There More to This?

God gave me a vision for using business to advance His Church and provide economic blessing in India, but was that all? Were there other Christians pursuing similar objectives through for-profit businesses? Was I unknowingly part of a larger movement of God? Was the model used at ET the only template for business as missions? What different approaches were Kingdom-focused believers using to effect economic and spiritual transformation, and where did these approaches work?

The questions were numerous, and I started to investigate.

CHAPTER 2

BUSINESS AS THE EMERGING MISSIONS STRATEGY

"Please don't send us money; it only creates division. But do send us business people who can create jobs for us, that we can build ourselves up." The Eastern European Christian leaders at a 2004 conference in Bulgaria were unified in their call for the Western Church to send Christians skilled in business to bless their nations economically and spiritually.

Rajesh, an Indian leader of an organization that coordinates the efforts of 15,000 Indian missionaries, agreed. "We need to learn how to live our faith in the workplace; how to work and witness," he said. "We need models of doing business and outreach."

Drazen from Croatia went so far as to say, "Sending us missionaries is good, but we'd prefer that you send us godly businessmen who can teach us and help us to start businesses and create jobs in a Christ-like way."[1] These Christian leaders were calling for Kingdom business.

This idea may seem unusual, but as long ago as 1857, missionary pioneer and explorer Dr. David Livingstone commented, "Those two pioneers of civilization—Christianity and commerce—should ever be inseparable." The African continent suffered from dark spiritual and economic conditions, and Livingstone believed the missions effort had to address both areas in order to achieve true transformation. The two pressing needs of Africans 150 years ago, to follow Jesus and to experience economic opportunity, remain the overriding requirements of much of the world today.

A common determiner of poverty is an income of less than two dollars per day. Half the current global population of 6.3 billion lives at or below this level.[2] Over the next 15 years, an estimated one billion will be added to the world population, and the majority of those will be born into households that live below the poverty line. Meanwhile, 2.3 billion live in people groups that are considered unreached (less than 2 percent evangelical, less than 5 percent Christian). The top 50 of the world's least-evangelized mega-cities all lie in the famous "10/40 Window," where average annual income is less than 500 dollars. Dark spiritual and economic conditions persist, and the Church is presented with a tremendous opportunity to offer God's solutions to these problems.

A Brief History of Missions

Throughout history, God has used the dominant political, cultural and economic forces of any given historical period to advance the gospel. For example, in the first century, the early Christians utilized the roads and trade ships of the Roman Empire to preach the gospel widely. In the fourth century, Christianity became the official religion of the Empire, allowing the gospel to be preached throughout the entire region. In the mid and latter part of the first millennium, God used the Catholic and Orthodox churches to convert the barbaric tribes of central and northern Europe. In the Age of Exploration (1400-1800), God used the great seafaring nations of Spain, France, England, Portugal and the Netherlands to take the gospel around the world.

The modern English-speaking Protestant missions movement began a few years prior to 1800 with William Carey. Carey made the case for missionaries to take the gospel to faraway peoples and established the first modern foreign-mission sending agency. Carey himself had a difficult, but ultimately very successful missionary career in India. Many others followed his lead, and the nineteenth century saw Christianity spread faster than at any time since the fourth century. In 1750, 22 percent of the world called itself Christian, 26 percent of the world was evangelized, and the Bible was available in 60 languages. By 1900, 34 percent of the world called itself Christian, 51 percent of the world was evangelized, and the Bible was available in 537 languages.[3]

But how has the Church done recently? To be sure, the investment in missions has continued. Since 1900, the world population has increased four-fold while the number of foreign missionaries has outpaced it, increasing seven-fold. However, despite an increase in the overall missionary effort, the last century has seen Christianity achieve no net gain, as 33 percent of the world now calls itself Christian (versus 34 percent in 1900).[4]

Current Situation in Missions

According to *World Christian Trends: AD 30-AD 2000,* 2 billion people call themselves Christians worldwide, and 650 million of these are considered practicing or evangelical Christians. There are 434,000 full-time foreign missionaries, 400,000 short-term foreign missionaries, and 4,150 missionary sending agencies, representing all Christian denominations, worldwide.

Of the $320 billion given annually to Christian causes, only $18 billion (6 percent) go to foreign missions. Moreover, the large majority of that missions funding is deployed in regions of the world that are already reached:

- $15.6 billion (317,000 missionaries) to the "Christian world" (27 percent of the world population; e.g., Brazil, Poland, United Kingdom);
- $2.1 billion (106,500 missionaries) to the "Evangelized Non-Christian world" (40 percent of the world population; e.g., India, Japan, China, Russia);
- $0.3 billion (10,500 missionaries) to the "Unevangelized world" (33 percent of the world population; e.g., Algeria, Cambodia, Turkey).[5]

The resources devoted to worldwide missions might seem considerable in aggregate terms, but evaluated in light of total populations, it is far less impressive. This corresponds to one Christian missionary per 14,000 people worldwide. The Church spends $3 on foreign missions for every person on the earth. However, the majority of that goes toward efforts to reach the Christian world. Almost 75 percent of the world population resides in the non-Christian world, which largely consists of developing nations. There are far fewer missions resources devoted to that region, where Kingdom business can have the greatest impact. In fact, that region only has one Christian missionary per 38,000 people and only $0.50 devoted in missions resources per person.

Furthermore, the amount of money going to missions (in constant dollars) has been flat in the past 30 years. Funds for foreign missionary work have barely outgrown the factor of inflation.[6] Part of the problem is gaining access to countries in the first place. Irrespective of the monetary constraints of recent giving, the doors continue to close for traditional missionaries. The present condition does not bode well for growing a mission presence in the rest of the world unless something changes.

Barriers to Missions

In many parts of the world, traditional missionaries are encountering significant barriers to entering a nation and conducting their work of evangelism. This is especially true in the unevangelized world where many countries are officially closed to evangelism. But even some countries in the evangelized non-Christian world are limiting the number of religious worker visas they issue, as traditional missionaries are perceived as bringing no value to the nation. Without legitimate alternatives, some missionaries circumvent these restrictions by entering the country disguised as tourists, students or business people.

Traditional missionaries soon discover that gaining access to the target country can be a relatively minor issue compared to the difficulty of conducting evangelism. In regions where evangelism and discipleship activities are either outlawed or strongly opposed by authorities, many missionaries are frustrated by the lack of a legitimate and natural venue for meeting and befriending locals. This difficulty is compounded by increasing social barriers, including a growing distrust of any Westerner (particularly any American) who has a source of overseas income that is not easily understood by local people. Full-support missionaries in poor nations are frequently accused of being everything from CIA agents to drug dealers; this obviously impacts their ability to share the gospel.

Traditional missionaries are also facing real dangers abroad from militant political and religious forces. In recent years, there have been reports of brutality and murder against missionaries in places like Vietnam, Colombia, India, Uganda, Panama, Afghanistan and the Philippines. Because of their positions as full-time Christian evangelists and religious workers, missionaries have become especially attractive targets in some regions.

The cost of fully supporting hundreds of thousands of Western missionaries is becoming an increasing burden as well. The average total annual cost per foreign missionary in the Christian world is almost $50,000. Even in the unevangelized world that almost entirely comprises Third World nations, the average total annual cost is nearly $30,000.[7] Furthermore, in countries where full-support missionaries in ministry can earn dozens of times the average local income, the huge income and lifestyle gap discourages local believers from giving to the local church ministry and thus serves to perpetuate the reliance of the local church on Western funds.

Some national and local governments are also limiting the amount of external financial support permitted for advancement of the local church. For example, the strongly pro-Hindu government that ruled India until recently made it increasingly difficult for Christian organizations to obtain permission to receive overseas funds under the Foreign Contribution Regulation Act. Given these restrictions, sources of funding from within the nation are becoming increasingly critical to the growth of the local church.

In light of these realities, many have sought an alternative missions strategy to the one of the past two centuries that relies on fully supported foreign missionaries. Of course, traditional missionary church-planters, evangelists, doctors, nurses, teachers and translators will always be important components of world missions. Any emerging missions movement like Kingdom business must be complementary to these. But the traditional full-support Western missionary model will continue to face increasing pressure.

If the age of the traditional full-support missionary paradigm is ending, what will the Lord use in the twenty-first century to spread His Kingdom? According to Billy Graham, "one of the next great moves of God is going to be through the believers in the workplace."[8]

The Emerging Missions Strategy for the Twenty-First Century

I expect that Kingdom business will be a primary tool that revolutionizes missions in the twenty-first century by providing an economically self-sustaining vehicle that will enable an increasing number of missionary Christians to be welcome in any country. Kingdom business professionals not only bring the blessing of the gospel, but they also bring the blessing of productive jobs and economic progress to the citizens of that country.

For centuries, Christian missionaries were welcomed in other nations when they brought with them expertise in areas badly needed by the host society, such as health care and education. Thus, Western knowledge, technology and assistance have opened doors for Christian missionaries in developing nations. In the twenty-first century, the top priority of most developing nations is to help citizens lift themselves out of the economic morass of endemic poverty. And most Third World governments now recognize that one of the key ingredients for sustained economic growth is Western capital and expertise. A surprisingly large number of governments that do not admit Christian missionaries under any circumstance *do* admit Western business people who happen to be Christian—as long as those people bring into the country needed capital and know-how that is likely to create greater economic opportunities for the people of those countries.

Current Trends and Dynamics

The current overriding need in developing nations. is for economic development, and Kingdom business professionals are a welcome solution. Consider the following observations about the world in which we live:

- Free market capitalism is the most powerful economic force in the world today and is the economic system of choice for the vast majority of the world's nations. Even those governments that pay lip service to other models (like China) are moving rapidly toward free markets.
- Investment has soundly overtaken aid as the preferred method for assisting developing countries. From 1990 to 2000, annual Official Development Assistance to developing nations remained flat at $53 billion. During the same period, net private capital inflows to developing nations nearly quadrupled, from $44 billion to $154 billion. Private business capital has become the largest source of funding for emerging economies.[9]
- Entrepreneurs are the foremost creators of new jobs, wealth and opportunity in the world today. Even in the United States, small businesses provide the majority of all new growth. From 1990 to 1997, U.S. small businesses added more than 75 percent of all new jobs in the nation's economy.[10] This trend is

even more pronounced in economically underdeveloped countries where the informal, small business sector is frequently 90
percent of a country's real gross domestic product (GDP).[11]

· Societal support for job and wealth creating entrepreneurs is
growing at both a local and a national level. As a result, job-
and wealth-creating entrepreneurs are welcome in almost all
countries today, and most command a place of influence and
respect in their local communities.

God desires to bless the nations spiritually and physically. It stands
to reason that He will use the current trends toward capitalism and economic development to further the establishment of His Kingdom. As
God used the dominant political, cultural and economic forces to
advance the gospel in the past—from the trade routes in the Roman
Empire to the naval expeditions in the Age of Exploration—He is poised
to do it again. Kingdom business as a missions vehicle speaks to the current needs and desires of governments and peoples around the world
who are desperately seeking business expertise and investment capital.

Business People in the Worldwide Missions Effort

The potential for business as a central component of the worldwide missions effort of the Church is enormous. In the United States, 21 percent
of all bachelors and masters degrees are in business.[12] If they have a similar religious profile as the general population (about 20 percent evangelical Christian), that means in the United States there are *as many*
evangelical Christians graduating in business *each year* as there are full-
time Protestant missionaries *in total*. And while there are 10,500 foreign
Christian missionaries in the unevangelized world, there are 50,000 lay
Christians residing abroad in closed countries.[13] Christians in business
constitute a largely untapped force for spreading the gospel and transforming the nations.

But what are the benefits of business as a missions strategy? Are
there any unique features that Kingdom business promises? I see at
least 10 reasons why business people are strategically important and
effective:

1. *Kingdom business is a model for fully self-sustainable missions.* Profitable businesses support Christians devoted to the Great Commission without tapping into monies donated to churches or missions agencies. Owned and managed by Verbo Church, Casa Bernabe Orphanage in Veracruz, Nicaragua has 35 arable acres of land that are leased for farming. The land yields fresh food for the 80 kids at the orphanage, enables them to develop vocational skills, and provides an income for the ministry of the orphanage.

2. *Kingdom business brings much-needed expertise, technology and capital.* A Kingdom-focused entrepreneur built the most advanced chip factory in China with Western technology and $1.6 billion in investment capital. Kingdom business professionals build local commerce by supplying the principles, training, advice and funding needed to grow businesses.

3. *Kingdom business creates jobs.* Unemployment is a major problem in most underdeveloped nations, and it often leads to unrest, chaos and even violence. The best way to aid those in need is to give them jobs. In many regions, Christians are disenfranchised and particularly subject to employment challenges. That is the case in India, where ET is providing employment to hundreds of Christians. Kingdom business professionals start and grow businesses that result in meaningful work for many people, Christian and non-Christian.

4. *Kingdom business builds the local economy and blesses the nation.* As biblical business principles are taught and the business infrastructure is enhanced, the country's economy becomes more robust. And as business and trade grows, more families earn incomes and standards of living increase. A Kingdom business was given Israel's highest industrial award and was commended by the government for blessing the nation of Israel. Kingdom business professionals are a blessing to nations by promoting successful business.

5. *Kingdom business provides access to many locations.* Even in countries closed to the gospel, Western business people who

establish and promote successful local enterprises are welcomed. Kingdom business professionals currently operate in
countries like Afghanistan, China and North Korea. They
can reach all corners of the world.

6. *Kingdom business presents the gospel by word.* Business is a wonderful context for personal evangelism. Successful capitalism
is based on biblical principles, and culture is transformed
through opportunities to teach both these principles and
their biblical source. People are changed through the saving
power of Jesus, and lives are transformed through opportunities to share the words and life of Jesus. The witness of
Christians at one Kingdom business in China resulted in 10
people each month deciding to follow Jesus. Kingdom business professionals speak the gospel of Christ to employees,
business leaders and the local community.

7. *Kingdom business presents the gospel by deed.* Jesus took His disciples, showed them by example, and explained the truth to
them separately. It is in the day-to-day activities that we
demonstrate Christ. Business provides the opportunity for
Kingdom business professionals to demonstrate the gospel
in everyday life and to model faith in the real world to a
broad range of people. When explaining the concept of
Kingdom business to a group of Christians, I was asked what
would happen if a business failed. My belief is that such
times of trouble present great opportunities to demonstrate
the true faith, which in good times is more difficult to do.

8. *Kingdom business enables local funding of the church.* As local
Christians earn incomes and build successful businesses,
they accumulate the financial resources that allow them to
support the mission of the local church. This is especially
important in areas where outside funding is blocked or curtailed, but any breaking of dependence on support from
Western sources is commendable. Kingdom business professionals empower believers in developing nations to assume
financial responsibility for the local church. For example, a

Kingdom business owner in Croatia was able to use his profits to fund the construction of his local church building.

9. *Kingdom business can be a valuable partner for other missions efforts.* In no way is Kingdom business considered a replacement for the work of church planters, translators and pastors. Those traditional missionaries will always be needed. In fact, profits from successful business ventures can be used to support those missionaries who are dependent on outside sources of funding. In some cases, as with a group of Kingdom businesses in China, the business itself can provide employment and income for foreign missionaries who also have church-planting or discipleship objectives in the local area. (But it is important that these missionaries perform competent and dedicated work for the business and that they do not sacrifice their obligations to the company for their evangelism objectives.) Kingdom business professionals generate resources and opportunities that can be deployed by other segments of the worldwide missions movement.

10. *Kingdom business taps into an underutilized yet highly capable resource in the Church.* Many business people have a deep desire to be more involved in the Church's missions effort. We need to give the business community an opportunity to be useful in Church and missions beyond the roles of check writing and church administration, for without capturing their hearts, we will not capture their souls. Kingdom business is not limited to those people who run large corporations. Everyone with business experience can add immeasurably to the body of business knowledge in most developing countries. CEOs, managers, small business operators and entrepreneurs have gifts, talents and experiences that can be used to take the gospel to and bless many nations. I am reminded of the story of a CFO who went on a missions trip to Mexico to build houses, a task for which he was hardly equipped. Imagine how much more he could have blessed the local people if he had

helped them improve their businesses or the country's financial system.

Responding to a Changing World

I believe that Kingdom business efforts do represent a massive sea change for the worldwide missions movement. Change is one of the only things we can count on. We are in a constant state of change. Therefore, how we deal with change is important. There are two different attitudes people have toward change, and they produce very different reactions.

- Some view change as a *difficult burden*. These people are reluctant to do something different or alter their behavior. Often this attitude results in resistance to suggestions of change.
- Some view change as an *opportunity*. These people can see the possibility of growth or redirection. For them, change creates an opportunity that was previously unavailable, and this attitude often leads them to anticipate the prospects of change.

Change comes as a result of trends that close doors to existing methods of doing things but create openings for new approaches. In order to take advantage of any change, these trends must first be recognized. In Henry Blackaby's influential book *Experiencing God,* he encourages those who want to witness Church growth to see what God is doing and to join Him. We should not seek His blessing on *our* programs and *our* methods. Rather, we should be attuned to *His* hand working in the world, and we should pull in that same direction.[14] How is God changing the world today? What should be our response?

Conclusion

In the past two centuries, the need for basic health care and education provided the opportunity for missionary doctors and teachers to take the gospel to faraway lands. While these needs still exist in the twenty-first century, the overriding current need is for economic development, and the opportunity is ripe for missionary business people to take the gospel to nations all over the world. The forces of the free market economy are winning over an ever-growing number of governments. These nascent economies are yearning for the business skills, technology and investment that are needed to propel them out of Third World status. The opportunity is ripe for Kingdom business.

Christians in business are an underutilized resource in the worldwide missions effort, particularly in an age when both the burden of supporting traditional full-support missionaries and the barriers to their effectiveness are being felt. Business people who bring expertise and investment capital are welcome in regions typically closed to traditional missionary efforts. They are able to preach the gospel by word and by deed, demonstrating it in the everyday challenges of the business world. They are able to sustain themselves through profitable businesses. And they are able to bless the nations by providing jobs, strengthening the economies, and increasing the standard of living. God is moving, and Kingdom business is becoming an important missions strategy that pulls in the same direction.

I have talked about Kingdom business as an important emerging missions strategy. What exactly do I mean by "Kingdom business"? Is it simply Christians engaged in business? Is it just another term for "tentmaking"? Let's see.

CHAPTER 3

DEFINING KINGDOM BUSINESS

Dan Carless is an American businessman with a passion to advance the kingdom of God. In his 33 years in business, this experienced real estate developer converted 30 condominium projects, primarily high-end properties in San Diego and Hawaii. Dan's company purchased existing apartment complexes, commissioned attractive upgrades and renovations to the units, and sold each one individually as a condominium. The business was a success. But was there a way to channel his business skills to advance the ministry of the Church? What if he could establish projects whose profits would finance Christian ministries? The wheels started to turn.

Dan turned his Kingdom focus on Colorado Springs, a city of 500,000 in which the housing authority reported that 30,000 frustrated tenants were unable to enter the market as homeowners. The plan was to bless that city's working poor physically, economically and spiritually. That was the example of Jesus' ministry. But rather than establish a ministry that relied on continual charitable donations, Dan sought to create a model that would yield recurring revenue and therefore require no outside gifts. Even better, it would be profitable, and investors would be encouraged to use part of their gains to promote other Kingdom efforts.

Having grown up in inner city Detroit as the son of a minister, Dan was familiar with the plight of the working poor. With little or no savings, the working poor of Colorado Springs would rather own than rent if they could get in with no money down and a monthly mortgage payment roughly equal to their current rent. Unfortunately, those favorable opportunities didn't exist—at least not until Dan put his business skills to use to provide a Kingdom business solution. He purchased a 111-unit complex with plans to upgrade and sell each unit at below-market entry points and formed alliances with select lenders that had programs with liberal underwriting policies designed for the working poor.

One unit was set aside for a couple to act as community advocates/pastors, called "life coaches," who would be commissioned to pastor the 110 resident families. The plan called for each resident to attend several classes taught by the community life coaches before he or she received approximately $3,500 in assistance for closing costs, funds that enabled a no-money-down purchase. The instruction would be of particular help to the working poor: personal finance and family budgeting, proper home care, good neighboring, and living with a long-term perspective. Following the project's completion, the life coaches would live in the community, guiding residents through life issues in a life-giving manner. The life coaches would also play a central role in the homeowners' association, combining an opportunity to plant a church and minister to people.

In order to fund his Kingdom-focused venture, Dan sought investors who shared his vision. After 14 months, the estimated profit to investors would be 25 percent, and investors were invited to donate some portion of the proceeds to the ministry of their choice. For example, a

Kingdom-focused investor might decide to give anything above the return he or she might have expected from a stock or money market mutual fund. In this way, the business venture would bless not only those receiving affordable housing but also others around the world.

Investors, the developer, the realtor, the renovator and the property manager would all be committed Christians, meeting a real need in the community. The church would demonstrate that it cares for the physical, economic and spiritual needs of the city, becoming a true friend of the city and its government. Dan Carless is using his business expertise and experience to further the kingdom of God.[1]

Expressions of Kingdom Business

Dan's business venture certainly has a number of noble objectives. But is it a Kingdom business? What do we mean by that term?

Kingdom business has several objectives, and a thorough discussion of it covers many facets. Yes, it is about missions, successful business practices, the integration of work and faith, economic development, spreading the gospel, transforming nations and transforming lives. Yet Kingdom business is not characterized by any of these alone. Like Dan Carless's development venture, it combines all of these factors in a refreshingly integrated missions movement.

A while ago, I talked to a person at a Christian organization about the organization's mission. He explained that they are engaged in work with the poor. The organization equips Christian business people to help the poor and each other through partnerships. I described some of the work in which I am involved, using overseas for-profit companies to advance the gospel. So few of the terms we used were aligned that we seemed to be talking past each other. It took us almost an hour to realize we were essentially speaking about the same thing.

There is an ancient parable thought to have originated in China in which three blind men are asked to describe an elephant. One man, grasping the trunk, says, "An elephant is like a large snake." Another, holding the tail, claims the elephant is more like a rope. The third man, his arms wrapped around a leg, observes, "An elephant is like a tree." Like that elephant, multi-faceted Kingdom business presents a diversity of appearances. Kingdom business is conducted with businesses of many sizes, from one-person enterprises to large corporations. It is pursued in roles inside and outside companies, from business manager to financial investor. It is happening in locations all over the world, from Ecuador to China.

In exploring how other believers have been called to use business to preach the gospel in word and in deed, I discovered that those engaged in business as missions are conducting their work in a wide array of capacities. Interacting with employees, negotiating with suppliers, advising entrepreneurs, creating useful products, and building local wealth are all vehicles for advancing the kingdom of God. A definition of Kingdom business must encompass the following ways in which God is using His people in the worldwide missions effort.

- *Founder or manager of a Kingdom business.* Those with entrepreneurial or managerial skills are building and leading successful businesses in developing nations. They provide employment, training, income and the gospel of Jesus to many. For example, Clem Schultz is one of many American businessmen who started a number of successful manufacturing companies in East Asia that have Kingdom objectives. His factories follow both a business plan concerned with economic results and a "Great Commission plan" concerned with spiritual impact goals.[2]
- *Lender to the poor.* Christians are extending microloans to those considered unbankable. They are also providing business and spiritual instruction to loan recipients who typically establish simple cottage industry ventures. Barclays Bank was started by devout Quakers in 1690 with a focus on the banking needs of the poor, a segment no other bank would serve. Today, Christian organizations like Opportunity International and World Vision are assisting the poor through loans and business training.
- *Mentor and financier of Kingdom businesses.* Christian business professionals are providing the necessary funding, advising

and mentoring to local Christians who are establishing or operating businesses in the developing world. Staffed largely by business professionals, Integra Ventures, for example, assists those running Kingdom businesses by providing the funding, consulting and discipling they need to succeed as part of the financing package.

- *Trainer in Kingdom business.* Some are training local managers in the basic skills and principles of business. These training courses typically include instruction in biblical values and principles that lead to successful business. For example, SERVUS, a Swiss organization led by Christians, offers biblical business training courses to managers in developing nations.

- *Short-term consultant to Kingdom businesses.* Christian professionals are engaging in short-term missions work that seek to bless business owners in developing nations. In connecting with specific Kingdom businesses on short-term trips, these Western business people are consulting with Christian managers on business strategies, managerial issues and spiritual matters. Led by Brett Johnson, Equip has been taking young Silicon Valley professionals on short-term Kingdom business missions trips. Their objective is to help South African businessmen and women re-purpose their companies as Kingdom businesses.

- *Expert advisor to Kingdom businesses.* Western Christians with relevant business experience are using their knowledge, expertise and contact network to assist Kingdom businesses in the developing world. Though they often reside on different continents and may even be retired from their careers, they are able to provide valuable help by lending their experience and by opening doors in the Western world. The Business Professional Network, led by John Warton in the United States, is an excellent example of an organization that connects experienced Western business people with Third World ventures.

- *Sales partner to Kingdom businesses.* Kingdom business professionals and organizations located in the First World are seeking to promote Kingdom business companies in developing nations. By marketing products or establishing sales channel partnerships, those in the West provide valuable assistance to Kingdom businesses. For example, a Christian wholesale distributor in the United States has become a sales partner of a company in China, adding a line of products the Kingdom business in China manufactures to the items he distributes. The Kingdom business organization EC Institute (Michigan) also assists Kingdom-focused companies overseas by connecting them with Western buyers for their products.

· *One-off support for Kingdom businesses.* Some Christians employed in the Western business world are in a position to open doors for Kingdom businesses. Simply acting in the interest of their own organizations, they can introduce the products or services of Kingdom business ventures. A Kingdom-focused friend at a major U.S. credit card company opened the doors for ET to present its call center services. This simple act made possible a business relationship that could potentially double the number of Indians employed at ET.

· *Investor in Kingdom businesses.* God has blessed some people with the financial resources to be major investors in Kingdom businesses around the world. These people are promoting Kingdom business by providing capital to companies led by expatriates or by local Christians. For example, Evangelistic Commerce, led by Thomas Sudyk, has invested in the creation of several Kingdom businesses in the developing world.

· *Manager of Kingdom business funds.* Though this role is still emerging, Kingdom business professionals can also act as private equity fund managers. Working within existing laws governing the establishment and management of investment funds, they can serve entrepreneurs, managers and investors by assisting and funding Kingdom businesses. For example, the Business Professional Network U.S. has started a small exploratory fund to invest in promising Kingdom business ventures.

Various individuals and organizations are actively involved in Kingdom business, yet in many ways, the terms commonly used to speak about and describe Kingdom business have yet to be codified. To date, the practice of Kingdom business has outpaced efforts to define or study it in a systematic manner. We need to define the language and structure so that professionals can communicate clearly. The most foundational of these terms is "Kingdom business" itself.

Simply Stated . . .

Kingdom business is for-profit business ventures designed to facilitate God's transformation of people and nations. Business becomes a missions tool for ministering to those with real needs, both economic and spiritual. Addressing both needs is important for either to succeed. Though the practice of Kingdom business takes on many forms, what unites these efforts is a commitment to sustainable transformation, captured by a three-fold objective: (1) profitability and sustainability, (2) local job and wealth creation and (3) advancement of the local church (the three-fold objective of Kingdom business is discussed in chapter 8). Kingdom business pursues each of these simultaneously.

Specifically, this book deals with Kingdom business in the missions field of the developing world. The term "Kingdom business" can and does apply to the many worthy efforts, like that of Dan Carless, to effect change in the developed First World, though they are not the subject of this book. For example, those Christians working with the poor in the inner city to build businesses and see spiritual and economic transformation are pursuing Kingdom business objectives. Although many ideas in this book may apply to their much-needed and laudable efforts, our discussion of Kingdom business is focused on missions to developing nations and will not deal directly with attempts to reform Western pockets of poverty.

Kingdom Business Professionals

Kingdom business professionals are authentic, skilled business people who use their talents to further the worldwide mission of the Church through Kingdom business.

They are called and equipped to use their spiritual gifts in a business context. Kingdom business professionals have hearts and minds both for growing businesses and for growing the Church. Rather than perceiving their work in business as a distraction from their ministry, Kingdom business professionals recognize it as the important vehicle through which they bring the gospel by word and by deed. Kingdom business professionals are so committed to meeting spiritual, economic and social needs in the driest places that they are willing to live and work in these locations.[3]

Kingdom business professionals see their mission as multi-fold: They seek to influence employees, partners, suppliers, customers and the local community for Christ. They use business itself to demonstrate biblical business principles and set values. They serve others through quality products and helpful services. They seek to provide a venue for people to use their gifts and earn a living. They desire to create a culture of light in and around the businesses that they develop through good, biblically based business principles and the love of Jesus Christ.

Kingdom Businesses

Kingdom businesses are for-profit commercial enterprises in the mission field of the developing world through which Christian business professionals are seeking to meet spiritual, social and economic needs. Kingdom businesses come in many sizes and shapes. However, we can point to some features that commonly characterize them.

As I noted in chapter 1, businesses are not Christian. People can be Christian; businesses cannot. Thus, the discussion centers around the characteristics of Christians in business, not about the characteristics of Christian businesses. It's a subtle yet important distinction. People can have right standing and communion with God, businesses cannot. People can be indwelt by the Spirit of God, businesses cannot. People can become sons and daughters of God, businesses cannot. Confusion about this can lead to questionable business decisions. Some people might seek to establish a Christian company by only hiring Christians. But how are they going to be salt and light in the workplace if they are surrounded only by fellow Christians?

Jesus taught that the nature of a tree is observed by the fruit it bears. The follower of Jesus who has the Spirit of God as his or her guiding force will exhibit good fruit—sanctification is the primary sign of the presence of the Holy Spirit. In fact, Scripture explicitly lists what characterizes that fruit of the Spirit: love, joy, peace, patience, kindness, goodness, faithfulness, gentleness and self-control (see Gal. 5:22-23). So what does the fruit of Kingdom business look like? R. Paul Stevens, scholar and author on the topic of faith in the marketplace, notes 10 characteristics of companies that are led by followers of Jesus whose goal is to advance the kingdom of God.[4]

1. *The presence of a Christian or Christians with a sphere of influence.* This does not necessarily mean that the Chief Executive Officer or the majority owner of the business must be a Christian. I am a board member of and minority investor in ET, an Indian company with few Christians in senior management but with a decidedly Christian influence. At Inmac, my partner was not a follower of Jesus, though we agreed that we would run the company on Christian business principles. The important characteristic is that Christians affect the policies and direction of the business.

2. *A product or service in harmony with God's creational purpose.* "Then God said, 'Let us make man in our image, in our likeness, and let them rule over the fish of the sea and the birds of the air, over the livestock, over all the earth, and over all the creatures that move along the ground'" (Gen. 1:26). God's command to fill the earth and rule over His creation includes development of the world. To be sure, there are business activities and realms, such as pornography and illegal drugs, which do not fulfill this mandate. But most commercial activities, from producing medical equipment to dry cleaning to selling groceries to farming, are helpful to society.

3. *A mission or business purpose that is larger and deeper than mere financial profit (though including it) so that the business contributes in some way to the kingdom of God.* For more than 25 years, my

personal life goal has been to be a witness to employees and the business community and to fund Christian work around the world. I have moved from entrepreneurship to venture capital to philanthropy, yet my personal mission statement has not changed.

4. *The product and service is offered with such excellence that it suggests the presence of the Kingdom and invites the opportunity to witness.* Though not situated in the developing world, Buck Knives is a prime example of this characteristic of Kingdom business. Located in Southern California, the company has been a manufacturer of high-quality pocket knives for more than 100 years. The company is renowned for the excellence of its products. In the warranty note to customers who purchase his knives, chairman Chuck Buck states, "From the beginning, management determined to make God the Senior Partner. . . . Each knife must reflect the integrity of management, including our Senior Partner."[5] Buck's outstanding products allow the company to point to Jesus, whose life and teachings motivate this excellent service.

5. *Customers are treated with dignity and respect and not just as a means of profit.* Outstanding service means that the customer is to be loved and respected as a person created in the image of God and that business transactions should be fair. "Welcome aboard," Buck tells its customers, "You are now part of a very large family. Although we're talking about a few million people, we still like to think of each one of our users as a member of the Buck Knives Family."[6] We are to treat others with love and respect. If business is our ministry, genuine service to the customer is part of following God.

6. *Employees and workers are equipped to achieve greater potential in their life and, if they are Christians, to work wholeheartedly with faith, hope and love.* God has gifted individuals with talents and abilities. A primary concern toward employees should be the deployment of those gifts in meaningful ways that allow them to glorify God through their work. Those who are

followers of Jesus should be fully committed to excellence in their work rather than neglecting their duties in favor of ministry. At Inmac, I saw my job in part as guiding the company and preparing people for larger roles in the company.

7. *All aspects of the business are considered to be potentially a ministry and the subject of prayer.* Kingdom business professionals think of their work in the marketplace as ministry, and guidance through prayer is an important aspect of surrendering the business to God. "The fantastic growth of Buck Knives, Inc. was no accident," Chuck Buck tells his customers. "In a crisis, the problem was turned over to Him, and He hasn't failed to help us with the answer."[7] Likewise, you will find recounted in these pages a number of instances in which God clearly answered prayers regarding aspects of my own work in business.

8. *The culture (values, symbols, governing beliefs) of the organization line up with God's word and Kingdom purposes.* There is a renewed recognition in business education that a company's culture is a key to its success. By explicitly promoting and adhering to biblical principles, such as integrity, service, justice, respect and trust, Kingdom business professionals can infuse both their companies and the local business community with values that bring honor to God. His Kingdom is advanced as individuals and their business practices honor God's teaching.

9. *The business runs on grace.* The business world is full of inequalities. Organizational position, economic position and social position all result in the potential for power to be exerted with respect to others. God invites us to operate on grace, for He extends grace when we fail. "If sometimes we fail on our end, because we are human," says Buck's message, "we find it imperative to do our utmost to make it right."[8] Likewise, we told Inmac employees to admit it if they made a mistake—we would support them. We extended grace to our customers by giving our customer service people the power to fix any problem on the spot, whether it was caused by our error or by the

customer's. The customer service people were guided by one simple principle: If you had this problem, what would you like the company to do for you to fix it? There will be mistakes and failures, but Kingdom business professionals should operate within a spirit of grace.

10. *The leaders are servants, dedicated to serve the mission of the business, the best interests of the employees, the customers and the shareholders because they are first of all servants of God.* Servant leadership has recently become a concept embraced by some academics, but its origins are not at all modern. Jesus taught that status and heroism are not required for leadership. In fact, He taught that to be a leader, one must be a servant. Rather than seek honor and position, servant leaders are committed to the common mission, and they empower their team members to excel. As a servant of God, I sought to serve others at Inmac. The letter I mentioned in chapter 1 that was displayed in the Inmac's lobby made it very clear that employees, customers and partners could expect to be treated with respect, fairness and integrity because I was a follower of Jesus.

Counterfeit Kingdom Businesses

Kingdom business is a powerful vehicle for meeting spiritual, social and economic needs, but this does not sit well with those forces opposed to God. The enemy has a way of taking what is good and offering counterfeits that do harm to Christians and the gospel. In fact, if God is using something to His glory, you can almost be sure this is happening.

Thus, it may come as no surprise that we can already witness the enemy usurping Kingdom business. In November 2003, United States FBI and Internal Revenue Service agents arrested a former missionary to the Philippines, several members of his family, and a minister. They were charged with operating a Ponzi scheme that bilked Christian ministries of $160 million. Under the name International Product Investment Corporation (IPIC), money was collected from Christians and ministries with promises of 25 to 50 percent returns in three to six months. IPIC ostensibly imported products manufactured in developing nations, primarily in Panama, and sold them through well-known U.S. retail chains such as Costco, J.C. Penney and Pier 1 Imports. In fact, a suspicious ministry executive who performed due diligence and visited Panama claimed to have found a small mom and pop operation that was entirely unable to sustain the level of sales claimed by IPIC executives. The United States Securities and Exchange Commission found that IPIC had no legitimate operations; dollars contributed by new investors were paid out to earlier investors. In addition, federal investigators claimed that those who ran the scheme bought houses a helicopter, and a yacht with investors' funds.[9]

I note this story to provide two words of caution: The first is illustrated by Jesus' parable of the mustard seed. While there are several interpretations of the parable, many believe it speaks of Satan's tendency to latch onto and exploit significant movements of God. "The kingdom of heaven is like a mustard seed, which a man took and planted in his field. Though it is the smallest of all your seeds, yet when it grows, it is the largest of garden plants and becomes a tree, so that the birds of the air come and perch in its branches" (Matt. 13:31-32). Earlier in the chapter, Jesus told the parable of the sower in which birds representing Satan eat some of the seed sown by the farmer representing Christ. Now the birds are nesting in the tree God has grown from the smallest of seeds. Unfortunately, when the Kingdom grows like that, the birds will come.

The second word of caution is that Christians cannot turn a blind eye toward bad business cases simply because there is a ministry aspect to the venture. We cannot justify support for poor—or illegal—business plans and inexperienced personnel under the guise of some ministry benefit. It is vital to work with knowledgeable professionals who operate within the law. A number of individuals and organizations that fit this profile are mentioned in this book.

Barriers to Kingdom Business in the Church

Many Christians hold views that represent significant barriers to the idea of Kingdom business being a viable missions tool. One barrier, as already mentioned, is the notion that only pastors or full-time Christian workers are engaged in God's work. I fell for that misconception myself. As I discussed in chapter 1, it took me a while to discover that the passions and talents God had given me were best used in the business world, and that is where He wanted me to serve Him. It also became clear to me that the most spiritual calling for each individual is that to which God calls and equips him or her. There is no highest calling, not even that of working in the ministry. My ministry was to serve people and bring them the gospel through business.

Because this notion is so widespread, it must be addressed for Kingdom business to be embraced as a laudable mission of the Church. Additionally, I have found that sincere Christians sometimes hold several other misconceptions that are barriers to Kingdom business. What follows are brief observations about transformation, work, business, profit and wealth. (A more detailed discussion of these concepts is found in appendix A.)

Transformation

Various segments of the Church today emphasize different aspects of transformation. Some Christians focus exclusively on spiritual transformation, demonstrating great evangelistic zeal but showing little compassion for the economically needy or socially outcast. Others emphasize social and economic transformation by fostering harmony and unity and curing social and physical ills. The ministry of Jesus demonstrates that God cares about transforming people's spiritual, social and economic conditions. He fed the hungry, called people to personal holiness, healed the sick, taught in the synagogue, preached to thousands, and affirmed the social outcasts. His was a comprehensive ministry, not one limited to a single realm. Likewise, Kingdom business is committed to transforming nations and advancing the kingdom of God through a comprehensive ministry. It addresses spiritual, economic and social ills that plague many people in developing nations.

Work

The hierarchy found in much of the Church today, in which vocational Christian professionals are thought to be following a higher calling than those in secular work, is not supported by Scripture. Christians need to adopt a paradigm that views work itself as ministry and God's holy call on their lives, whether or not they are employed by the Church. All believers, with a multitude of God-given gifts, are called to ministry (or service) and can be said to be in full-time Christian work. Work is inherently good and mandated by God. It is ministry, be it in a business, in a school, in a home or in a church.

Business

Christians are gifted for and called to vocations of every type, including those vocations in the business world. Though media and entertainment portrayals of business people might lead us to conclude that there is nothing redeeming in their profession, business can be a very noble pursuit. Successful commerce is about serving one's fellow man and increasing his standard of living. It is about discovering people's needs and meeting them. Business brings glory to God when it blesses man through the creation of needed products, the delivery of outstanding services, and the increase of society's living standard.

Profit

The wide-standing perception is that business is primarily about maximizing profits. However, the true purpose of business is to provide a vehicle for serving others through efficient delivery of useful goods and services. When this objective is pursued, there will be an opportunity for profit. Profit is like oxygen—it allows a company to grow and continue to serve others effectively. Another prevailing notion is that nonprofit organizations are inherently nobler than for-profit organizations. But there is no direct correlation between lack of profit and benefit to society. In fact, the greater the product or service's benefit to the recipient, the greater the potential for profit. We cannot consider business ignoble or unspiritual because it is profitable.

Wealth

Some Christians consider poverty and austerity to be more spiritual than wealth. Others believe health and financial blessing will necessarily follow from sincere faith. Both the "poverty gospel" and the "health and wealth gospel" fall short of the rich biblical teaching about prosperity. Wealth (material, physical and spiritual) is given by God, and He expects us to manage it for His purpose. He also wants us to enjoy it. To be sure, both poverty and wealth pose potential pitfalls. But poverty is a disease, and a large segment of the world suffers from the cycle of despair that accompanies it. On the other hand, economic improvement brings with it a cycle of success that propels a nation to aggregate increases in wealth, self-esteem, health and the development and use of gifts.

Such attitudes in the Church, some prevalent and some less widespread, create real barriers to the acceptance and growth of Kingdom business as an effective missions movement. Those who devalue economic or spiritual results, consider work in the marketplace as second rate, see business as ignoble, view profit as dirty, or consider wealth as the enemy may have difficulty accepting Kingdom business as a laudable part of the missions movement. Kingdom business rests on notions that God cares about people's spiritual, social and economic transformation, that work in the business world is both a ministry and a calling, that profit is both necessary and a sign of useful service, and that poverty is a social disease to be addressed.

Relating Business to Missions

It is important that Christians, especially those in business, have a framework for connecting business and missions. There are three ways of relating business to missions: business *for* missions, business *and* missions, and business *as* missions.[10]

Business for *Missions*

Those who hold the notion that business should serve solely as a source of assistance to missionaries and evangelistic efforts view missionaries and vocational ministry professionals to be uniquely qualified to reach the world, and they believe the role of business is to support them. There are several variations on this notion of business *for* missions.

Support functions for missions. Some Christians see the role of business people in missions as providers of the professional and technical expertise needed for worldwide evangelism. For example, Christian computer consultants and publishing companies can assist missions agencies and missionaries in their work of spreading the gospel. While these are indeed important functions often best filled by business professionals, a definition of Kingdom business that limits its role to professional support for missions agencies falls short of the concept presented here.

Front for missions. Some missionaries view a business as a helpful cover that provides much-needed visas. The business is a vehicle for gaining entry and maintaining residence, and the title of "businessperson" can be helpful in certain circumstances. Of course, the business is a distant second in the priority of the missionary. Lack of expertise, training and interest in business matters almost guarantees the business's economic failure, but somehow the missionary manages to stay "in business" for years. This is certainly not the idea behind Kingdom business.

Kingdom business professional Clem Schultz has been founding and operating companies in East Asia for a number of years, and he is often approached by those who wish to use his businesses as a cover for their evangelism work in a region. Clem stipulates that those missionaries work no less than 20 hours per week in the business, and that they be competent, trained and fully committed to their jobs in his companies. He even mandates that there be no witnessing with fellow employees on the job, stipulating that it can be done after hours and that the believer must demonstrate a proper work ethic during the working hours he or she has committed to the company. The Kingdom business is a vehicle for missions, but it is not to be used as a front for missionaries who have no interest in working there.

Funding source for missions. Some Christians, not perceiving the intersection between work in the marketplace and work in missions, see the redeeming value of business in its ability to provide funding for missions work. Business is not really virtuous work, the thought goes, but money earned through business can be used to support spiritual work.

This, too, falls short of the full definition of Kingdom business. Whether in Canada or in Croatia, business continues to be an important source of funding for the local church. But to limit business to this role in the missions effort of the church is shortsighted. Business must not be relegated to the sidelines, because it is where everyday people are encountered and transformed.

Business and Missions

Others admit that there is a legitimate missions role for the businessperson himself in the world. The mission field is not just for church-funded missionaries. Especially in regions that are difficult for traditional missionaries to access, why not have Christians relocate there through employment? Their work in business grants them both the funding and the legal status to remain in the country, and they can do ministry outside of work hours. They can fulfill both purposes: They can engage in business *and* missions.

This concept, which has been termed "tentmaking," should not be confused with the practice of Kingdom business described here. Tentmakers International Exchange defines this business and missions idea as follows: "Tentmakers are Christian witnesses from any nation who, using their vocational skills or experience, gain access and maintain themselves in another culture with the primary intention of making disciples for Christ Jesus and, where possible, establishing and strengthening churches."[11] Instead of the three-fold objective of Kingdom business (profitability and sustainability, local job and wealth creation, and advancement of the local church), the goal of tentmakers is typically limited to spiritual results. Tentmakers are usually job takers, and the job is the means for gaining access to the country for evangelism purposes. The primary intention is making disciples for Christ Jesus. While Kingdom business professionals likewise seek to develop followers of Jesus, their mandate includes raising the standard of living and creating a better life for all by providing employment, financial resources, goods and services.

Tentmakers often find it difficult to deal with the tension between their secular employment and their real purpose, missions work. Operating in a framework that ascribes little eternal value to their jobs, tentmakers often view their nine-to-five work as a hindrance to ministry.

It is the entrance fee that must be paid for access to the mission field. By contrast, Kingdom business professionals don't consider their work as a hindrance to ministry—it *is* their ministry.

Tentmaking has achieved some level of popularity in recent decades, especially in countries less open to traditional missionaries. This approach has yielded some positive results, but there have also been failures along the way. Tentmakers have a critical role to play in the furtherance of the gospel worldwide, but the idea of Kingdom business goes beyond taking a corporate job to gain access to a foreign country for ministry purposes. Kingdom business does not consider commerce and ministry as separate spheres of operation.

Business as *Missions*

The concept of Kingdom business sees business *as* missions. It considers business activity itself the missions work. Kingdom businesses are for-profit businesses that meet spiritual, social and economic needs. Kingdom business professionals work with real-world problems with which they can demonstrate the gospel in action. Perhaps most importantly, Kingdom businesses provide a powerful platform of respect for the furtherance of the gospel both within the enterprise and outside of it.

Individuals engaged in Kingdom business see their role as job-makers who provide work opportunities for those who are desperately lacking them (frequently, these are local believers). Their companies produce valuable goods and services. They create long-term value for all stakeholders: employees, partners, customers, investors and community members. And they effectively further the gospel in the local community in which they operate at no cost to the local or worldwide church. They are missions vehicles for sustainable transformation.

Conclusion

Kingdom business is for-profit business ventures designed to facilitate God's transformation of people and nations. The objective of Kingdom business in the developing world is to foster sustainable companies that both further the mission of the local church and provide jobs and financial resources. By leading, shaping, advising, funding and growing businesses, Kingdom business professionals are able to guide the culture, vision, hiring, compensation and business practices of organizations— all of which are important components of ministry to the nations. Though perhaps lacking formal training in theology or preaching, Kingdom business professionals are ideally suited to teach the gospel by word and by deed. By speaking truth and living out their faith in the workplace, they are able to lead many to Christ. They seek to bless the nations through business. They consider their work in business as ministry, not as a support or access vehicle for ministry. Kingdom business *is* missions.

The power of business to transform nations is illustrated by the following statement from former Chinese president Jiang Zemin: "I would make Christianity the official religion of China."[12] Why would the communist leader of the world's most populous country make such a statement? Is he convinced by apologetic arguments that Christianity is the truth? No, I'm afraid his astonishing statement does not flow from personal faith or theological analysis. But Jiang Zemin has noticed something about Christianity that makes it highly attractive to him. We will explore that next.

CHAPTER 4

SUCCESSFUL CAPITALISM AND BIBLICAL PRINCIPLES

In the very early days of Inmac, we received a shipment of tear-resistant envelopes from a supplier. During the unpacking, I accidentally sliced into one-third of the envelopes. It sickened me, because those envelopes represented 5 percent of the money for our fledgling company's inventory. Having counted the economic cost, I simply couldn't get up the courage to remove the damaged items from the inventory. When the first order for these envelopes arrived, I shipped a number of the defective ones without thinking twice about it. Suddenly, all of our orders stopped. Not a single call for three days.

As I was praying that night, I remembered those envelopes and I sensed that God was trying to get my attention. I asked Him to forgive me for cheating the customer that I had sent them to and I vowed to make it right. First thing the next morning, utterly embarrassed, I apologized for my mistake to my bewildered part-time employee. Then I rushed out a replacement shipment to the customer. Normally, we experienced our lowest volume on Thursdays, but that day the orders came pouring in again—so much so that we made up the entire shortfall from the beginning of the week on a single Thursday! I believe the Lord was saying to me, "Ken, if I can't trust you in the little things, how can I trust you in the big ones?"

By knowingly sending defective products, I had violated the biblical principles of integrity, honesty, service and quality. Although one would not normally expect that incident to have produced the immediate and drastic economic consequences that followed (even if it had undermined future sales), it was a good way for God to get my attention. The marketplace rewards adherence to biblical values and penalizes those who act contrary to them. Biblical principles are the basis for successful capitalism.

Capitalism

In 1982, former *Christianity Today* editor Harold Lindsell stated that the whole world was engaged in a massive struggle between the two opposing forces of capitalism and socialism. He viewed socialism as a dangerous concept that was on the rise in spheres from economics to religion.[1] The tide has certainly shifted since then. Today, the communist policies of the Soviet Union are generally viewed as a failed experiment, and even hybrid economies with strong socialist components are falling behind. (For a more extensive discussion of socialism, see appendix B.) Increasing numbers of developing nations have turned their gaze toward capitalism as a solution to prevailing economic problems.

It has been said that capitalism is not a good system—except when compared to all others. Many Christians are moved by the economic disparity found in the world, and the conditions in many regions are troubling to the Church. Author, philosopher and theologian Michael Novak, said:

> If one keeps uppermost in mind the material needs of the poor, the hungry, and the oppressed, rather than one's own state of feelings, one asks: What is the most effective, practical way of raising the wealth of nations? What causes wealth? I have come to think that the dream of democratic socialism is inferior to the dream of democratic capitalism, and that the latter's superiority in actual practice is undeniable.[2]

If there is one principle that underlies the economic system of capitalism, it is the notion of inalienable property rights. This involves the intrinsic right to own, control and use private property, in particular, the means of production. Land, equipment, money and labor are all means of production. Other property includes ideas, trademarks and products. All may be owned by the individual or a group of individuals, and they may be freely exchanged for other property in a manner agreeable to both parties. An aggregate benefit is derived from such a transaction, and the sum of all such transactions leads to the creation of a society's wealth.

Capitalism and Scripture

Like no other economic system in the history of mankind, capitalism is producing needed goods and services and is improving the world's standard of living. But is there any biblical support for capitalism? The answer is yes on a number of levels. Unlike the modern examples of socialism, capitalism rests on the biblical principle of personal freedom and responsibility. Man is free to use his gifts in the manner in which he chooses; he is free to pursue the vocation to which God leads him. Capitalism also fulfills more effectively the mandate God issued in the Garden of Eden: "to work it and take care of it" (Gen. 2:15).

In the Old Testament, God's people owned private land, animals and money. It was a "capitalist" system. The Israelites were free to do with their property as they chose. The sole exception was a limitation on the perfect liquidity of land assets. God had promised the land of Canaan to the Israelites, and they were to be its stewards. Every family was given specific property. The Jubilee law mandated that real estate could only be leased rather than permanently sold. Every 50 years, all leases were to end, and the land would revert back to the original owner or his heirs. Of course, the price paid for the use of a piece of property would take the remaining life of the lease into consideration, and those who leased the land were free to benefit from its use. In Israel's agrarian economy, the Jubilee law was a way of giving everyone the opportunity for a fresh start. Much as modern bankruptcy laws are, it was designed to keep the society free from perpetual slavery or failure. But in no way was the Jubilee law considered a means for redistributing wealth. In essence, the Old Testament depicts free enterprise with a somewhat illiquid real estate market.

The Bible does acknowledge that human weakness can manifest itself in the marketplace. Greed can result in the use of private property for ignoble purposes. In the Old Testament, this was dealt with through usury laws. For example, the law given to Moses stipulates that if money is lent to one of God's people who is needy, no interest is to be charged, and collateral that is essential to the borrower's well-being is not to be held (see Exod. 22:25-27). In other words, help is to be extended to a brother or sister who is in dire need. It should be considered a gift, not as an opportunity to profit from the situation.

It is important to distinguish the situation of desperation described in Exodus from someone's seeking a loan to start or expand a business. God was not outlawing the practice of lending or charging interest altogether. Consider the scriptural prophecies forecasting that in its prosperity Israel "will lend to many nations but will borrow from none" (Deut. 15:6; 28:12). In the parable of the talents, Jesus commends those who grow what God has given them by earning a return on their investments. Thus, the law given to Moses should not be interpreted as prohibiting those engaged in Kingdom business from receiving a fair return on their investments.

Though the teachings and parables of Jesus provide ample opportunity to speak out against private property, there is no clear passage to this effect. In story after story, Jesus affirms the right of a landowner to collect a lease, the right of a son to inherit the property of his father, the right of a farmer to do with his wealth as he chooses, and the right of a nobleman to expect a return on his investments. While He denounces the unwise use of resources, Jesus affirms the ownership, control and use of private property.

Success of Capitalism

Many democratic capitalist systems have witnessed astounding success in raising the standard of living and wealth of nations, thereby blessing all the people materially. Indeed, of the 50 wealthiest economies in the world, only one has a socialist history (Slovenia, which is no longer socialist). The rest are nations that have been strongly committed to capitalism.[3]

The starkest comparative example might be observed in Germany. Before World War II, East Germany boasted a GDP per capita 7 percent higher than West Germany's. After the war, West Germany flourished under democratic capitalism and became an economic power. Under socialism, East Germany languished. When the two were reunified in 1990, West Germany's GDP per capita was 82 percent higher than East Germany's![4]

There is no doubt that capitalist economies are succeeding in providing increasing benefits. Society is being served through more effective treatments for disease, an ample food supply, and overall improved standards of living. A $5 digital watch contains more computing power than the largest corporation in the world could have afforded less than two generations ago. Even members of lower economic standing in the developed world can afford automobiles and televisions, aspirin and electricity—resources and products that Solomon could not have imagined—and their life expectancy today is far beyond that of the kings and queens who reigned in Europe several hundred years ago.

Three Connected Systems: Economic, Political and Moral-Cultural

Capitalism is an economic system, one of three components of a society's governance. The economic system cannot be separated from its two siblings, the political system and the moral-cultural system, which determine the rules of the game in a society. Douglass North, a secular economist, won a Nobel Prize for his work demonstrating that these rules, which he termed "institutions," have a strong effect on economic performance.[5] He showed that both the formal rules of the political system (constitutions, laws, regulations) and the informal rules of the moral-cultural system (morals, conventions, social norms) play a large role in economic outcomes. We would be unwise, therefore, to offer solutions that fail to address shortcomings in a nation's political or moral-cultural systems.

The three systems are intertwined, and the most effective outcome requires them to work in conjunction. The economic system of capitalism operates best in an environment of freedom, and the political system must support that. However, it does not follow that democracy is a necessary ingredient for successful capitalism. In Singapore, though elections are held, Lee Kuan Yew and his political party control the government to such a degree that it is essentially a benevolent dictatorship. But even while exercising tight political control, the government grants the economic freedom necessary for Singapore's capitalist system to flourish. Monaco is technically a monarchy, but economic freedom and a respect for property rights have yielded economic success. Although a democratic political system is not a requirement for successful capitalism, a stable government, a respect for property rights and a moral-cultural system aligned with Judeo-Christian values are essential.

While there is some support for exporting both capitalism and democracy to developing nations, very little attention is paid to the moral-cultural system that is necessary for them to thrive. Yet the moral-cultural arena is precisely where Christians have much to offer. "It is all well and good to teach economic principles that will benefit the developing world, but don't impose any specific moral system on it," the secularists preach. However, effective capitalism requires a moral system that nourishes certain values and virtues, and often these are lacking in the cultures of the developing world.

The absence of an accompanying morality to balance unbridled capitalism has yielded disastrous outcomes. Capitalist systems without moral underpinnings result in commerce that is unhealthy and unprincipled. These systems can lead to slave trade, such as that found in Africa and the Americas several hundred years ago.[6] They can lead to a business environment marked by corruption, such as that found in Eastern Europe. They can lead to abuse of workers, such as that found in many parts of Asia. Without a solid moral-cultural system that enhances trust in the economic system, capitalism will not truly thrive.

Capitalism and the Judeo-Christian Moral Authority

Every business school program acknowledges that company culture is an important factor in the success of a business. Any deficiencies in company culture must be remedied. However, there is a somewhat baffling reluctance to acknowledge that a nation's prevailing culture is an important factor in the success of a nation's business. Nevertheless, moral-cultural systems that are incompatible with successful capitalism must be addressed.

A nation's business practices can be characterized by three possible moral attitudes: immorality, amorality, or morality.[7] *Immoral* business is that which operates contrary to the established laws of God and the nation. Illegal drug trafficking, organized crime and child pornography fit this category of business activity. Fraud, violence, bribes and extortion are the byproducts of immorality. If not completely controlled by the forces of illegality, government agencies will work to punish or shut down immoral business activity. Even if the government does not step in, immoral business that violates a nation's laws must operate underground, outside the public marketplace. Therefore, immoral business provides no sustainable solution for a nation's economy.

Amorality is an attitude often found in modern Western business. Its mantra may be summed up as follows: maximize profits. While staying within the law, amoral business remains unconcerned with moral principles. The question is not "right or wrong?" but "legal or illegal?" The rule of law takes the place of morality. In many respects, the United States is adopting a standard of amorality, as the moral fabric behind the Constitution is replaced with more and more complex legislation. But laws cannot replace morality. "Show me the law," lawyers have said to me, "and I will show you a way to get around it."

Trust and loyalty are foreign concepts in an amoral system. Promises made to employees and customers can be broken if economic conditions make keeping them less profitable. The result is a cold, calculating, and bleak business environment in which employees find very little joy and customers operate in suspicion. Furthermore, where there is no trust there is a greater need for oversight, for legal checks and balances. This increases the transaction costs of doing business and puts the society at a distinct economic disadvantage. The number of laws being developed to regulate commerce in the United States is growing exponentially, all of which adds cost to the system and thereby reduces the economic value.

The third option is a business environment that operates within a *moral* standard. Values such as service, integrity and loyalty are observed not because they are mandated by the law (they are not) but because they are morally right. In this environment, the value of the individual is not solely equated with the individual's perceived contribution to the bottom line. This is an environment in which the human spirit thrives. Trust follows when other members of an economic system are known to operate under such a moral standard. Where there is full trust, lengthy contracts may be replaced by a handshake. There is less need for costly security measures that guarantee performance. In a moral business environment, transactions are simplified and the cost of doing business decreases. In short, a moral standard is a vital component of long-term successful capitalism.

Which Moral Standard?

Capitalism must be coupled with a culture of morality that acts as a counterbalance to immoral or amoral versions of the economic system. But what should be the basis of morality? That's not a trivial question. Former SEC Chairman John Shad offered to donate $20 million to Harvard Business School to establish an ethics program. He gave an initial $250,000 to the university and commissioned it to first define "ethics." Harvard's intellectuals could not come to any agreement on a definition, and the project was scrapped. Even with the prospect of a huge grant for an ethics program, they hit a dead end. In the university's prevailing atmosphere of philosophical relativism, a single source for ethics has no place. So the question arises, what should be the source of that moral standard? Here again, we will discuss three alternative sources: self-interest, a secular universal ethical code, or the revelation of a higher Judeo-Christian moral authority.[8]

Those who advocate the selection of a moral standard based on *self-interest* assert that the world of business rewards those who are perceived to operate morally. A reputation for honesty, fairness and quality is an economic asset that a company protects in its own self-interest. There is some truth to this, but the façade can quickly fade when the potential for greater economic interest lies in dishonesty or unfairness. Richard Whately, the nineteenth-century Anglican archbishop of Dublin said, "Honesty is the best policy; but he who is governed by that maxim is not an honest man."[9] An honest man is governed by the maxim "honesty is the *only* policy." The man who believes honesty is the best policy will abandon honesty as soon as it appears not to be the best policy. The famous case of the U.S. energy company Enron illustrates this well. The company touted its moral and ethical environment, but it soon became clear that self-interest was the ultimate source of that morality.[10] When self-interest in the form of enormous financial gain dictated it, Enron chose to follow a path that most people consider highly unethical.

Self-interest as the source for morality results in situational ethics that are guided by the degree of personal gain. When Israel had no king and respected no higher moral authority, people acted in self-interest, and "everyone did as he saw fit" (Judg. 17:6). In the end, self-interest is neither a robust enough nor a powerful enough source of moral authority.

Others seek to appeal to some *universal* morality that may be derived from the wisdom of the world's religious or ethical traditions. This approach finds much support in international institutions, and efforts to define a global ethic have been made by groups such as the Council of the Parliament of the World's Religions (1993) and the Interfaith Foundation (1994). Never mind the inherent difficulty in constructing such a code, the real problem with this approach lies in its inability to transform individuals into adherents of the moral standard. What will motivate people to internalize this universal morality? What will drive adoption of a universal ethic? While this approach recognizes the need for a moral norm based on transformed consciousness, it lacks any mechanism to achieve the necessary conversion of the heart.

The third source of moral standards, the *higher authority of God*, provides a robust moral culture. The revealed Word of God also has the power to transform man's consciousness. Followers of the Judeo-Christian faith choose loyalty, honesty and fairness not just because it is in their best interest to do so, but because they are ultimately accountable to the Almighty. When people turn to God as the source of moral wisdom, they avoid the trappings both of a changeable morality based on self-interest and of a universal morality to which they have no personal allegiance. Lord Brian Griffiths concluded that the Judeo-Christian faith "which sees business as a vocation or calling, so that a career in business is perceived as a life of service before God, is a most powerful source from which to establish, derive, and support absolute moral standards in business life."[11] Only a moral standard that subjects itself to the authority of God has lasting power.

The Law of God Written on the Hearts of Men
The United States was founded over 200 years ago on three small yet important documents: the Declaration of Independence, the Constitution, and the Bill of Rights. Those three documents reflect the values that were written on the hearts of the men who founded the country. John Adams, the second president of the United States, said it this way:

> We have no government armed with power capable of contending with human passions unbridled by morality and religion. Avarice, ambition, revenge, or gallantry would break the strongest cords of our Constitution as a whale goes through a net. *Our Constitution was made only for a moral and religious people. It is wholly inadequate to the government of any other.*[12]

Adams knew that the Constitution worked only because it governed a moral and religious people. The founding documents outlined biblical values and principles that were already ingrained in the society of the day, and those deeply held convictions were the building blocks for the nation.

The French Revolution took place about the same time as the American Revolution, and though the revolutionaries had similar goals, there was one significant difference. In spite of the motto *"Liberté! Égalité! Fraternité!"* the French did not share the same passion for personal righteousness and subjection to the authority of God. They sought to introduce a godless and humanistic government, and the result was vastly different from the American experience. "Instead of the liberty, justice, peace, happiness, and prosperity experienced in America, France suffered chaos and injustice as thousands of heads rolled under the sharp blade of the guillotine," notes W. Cleon Skousen.[13] Christian virtues were not part of the French revolutionaries' DNA, and the result was a nation not fashioned "under God."

Alexis de Tocqueville lived through the chaotic and bloody aftermath of the French Revolution. As a jurist, he was intrigued by the different society emerging in America. In 1831, he visited the United States to study its system of government and the culture of its people. De Tocqueville's observations were famously documented in his book *Democracy in America.*

"The sects [denominations] which exist in the United States are innumerable. They all differ in respect to the worship which is due from man to his Creator, but they all agree in respect to the duties which are due from man to man. Each sect adores the Deity in its own peculiar manner, but all the sects preach the same *moral law in the name of God.* . . . Moreover, almost all the sects of the United States are comprised within the great unity of Christianity, and Christian morality is everywhere the same. . . . There is no country in the whole world in which the Christian religion retains a greater influence over the souls of men than in America.[14]

De Tocqueville discovered that the key to understanding the success of American democracy and society was the Christian moral law held in the souls of men. "Thus whilst the law permits the Americans to do what they please, religion prevents them from conceiving, and forbids them to commit, what is rash or unjust," he noted.[15] Behind the three small founding documents was the law of God written on the hearts of American men and women.

While in America the Church-state separation was established to prohibit the state from interfering with the free exercise of religion, France's firewall between Church and state, called *laicité*, sought to protect the political sphere from the Church. Today, France is as committed as ever to secularism and to ridding the nation of religious influence. "Secularism is not negotiable," stated President Jacques Chirac. Secularism stands as the only acceptable religion in public life. In the process of sweeping the house clean of religion, liberties are being trampled. A recent law banning all religious symbols such as Muslim veils, Jewish skull caps and conspicuous Christian crosses from public schools was met with protest, most notably from Muslims who now make up 10 percent or more of the population. "Just as the house swept clean of a demon but not refilled with God will attract seven worse demons (Matt. 12:43-45), so too the slogans of liberty and tolerance cannot stand before the aggressive march of Islam," opined *World Magazine*'s Andree Seu.[16] Led by the creed that there are no absolutes and that all religions and cultures have equal value, secularism is leaving a dangerous vacuum in French society.

Adopting the Moral Standard

While socialism has fallen into disfavor and capitalism is carrying the day, the question before us is this: Will developing nations adopt a secular capitalism devoid of a higher moral authority or will they adopt a Judeo-Christian capitalism infused with the moral values of Scripture? Secularists are promoting either an amoral capitalism that is concerned only with laws and profits or a universal morality that lacks conviction. Neither one offers a mechanism for transformation of man's consciousness, for conversion of his heart.

The capitalism found in post-communist Russia is hardly considered a success. Its greatest shortcoming is that it lacks the necessary moral fabric. Between 1994 and 1999, illegal drug trafficking and economic crimes in the banking sector quadrupled, and by 2000 an estimated 80 percent of the nation's enterprises were offering protection money to racketeers. Corruption also runs rampant in the judicial and political systems. The country's wealth has been privatized into the hands of a few oligarchs. In the late 1990s, the seven wealthiest of them were thought to control 50 percent of Russia's economy. The adoption of capitalism devoid of a moral authority has left Russia in such a bleak economic situation that many are wishing for a return to communism![17]

De Tocqueville credited the success of the United States to the law of God written on the hearts of men:

> In the end, the state of the Union comes down to the character of the people. I sought for the greatness and genius of America in her commodious harbors, her ample rivers, and it was not there. I sought for it in the fertile fields, and boundless prairies, and it was not there. I sought it in her rich mines, and vast world commerce, and it was not there. Not until I went into the churches of America and heard her pulpits aflame with righteousness did I understand the secret of her genius and power.[18]

The power of God's moral authority over a person produces good character, and this is the only source of morality that yields true robust internalization of the virtuous life. Exporting capitalism alone is insufficient. It needs to be coupled with biblical values. In fact, those engaged in Kingdom business are presented with a wonderful opportunity to demonstrate in word and in deed how the ethic that leads to business success is found in the Bible. Christian principles and attitudes are the underlying values of successful capitalism. A person who adopts these virtues is brought closer to the ultimate transformation of adopting the Christian faith. Those in Kingdom business must not shy away from acknowledging the ultimate source of their principles. While it is good to produce business people who think honesty is the best policy, it is better to produce honest business people who operate with a sense of responsibility toward God.

Biblical Values of Successful Capitalism

Writing at the beginning of the twentieth century, Max Weber reflected back on the origins of the successful spirit of capitalism that he observed in parts of Europe and especially in the United States. Why, he asked, did capitalism thrive in certain regions? His conclusion was that the countries that had adopted predominantly Protestant values of vocation, hard work and personal piety experienced much better economic success than their neighbors who had similar resources and people groups. While in Catholic nations the pious served in the Church, in Protestant nations the spirit of personal piety was present in the marketplace. It was the internalization of biblical values and the emphasis on personal character that led to successful capitalism.[19]

Before setting out to write his popular book *The Seven Habits of Highly Successful People*, Stephen Covey surveyed the literature on success that has been published in the United States since its founding. He discovered that *character* was identified as the dominant success factor in the first 150 years. Benjamin Franklin and others promoted a character ethic that espoused virtues such as integrity, temperance, humility, courage and fidelity. In the past 50 years, Covey concluded, that character ethic has been replaced by a personality ethic. What is inside is deemed less important than what is outside. Success is now a function of dressing right, understanding corporate politics, speaking eloquently and excelling in social situations.

Covey's and other management books are popular today because they speak of character as the long-lost ingredient of successful capitalism. Rather than techniques or mental attitudes, biblical principles remain the underlying values of the character ethic.

Grover Cleveland, the twenty-second and twenty-fourth president of the United States, once noted, "The citizen is a better businessman if he is a Christian gentleman and, surely, business is not the less prosperous and successful if conducted on Christian principles." What are the biblical values of successful capitalism? Here are some of the more obvious ones that relate to personal character, interpersonal relationships and the performance of work.

FIGURE 1

Personal Character Values	Interpersonal Relationship Values	Performance Values
integrity	humility	service
honesty/truthfulness	service	excellence
loyalty/faithfulness	respect/dignity	value
trust	justice/fairness	quality
commitment/diligence	grace/compassion	
order/cleanliness	forgiveness	
hope	consideration	
	trust	
	accountability	
	interdependence	

Biblical Principles in Action

We have noted that successful capitalism starts with the Bible. But how do these biblical values affect the way business is conducted? How do biblical principles play out in the marketplace?

Honesty, fairness and integrity. Businesses that have a culture of honesty, fairness and integrity benefit from their reputation. Customers, partners and employees are drawn to them. If there is any doubt that a reputation for doing what is right has economic benefits, ask those who sell their products through eBay. Buyers are able to evaluate the service they receive and leave feedback on the transaction. If the seller has failed to deliver a product, inflated the description of a product, or shipped a product inappropriately, the buyer will leave negative feedback for all future potential buyers to see. If a product arrives as advertised and on time, positive feedback will result. Because they know buyers take this into account when bidding on their products, eBay sellers are extremely protective of their feedback rating, and they work feverishly to maintain and improve it.

Service. Effective capitalism is serving one's fellow man—who evaluates with his wallet how well he is being served. Goods and services must be helpful to the buyer, and the more value they represent, the more the buyer will be willing to pay. At Inmac, excellent service was a top priority. In the early days, we managed to fend off competition from larger companies by taking care of customers better than they did. We established the innovative practice of same-day shipping; our customers loved it and remained very loyal to Inmac. Serving others through useful products or helpful labor is at the core of successful business.

Grace and forgiveness. One of the reasons Silicon Valley is such a dynamic breeding ground for new ideas and ventures lies in the prevailing attitude toward failure. Rather than rejecting entrepreneurs whose ventures do not succeed, Silicon Valley has a remarkable sense of forgiveness and grace for those who courageously pursue a dream. People are seen as more valuable after a failure experience than before it. Contrast that with other regions of the country where a failure in one area will ruin a career. Grace feeds the entrepreneurial spirit by giving it the freedom to fail.

Humility, dignity and service. "Almost every executive . . . says the old command-and-control style of leadership no longer works," said David Bradford of Stanford's Graduate School of Business.[20] The management concept of servant leadership (or post-heroic leadership) is being touted in leading business schools, but it really dates back to the first-century example of Jesus. Simply put, it posits that the most effective means of relating to employees involves both an attitude of humble service and a recognition of others' gifting.

Bradford likes to tell the story of Henry Ford. Exasperated, Ford asked, "Why, when I want to hire a pair of hands, do I get an entire person?" The servant leader considers the whole person valuable and affirms his or her dignity and gifting. He seeks to utilize the person's full set of abilities. Instead of reinforcing the hierarchical structure of superiors and subordinates, Bradford says that the organization should think in terms of "senior partner" and "junior partner." Rather than functioning as a lone ranger who lords it over others, the servant leader should look for ways to serve and support other members of the group. Effective leadership is based not on position or academic degree but on service to and acceptance within the organization.

Excellence and quality. Other recent business trends have recognized biblical work performance values as the keys to success. In the book *In Search of Excellence,* Tom Peters and Robert Waterman describe the characteristics of companies dedicated to excellence. It is one of the most popular business books of all time.

Another success factor is quality, and thousands of organizations are making a commitment to Total Quality Management (TQM). As a member of General Douglas McArthur's staff charged with rebuilding post-war Japan, W. Edwards Deming has become synonymous with TQM. When Deming spoke to Japanese managers on quality control methods in 1950, "Made in Japan" meant anything but high quality. Deming advocated Quality Circles in which volunteer members were trained in statistics and teamwork. In the next decades, the commitment Japanese companies made to quality was evident. Automobile makers such as Toyota and Nissan found the quality of their products to be a competitive advantage over American brands. Today, the Deming Award is the most prestigious award for quality in Japan.[21]

Biblical Principles Redeeming Business

Though perhaps not out of personal faith, many educators and business people have identified certain moral principles that lead to successful business. However, the Christian in business can do even better. Going well beyond a basic moral code, he or she can redeem the marketplace through the power of the Holy Spirit. A business can truly become a venue for ministry in which others are served and in which real economic, physical and spiritual needs are met. Riverview Community Bank in Otsego, Minnesota, is doing just that.

"Is this the bank that prays with people?" asks the caller. "Yes, it is," replies Chuck Ripka, Senior Vice President of Riverview Community Bank. Chuck and several other Kingdom-focused business people founded the bank in March 2003. Eighteen years earlier while working at a furniture business, Chuck felt the Lord's leading to pray with a specific customer for the first time. Unknown to Chuck, the customer was going through a personal crisis. A little later he returned and bought a mattress. Through that incident God spoke to Chuck. "He showed me that I could do ministry and prosper in the marketplace at the same time," he says.

Prayer is now a daily, regular occurrence at the bank, and the results have been tremendous. Chuck himself prays with two or three people a day. During the bank's first 15 months of operation, 72 people became followers of Jesus, including customers, employees, family members, waitresses at nearby restaurants and others. Almost 60 individuals have experienced healings, some of them quite dramatic. Word has spread, and people have driven up to three hours to visit "the bank that prays with people."

Riverview Community Bank's 48 investors are not all Christians, but several times the bank's business plan explicitly notes a strategy and vision "to bring Christianity to the marketplace." Eschewing the notion that prayer and ministry belong only in the church or the home, the bank's leadership is following through on the vision of meeting people's economic, physical and spiritual needs in the marketplace. And they are establishing a successful business in the process. The bank set a goal in its business plan of $3.5 million in deposits by the end of its first quarter of operation. However, the first quarter's $20 million in deposits actually exceeded the projection for the entire first year! At the end of one year, the bank had deposits of $50 million, more than its five-year goal.

Seeking to live out Christian principles in dealing with customers, bank employees minister to the customers through excellent financial services, personal sincerity and love. "The attitude of management is that if a customer is struggling to make his payments on time, we are not going to send out the collectors, but we will call him to ask how we can pray for his situation," says Chuck Ripka. Riverview Community Bank is going beyond moral principles to bring the fruit of the Spirit to bear in the marketplace. (It is building spiritual capital, the subject of the next chapter.) The bank is redeeming business for the Lord. "I believe God is using the bank as a model for what He can do," Chuck concludes.[22]

Biblical Principles in Business Transforming a Nation

The biblical principles in business that are being rediscovered today were instrumental in the transformation of the business culture in London in the Middle Ages. The example of the Livery Companies illustrates the power of biblical principles in action. It is a story of how moral standards and mutual accountability can revolutionize a nation's business climate.[23]

With roots in the eleventh and twelfth centuries, Livery Companies are trade organizations that unite workers in various occupations from skinning to clothworking. King Edward III granted the first charters in the fourteenth century, and the original 12 Great Companies included the mercers (dry goods merchants), grocers, drapers, fishmongers and goldsmiths. (Several Livery Companies have also been formed in the twentieth century, including the Scientific Instrument Makers and the Air Pilots and Navigators.) The origins of the Livery Companies were as much religious as they were the protection and promotion of trade. The Livery Companies were closely linked to the Church, and court meetings were typically preceded by prayerful worship. They carried names such as "The Most Worshipful Company of Goldsmiths" and mottoes like "Praise God for all" (bakers) and "In God is all our hope" (plumbers).

At a time when dishonest scales and commerce were commonplace, the London Livery Companies were established to promote honest and excellent business practices. The charter of the Worshipful Company of Plumbers states that it is expressly intended to be "for the utility, advantage, and relief for the good and honest, and for the terror and correction of the evil, deceitful, and dishonest." The tenets of the Livery Companies were based upon Biblical principles, and every person who wanted to become a member had to agree to uphold them. Even today, every Freeman of the City of London (prerequisite to becoming a liveryman) receives a book titled *Rules for the Conduct of Life*, which outlines 36 biblical principles penned by the Lord Mayor of London in 1737. The timeless principles of the Livery Companies can be summed up as follows: energy and purpose through shared philosophies, integrity through shared values, excellence through shared example.[24]

The Livery Companies verified weights and measures and certified high standards of excellence and service in their trades. While those who engaged in honest trade benefited from the mutual accountability system they created, those who violated the ethical standards demanded by trade association membership often faced strict penalties. In fact, the term "baker's dozen" originated from the practice of including more bread as insurance against discipline from the Worshipful Company of Bakers.

Businesses that subjected themselves to these biblical principles were rewarded by the trust, loyalty and satisfaction of customers. Every participant in the marketplace sought to belong to a livery company. In due time, virtually every trade adopted the set of standards, and the Livery Companies became a central part of London life and government. By the fifteenth century, these trade associations elected the city's mayors and sheriffs from among their ranks. The Livery Companies prospered and set up schools and charitable arms. These trade associations have continued to this day and now number over one hundred.

"The essence of the commitment that a person makes in taking on the Livery," notes The Worshipful Company of Builders Merchants, "is that one will conduct one's own personal life and business or trade life to a given standard and that because, by so doing, one has no doubt obtained a certain affluence, one will share a portion of that affluence with those who are less fortunate, starting with those in one's own trade and then widening the circle to charities related to the environment in which that trade is conducted."[25] Biblical principles in business led to the transformation of the nation.

Christian Culture and Economic Development

A business environment characterized by heartfelt biblical morality will be far more successful than one that is characterized by dishonesty, disloyalty, distrust and disorder. We must realize that where these biblical values are not present, capitalism will fail to live up to its potential. In fact, the degree to which economic development can advance is directly related to the degree to which a culture that is compatible with successful capitalism is adopted. This is the reason the issue of culture is so critical to the quest for economic improvement. Societies marked by chaos, dishonesty, poor work ethics or distrust need cultural reforms to pave the way for better commerce. As illustrated by the crippling corruption in Russia and elsewhere, promoting capitalism alone without the moral-cultural values necessary for its success is like building a house on sand.

It is not by chance that democratic capitalism flourished first and foremost in countries with a strong Judeo-Christian worldview. Scriptural principles include the equality of each person before the law, the sanctity of property rights, the ethical demand to be fair and compassionate employers, the injunction to work diligently and honestly, the grace to undertake new endeavors, and a hope for the future. In short, the cultures that experience business success are those infused with these biblical values.

As noted earlier, Max Weber attributed the economic success of Protestant nations to a personal piety and a sense of vocational calling not found in other countries. Regarding the United States, de Tocqueville is said to have put it this way more than 150 years ago: "America is great because America is good. If America ever ceases to be good it will cease to be great."[26]

Even today, we see the relationship Weber observed between faith and the work ethic. Oxford fellow Niall Ferguson notes that "the experience of Western Europe over the past quarter-century offers an unexpected confirmation of [Weber's thesis]. To put it bluntly, we are witnessing the decline and fall of the Protestant work ethic in Europe."[27] At the same time that God became less important to Europeans, and especially to those who were once predominantly Protestant, there was a dramatic decline in working hours. There has been no corresponding decline in the United States, where a much higher proportion of the population considers God to be very important. Ferguson observes today the correlation between an increasingly work-shy population in Europe and Godlessness on that continent.[28]

Almost every economically developed nation has a history steeped in Judeo-Christian culture. With the exception of Japan and Hong Kong (a long-time British protectorate), every nation at the top of the GDP-per-capita list has a long Christian tradition. Interestingly, it has been observed that the Japanese Shinto-Buddhist culture shares some key values with Christians that lead to business success. Honesty, trust, commitment and order are Japanese cultural traits that are highly important to successful capitalism. In key aspects, Japan's moral-cultural fabric includes biblical values and provides confirmation of the connection between culture and economic development. It is rather astounding to note that virtually every one of the most developed nations has derived its culture from a Judeo-Christian tradition. No wonder Jiang Zemin said that he would make Christianity the official religion of China!

Conclusion

Developing nations are turning toward capitalism as the answer to economic problems. The question is whether they will adopt a secular capitalism that lacks a robust morality or a Judeo-Christian capitalism that is infused with the moral values of Scripture. Exporting capitalism alone is not the best solution. Biblical principles are the foundational values of successful capitalism, and there exists a direct correlation between economic prosperity and the presence of biblical principles within a culture. Not all Christians who are involved in economic development see the connection between the promotion of commerce and the promotion of a biblical morality. However, in order for an economy to be truly blessed, Judeo-Christian virtues must be ingrained in the society's culture.

Biblical principles lead to successful capitalism. But how does that happen? How does a culture ingrained with biblical values achieve more business success? How does a developing nation that lacks a Judeo-Christian history build the cultural strengths needed for successful capitalism? We will explore this next using a concept called *spiritual capital*— the key to economic growth.

CHAPTER 5

SPIRITUAL CAPITAL

A friend of mine is a small businessman who distributes phone cards to convenience stores in the United States. A Christian, he is known for his honest dealings in a field that is sometimes served by people who do not have the same moral values. A number of his customers are not from the culture of the United States and do not ascribe to his Christian values. In casual conversations, these customers have told him that they laugh at our culture because it allows them to acquire businesses but cheat on their records and avoid paying taxes. If they are caught cheating, they excuse it as an accounting mistake, and, amazingly, their explanation is accepted.

The convenience store owners mentioned that they could purchase the phone cards from immigrants from their own culture. So my friend

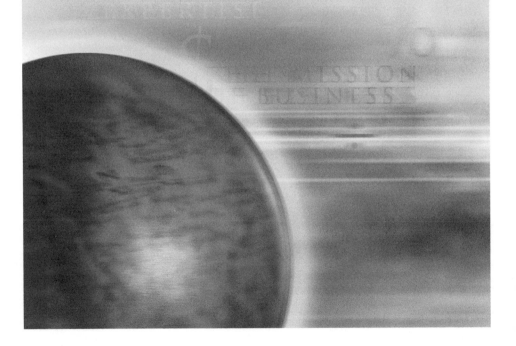

asked why they buy the cards from him. "You are a Christian, an honest person. We know we can trust you," was their immediate and unhesitating answer. "We would rather buy from you at a little extra cost and know we are not being cheated than to buy from someone who may come from our own country but who we don't trust." Although these customers value my friend's honest dealings and even acknowledge that they won't do business with people like themselves, they see no reason to be honest in their own business dealings.

What Is Spiritual Capital?

My friend's honest dealings yielded a higher price than his competition could capture. The supply and demand analysis of classic economics, which assumes that buyers will always choose the lowest price offered, cannot explain this. While game theory has been used recently to attempt to provide an explanation, classic economists cannot measure what factors contribute to deviations from their basic assumption about price and demand. And what can't be measured can't be studied.

In addition to the combination of item, quantity and price measured by economists, it is often the intangible or interpersonal aspects of the transaction that generate further economic value to the buyer. (In the business world, we use terms such as "goodwill" in accounting and "brand preference" in marketing to describe this surplus value.) While these aspects add to the value of the transaction, honesty and trust reduce the need for costly oversight and lower the transaction costs of doing business; this, too, generates economic value.

Why would someone pay more than the lowest price available? Several reasons come to mind. An established personal relationship with another person might lead to a preference for doing business with that person. Trust in someone's honesty might result in a willingness to pay a premium. Caring, heartfelt, selfless service or a commitment to consistent quality might make customers prefer a particular business or partner, which serves to lower the cost of doing business. Friendship, trust, honesty, love, service, commitment and quality—these are all biblical principles that constitute value. When these principles emanate from a heartfelt conviction, they amount to *spiritual capital*.

The concept of spiritual capital explains why there is a relationship between economic prosperity and the pervasiveness of biblical values in the culture. Think of spiritual capital as the faith, trust and commitment that others will do what is right—not only what is right in their own eyes or what benefits them the most, but what is right in the eyes of God. Showing integrity, being accountable and honest, offering hope, being loyal and trustworthy, loving and encouraging others, exhibiting good stewardship, being fair, creating order and serving others—these are not, for the most part, covered by the laws of the land. We have no legal compulsion to love others, exhibit good stewardship, create order or serve each other. There is no legal compulsion to encourage one another to pursue new ventures in hope and faith, trusting that God will go before us.

Those who build spiritual capital do what is right and do it to the best of their ability because they are doing their work "as unto the Lord." They perform to God's standard rather than to society's standard. Quality, service and guarantees are not based on an external scale that might yield a favorable comparison to someone else's performance. Instead, they are based on work that comes out of one's giftedness and the desire to do one's best, regardless of the competition or the level of expectation by one customer or another.

How often have you heard that personalized service is not the same as it used to be? Sure, competition has produced some improvements, such as 24-hour delivery and Internet ordering. But it seems rare and extraordinary when someone goes out of his way to provide the best. Often, people seem less caring about the quality of their work, instead simply seeking to meet or slightly exceed the minimal baseline requirements. As a result, rules are codified and applied with impersonal strictness. Consumers are often out of luck if defective items are not returned within 30 days, regardless of the particular issue or circumstance. Rules are replacing the personal morality that comes from faith.

How the Spiritual Capital Account Grows

If spiritual capital is the faith, trust and commitment that we and others will do what is right, it then follows that spiritual capital can increase or decrease based on personal experiences.

Imagine that there is a spiritual capital account that accrues to the individual and to the country. Like a bank account, it can grow or shrink due to deposits to or withdrawals from the account. The spiritual capital currency that is deposited (or withdrawn) is the exercise (or lack of exercise) of biblical principles: integrity, accountability, honesty, hope, love, trust, stewardship, fairness, order, loyalty, service, and so forth. For example, if one sells something with true weights and measures, then he has completed an honest transaction and has added spiritual capital to his and the nation's account. However, if one fails to fulfill his commitment to replace any defective products he sells, then he has proven untrustworthy and dishonest and has withdrawn spiritual capital from his and the nation's account.

Bill Child is chairman of R. C. Willey Home Furnishings. A devout Mormon, Child built R. C. Willey from a single 600-square-foot store into the biggest U.S. furniture retailer west of the Mississippi. A large, attractive product offering of appliances, electronics, and furniture certainly contributed to the growth, but Child says the company's reputation is its most valuable asset. He has spent years building R. C. Willey's spiritual capital, and he knows that is the reason for his success. His 2,000 employees are instructed to be perfectly honest, even when masking the truth might appear to influence a customer toward a purchase. He stands behind every product, accepting returns without questions.

R. C. Willey once sold thousands of product warranties to an insurance company that subsequently went bankrupt. Recognizing that the company needed to honor its commitments to customers, Child stood behind the warranties even though it cost the company more than $1.5 million. Other retailers affected by the bankrupt insurer informed customers that the warranties could no longer be honored. "We just felt it was the morally right thing to do," said Child.[1] R. C. Willey's long history of adding to the company's spiritual capital account has led to its economic success.

A Nation's Spiritual Capital Reserve

When people in the marketplace constantly do what is right, the nation's spiritual capital account grows, and there is much goodwill and trust in the general honesty of the system. The result is a healthy business climate in which goods and services are freely exchanged with little distrust or perceived risk. A nation that demonstrates a long pattern of being truthful, of following the rule of law, and of treating others with fairness builds up a huge reserve of spiritual capital. In the United States, the founders and citizens set the country on a path that resulted in much spiritual capital accruing to the nation's account. As a result, when corrupt and dishonest practices at corporations like Enron and Global Crossings were recently exposed, an overall trust in the system remained. These companies took from the nation's spiritual capital, but they didn't bankrupt the account.

In Scripture, God promises to heal the land if His people turn from their wicked ways and in humility seek Him (see 2 Chron. 7:14). The law of spiritual capital applies to all people whether they are operating in faith or not. God will bless the just and the unjust alike for the sake of the righteous. Jesus said, "He causes his sun to rise on the evil and the good, and sends rain on the righteous and the unrighteous" (Matt. 5:45; see also Isa. 55:10,11). As witnessed in the experience of my phone-card-distributing friend, sometimes the unjust live off the spiritual capital deposits of the just. They cut corners and draw down spiritual capital for the sake of potential financial gain. They enjoy the environment of trust developed through the spiritual capital account.

While I have only anecdotal evidence for this, it seems that once the level of a nation's spiritual capital reaches a state of depletion, its economic system fails. At some point, the capital base becomes so eroded that the economic system crumbles under its own weight and lack of fundamental support. The United States is not impervious to this problem, and arguably the West is now living off spiritual capital amassed in previous eras. If not checked, corrupt and heartless business practices could erode the spiritual capital reserve of the West.

Spiritual Capital in Developing Nations

In most developing nations, the situation is much more critical. Most of these nations have little or no reserves in their spiritual capital accounts, and often a lack of integrity in business is pervasive. They have neither a history of consistent integrity in commerce nor the necessary business practices and institutions to grow their spiritual capital.

In some countries, cultural characteristics mark this lack of spiritual capital. Harold Caballeros, pastor of Iglesia El Shaddai in Guatemala City, Guatemala, notes that the Spanish language has no simple words for some important concepts. For example, there is simply no translation to describe "procrastination" (or the absence thereof), and it takes two or three words to express the meaning of the words "commitment," "accountability" and "compromise"—these are spiritual capital words!

In some developing nations, the low level of spiritual capital means that simply buying and selling is a big deal. Buying on credit or advance payment is out of the question, and the only way two parties will conduct a transaction is by exchanging cash and goods at the same time. Sometimes, spiritual capital is so low that even the currency is not trusted, and the result is a barter-only economy in which goods are traded for other goods.[2] That was essentially the case in the Weimar Republic (1920s Germany) when hyperinflation made the currency worthless. The economic situation was so bad that people pushed wheelbarrows full of paper money to buy bread. Workers insisted on being paid twice a day and given an hour break to spend their wages before they devalued more. We see barter-only economies in some African nations today. The currency has become worthless in Congo, which is saddled with an insurmountable debt thanks to corrupt rulers who stole funds lent by international organizations. The country has reverted to a system of barter in which business transactions are stifled.

Most developing nations are trying to build their economies with very little spiritual capital, and they lack the business practices and institutions necessary to grow that capital. In these situations, people who draw on the nation's spiritual capital account can bankrupt it. After the fall of communism, Western corporations rushed into the former Soviet Union, attracted to cheap labor, an educated workforce, and a large market. However, many were stung by corruption and lost millions of dollars in the process. Russia is not an isolated case. Companies have encountered similar situations in China and other emerging economies.

"Most have been dismayed by the adverse business environment fostered by corruption," observed Askold Krushelnycky, a British-born journalist to Eastern Europe. "Many western firms and investors have withdrawn or reduced their activities because they are fed up with becoming the targets of corrupt officials demanding bribes, of being cheated by corrupt businessmen, of being at the mercy of a corrupt legal system. . . . In sum, corruption corrodes a society. When nepotism replaces merit, when cunning and cheating replace trust and honesty, when force and murder triumph over the law and a sense of decency—then the threads binding together a civil society are weakened and eventually destroyed."[3] A nation that has little or no spiritual capital reserve runs the risk of bankrupting the account and freezing the nation's economy.

Even within a country, an individual business or market can suffer the economic consequences of drawing down more spiritual capital than it has. Several years ago, a friend invested in a small public company whose managers turned out to be corrupt. They misled investors by fraudulently claiming to own certain assets. It was the first small-cap stock my friend had owned, and the negative experience soured him from venturing into other small-cap investments. Now, there are certainly many small-cap companies that are run by honest management, but for my friend, it took only one experience with a crooked company to bankrupt that market's spiritual capital account for him. One corrupt business ruined it for all others, honest or not.

Institutionalizing Spiritual Capital

If most developing nations are starting with very little spiritual capital, how do they build the necessary infrastructure for economic development? Simply put, the infrastructure is built from the bottom up, one businessperson at a time. Let's say there are five people who wish to trade with each other. They operate on a shared set of principles derived from their faith. Because of their shared deep-seated beliefs, they work well together. Eventually, there is a need to codify the established rules of engagement in some way for others who wish to do business with this group. In other words, they institutionalize their spiritual capital. These institutions form the basis for successful commerce and economic growth. The Livery Companies in the previous chapter provides a wonderful example of institutionalizing spiritual capital. When the London merchants agreed to deal honestly and to be accountable to each other, they laid the foundation for what Douglass North calls institutions, which codify the heartfelt beliefs of the participants.

Leges Sine Moribus Vanae

There is a danger in seeking to transition a developing nation to a capitalist system without first a clear understanding of why it worked in the West. In the West, it was not the laws of the land, the structure of capitalism or the rules of capitalism that led to its success. The system worked because the laws of God were written on the hearts of men and women. It worked because biblical principles were ingrained into the collective DNA of the society. It worked because it started with both a large initial deposit of spiritual capital and a strong set of biblical values to grow the account.

The University of Pennsylvania, founded by Benjamin Franklin in 1740, has the following motto: *Leges sine moribus vanae*, "Laws without morals are useless." That was the belief of Franklin, Adams and the other founding fathers of the United States. They believed that the only way a nation could have a pervasive morality was if that morality originated in a power greater than the nation, that is, in a personal transcendent God. Without a morality that is written on the heart of mankind, laws that are written on paper are useless.

In the case of Russia, we have in our present age a stunning example of an attempt to export capitalist ideas without addressing the deficiency in the hearts of the people. Russian analyst Ajay Goyal noted that after more than 10 years of transitioning to Western-style business, 80 percent of Russia's businesses are in private hands. Thousands of foreign corporations have opened offices in Moscow alone. Top consultants and auditors from the West have exported the best of business to Russia. Auditing and law firms have organized training courses and seminars costing millions of dollars in order to lend direction on conducting business in a free market. "Why, then, is capitalist Russia still so corrupt?" asked Goyal. "Because western capital has not been able to bring one key ingredient of business to Russia—the honor that comes with integrity."[4]

Kingdom business professionals are uniquely qualified to speak about integrity in business, and we would be remiss to repeat the mistake of focusing on transforming economic systems without paying attention to the requisite underlying moral and spiritual transformation that is needed. We are also uniquely equipped through the Holy Spirit and the power of the gospel to help a nation develop the spiritual capital that leads to true blessings on the nation.

Ultimate Inadequacy of Moral Capital

What if a nation simply adopted moral ways without spiritual transformation? Can't we just dispense with the Christian faith and advocate correct behavior instead? In essence, this is encouraging the development of what might be called moral capital, adopting some of God's moral laws without achieving the spiritual transformation that yields spiritual capital. Moral capital produces moral outcomes, but ultimately it is an inadequate subset of spiritual capital. Spiritual capital goes beyond moral capital to include hope, love, commitment and faith. It only comes from God's Spirit transforming the spirit of man.

Moral capital is merely a shadow of spiritual capital. Often captured in laws and rules, moral capital is derived from spiritual capital that historically stresses right and wrong. The usual pattern seems to be that a spiritual foundation that builds spiritual capital leads to traditions and culture. These residual values, held by people without a spiritual foundation, form the society's moral capital. It can endure for some time, even when those who embody the spiritual foundation are dead. With moral capital, the compulsion to act a certain way stems from economic and legal considerations rather than from a commitment to God's precepts. For example, the motivation for honesty, quality and service is usually economic benefit rather than any notion of doing what is right, blessing others and honoring God.

While a focus on moral capital may produce some desirable results, it ultimately sells developing nations short of the true blessing they could experience. There are several reasons for this. First, moral capital needs a spiritual capital or "tradition" base. Moral capital usually evolves from spiritual capital or tradition, and it is unlikely to find fertile ground in a nation that does not have a Christian tradition. On what basis should a nation adopt a new set of moral principles that are foreign to its culture? Unless the culture's DNA is predisposed to the moral capital that can develop the required Judeo-Christian institutions, there is no foundation on which moral capital can grow. (I believe that the countries so predisposed have largely developed those institutions already. The remaining nations more than likely do not have the necessary cultural DNA to develop the moral capital that leads to economic success.) The approach that seeks to instill a set of beliefs that produces moral outcomes without spiritual transformation is unlikely to work and is more difficult than the approach that seeks to build spiritual capital.

Second, those who focus on moral capital through legally correct behavior are advocating nothing less than the amorality discussed in the previous chapter. In an amoral system, the focus is on what is legal rather than on what is right. The rule of law replaces morality. But in an amoral system that concerns itself only with establishing and enforcing laws, participants do not really trust each other. An amoral system creates a cold, calculating and bleak business environment in which love, faithfulness and respect have no solid ground on which to stand. In short, laws written on the hearts on men and women are more effective than laws written on official documents.

The third reason a focus on moral capital is insufficient is that, unplugged from the Source, it erodes. As a residual vestige of spiritual capital, moral capital consists of values and beliefs derived from tradition rather than from the Holy Spirit's core transformation. Therefore, it is like unplugging a society from the power supply and having it run on battery power. Moral capital may maintain order in society for a while, but it will run down.

Some emphasize proper economic incentives rather than spiritual capital as the primary factor leading to economic development. Those who focus on simply providing an environment with proper economic incentives point to the significant and recent reforms in Chile that have brought a burst of economic growth.[5] But while the right incentives are certainly necessary, real development and transformation appear to require a culture that builds spiritual capital. The evidence seems to indicate that Chile, as a Christian nation, was already predisposed to a fundamental Christian belief system. According to Transparency International's 2003 Corruption Perceptions Index, Chile is by far the least corrupt nation in South and Central America. Worldwide, it ranks right behind the United States and immediately ahead of Israel, Japan and France. It seems that cultural conditions in Chile contributed greatly to the successful response to economic incentives. Proper economic incentives are always important, but they are most effective in a culture that embraces biblical values and builds spiritual capital.

The true model of serving and relating to one's fellow man comes from heaven. There will be at best a parroting of what really worked in the West unless there is a clear understanding and internalization of the principles that led to its success. There must be ownership of the meaning behind the words. Forgive the analogy, but macaw parrots can learn hundreds of words, and modern technology has succeeded in teaching robots a fairly large vocabulary, but neither the macaw nor the robot really understands what the words mean. True internalization of the concepts at the core level is necessary in the long run to build a strong and blessed nation.

Blessing a Nation: Why Faith Works

Scripture promises blessings on a nation that is obedient:

If you fully obey the Lord your God and carefully follow all his commands I give you today, the Lord your God will set you high above all the nations on earth. All these blessings will come upon you and accompany you if you obey the Lord your God:

You will be blessed in the city and blessed in the country.

The fruit of your womb will be blessed, and the crops of your land and the young of your livestock—the calves of your herds and the lambs of your flocks.

Your basket and your kneading trough will be blessed. You will be blessed when you come in and blessed when you go out (Deut. 28:1-6).

God wishes that His people keep all His commands always "so that it might go well with them and their children forever" (Deut. 5:29) and so that other nations will recognize the wisdom and understanding of the commands and the root of the blessings (see Deut. 4:5-8). God promises a multitude of blessings to a nation that follows His commands. But there is also a corollary to this. Right after the list of blessings, a parallel section describes the curses that befall a nation that fails to obey the Lord (see Deut. 28:15-19).

While the text in Deuteronomy is very specific about what God expects from the people of Israel, and indeed, from any nation that seeks to be blessed, God also exhibits mercy and grace. He recognizes that there is sin in the world and that all men will fail to reach perfection on Earth. As the Israelites ebbed and flowed in their relationship with God, we can correlate the spiritual life of the nation with its physical well-being. When the nation walked away from God, things did not go well for the people politically or materially. Individuals may have prospered, but the nation as a whole did not succeed in times when the people were not walking with their God.

Does a nation need to be wholly Christian to experience blessings? The answer is no. God has created physical laws and values that are also at work. A nation does not have to be Christian to receive economic blessings, but it does need to respect those laws and values. A case in point is Japan, a nation that is less than two percent Christian but embraces certain economic Judeo-Christian laws and values in its culture. However, because of the lack of spiritual transformation, the

Japanese have not experienced the fullness of God's blessings. Transformation needs to take place in all areas of life.

In Guatemala, 49 percent of the population considers itself evangelical.[6] However, while many Guatemalans have experienced spiritual transformation, transformation of their business life is what is needed. The country continues to be a developing nation that experiences limited progress precisely because many biblical values have not been fully internalized in the culture and economy. In his MBA thesis, Guatemalan pastor Harold Caballeros studied the influence of Korean Christians who came to his country to establish textile factories. The Guatemalan culture had not emphasized principles like savings, cleanliness, punctuality and quality, but that changed when Korean managers exhibited and taught these virtues. Caballeros observed a marked economic improvement in the communities whose culture was influenced by the Korean believers.[7] Though it is perhaps the most "Christianized" nation, Guatemala retains many cultural attitudes that run contrary to biblical values. Thus it fails to experience the fullness of God's blessings.

Because there is sin in the world, it is doubtful that any nation, even a fully Christian nation, will receive the fullness of the rich blessings God has in store for it. Jesus said, "You will always have the poor among you" (John 12:8). Short of His return, that is the condition of our fallen world. It would be unreasonable to state that the United States was ever the pinnacle of virtue. Still, as the United States has looked toward God throughout its history, He has blessed the nation. In contrast, as America has become increasingly less Christian at its core and experiences greater lawlessness or rebellion to God's laws, the nation has enacted more laws. Today, new legislation grows annually (yet, ways around the laws have developed just as fast—if not faster).

At a national level, we can see a link between the material blessings of God and the spiritual condition of the people. This link is not politically correct, but it is fundamental to the development of long-term economic welfare of the people. God's blessings involve both restoration from trespasses and guidance in progress. Grace and mercy provide defensive cover, while love provides offensive strength. In our times of failure, we need the merciful forgiveness of God to give us a new start.

God continually picks up the believer, dusts him off and, with grace, starts him anew on his journey. The love of God frees us from the chains of sin and allows us to move ahead, introducing transformation and opportunity to others.

God's Blessings: Moral Capital Provides Defense Only

The analogy of an athletic team is helpful in explaining God's blessings in terms of moral capital and spiritual capital. An athletic team needs both an offense and a defense to succeed. Moral capital provides a defense—but not an offense. Without an offense, the world's best defensive team will not win. Spiritual capital provides both a defensive and an offensive mechanism.

A system that relies on rules and laws may result in moral capital, but it is only a defensive system. Most of the moral code tends to focus on what is illegal, what cannot be done. It sets the lower boundary on what behavior is acceptable. While it sometimes includes traditions that may have positive aspects, these traditions do not go as far as the gospel does in teaching a proactive and offensive attitude of readily going above and beyond the moral code. The moral code merely holds people to a minimum requirement, expecting nothing more.

For example, hospitality is a well-known trait of those in the Middle East. Guests can be sure of being well-fed and well-treated; nothing will be lacking to the extent their host can provide it. But this incredible hospitality is based on tradition. One must provide this hospitality or suffer lack of respect in the community. Note the negative aspect: The price of failing to show such hospitality is lost respect. This is essentially a defensive posture. The motivation is a fear of negative consequences rather than love for the guest. Jesus holds us to a higher standard. The gospel's idea of love and motivation for hospitality goes much further.

The Palestinian refugee situation is another case in which this limited notion of hospitality can be seen. During the creation of the state of Israel, there was much unrest and upheaval in the Arab world. Some Arabs in the region feared the Israelis and fled, while others left due to warnings they received of their possible death during the impending Arab annihilation of the Israelis. Whatever the reason, 450,000 people became unsettled at that time. Decades later, many Arabs, most notably the Palestinians, still live in refugee camps. While the United Nations and others have spent millions of dollars to help these refugees, there has been little progress for them. Limited help has come from their Arab brethren, who have hesitated to welcome them. The Muslim culture has no set of spiritual values that obligates them to care for their refugee brethren. By contrast, during the same period and at no small expense, Israel has welcomed millions of Jewish refugees coming out of Europe and Russia. The Jewish people have done this because their culture (from which the Christian culture has grown) was founded on highly motivating spiritual values: love God with your whole being and love your neighbor as yourself. Where this kind of love is lacking, there exists a vacuum that leaves a spiritual capital deficit.

Moral capital provides a good defense, but it ties us to a limited vision—the law and a system of values that do not take the offensive. It is captured in a system of laws that protect rights, set rules for transactions, and deal with aspects of operating around our neighbor. But moral capital only constitutes a fraction of the blessing.

God's Blessings: Spiritual Capital Provides Offense and Defense

Spiritual capital is broader than moral capital and includes a number of biblical concepts not covered by a nation's laws: showing integrity, being accountable, being honest, offering hope, loving others, encouraging one another, being trustworthy, exhibiting good stewardship, being fair, creating order, being loyal and serving others. As I said at the beginning of this chapter, there is no legal compulsion to exercise most of these. Exercising these virtues is an offensive action that exceeds the bounds set by a moral code of laws. Those who are spiritually transformed by the gospel of Christ pursue these virtues not because they are included in man's laws (for the most part, they are not) but because they reflect God's precepts and character. That is especially the case with love. "We love because He first loved us" (1 John 4:19).

Love is the offensive strength of spiritual capital. Love is not restricted to a set of do's and don'ts. It reaches out, without limitations, offering assistance to anyone, no matter what the cost. "Love compels us to serve a cause greater than our own self-interest," said U.S. President George W. Bush.[8] Love causes us to give when others do not see the value in the giving. Love causes us to sacrifice above and beyond what is comfortable and moral. Love causes us to do the extraordinary and to go beyond cultural and traditional boundaries.

For example, in 2000, civil strife erupted in Fiji between the Indians and the native Fijians, each of whom make up about half the population. Many native Christians went to the homes of Indian Hindus and offered to protect them from the rioting and looting Fijians, who saw the Indians as outsiders. These Christians were prepared to pay the price for people who were of a very different faith. It was an act of love that went well beyond what moral capital would dictate through the laws of the land. It was a love motivated by the spiritual transformation of the gospel.

While moral capital provides a defense against immorality, spiritual capital goes well beyond the minimum standards of the moral laws, allowing people to put faith in institutions, for the good of all. Love takes the idea of success and asks why others can't enjoy it as well. Spiritual capital calls people to pass on physical and spiritual blessings by bringing peace, providing for fundamental needs and loving others we do not know. As people surpass their traditions and reach out to help others, the nation begins to be blessed. The blessings include the following societal benefits: prosperity, loving one's neighbor, trusting others, providing for others, and feeling compelled to help those who are less fortunate.

Without Christ, a nation is forced to rely on a defensive strategy: moral capital. While helpful, it will not take the nation to the heights of blessings God has in mind for it.

Kingdom Business and Spiritual Capital

While primitive economies are filled with microenterprises and small businesses, advanced economies involve more sophisticated organizational structures and business transactions. These generally require that people who do not have lengthy personal relationships trust each other enough to do what is right. In other words, they require spiritual capital. This is what allows people who are less familiar with each other to enter into the types of larger business relationships that characterize a developed economy.

In the West, we might take this business environment for granted. But the spiritual capital necessary to advance the economy simply does not exist in many developing nations. Economist Timur Kuran notes that in Muslim countries, specific characteristics of the prevalent culture have caused those countries to fall behind economically.[9] While not all Muslim countries follow Islamic law (some are more secular), cultures are still influenced by tenets of the dominant religion. Islamic law spells out exactly how partnerships and inheritances must be structured. Partnerships are to be between individuals only, and only an individual, rather than the partnership, has legal rights. There is no allowance for the modern corporation, an entity with legal rights separate from those of its individual members. Islamic law also dictates the proportion of a person's assets that must go to each heir, and to be equitable, inheritances must be paid out in currency. Thus, when a partner dies, the partnership must be liquidated. Obviously, this impacts the duration of the partnership, the nature of the partnership, and the size to which the partnership is willing to grow. A partnership with more members has greater complexity and shorter longevity.

Imagine how difficult it is in this environment to build a long-term illiquid-asset-based company, such as those needed to develop the infrastructure in a nation—telephone companies, power companies, construction companies. In fact, most of the infrastructure development work is done by foreigners or by state-owned agencies. As a result, the wealth leaves the nation, or in the case of government activity, it does not add as much to the wealth of the nation as it could.

Guided by Islamic partnership and inheritance laws, Middle Eastern commercial enterprises historically have remained small and ephemeral. "The upshot is that European enterprises grew larger than those of the Islamic world," Kuran summarized. "Moreover, while ever larger enterprises propelled further organizational transformations in

Europe, persistently small enterprises inhibited economic modernization in the Middle East."[10] These aspects of Islamic law constitute only one of many cultural barriers around the world that are inhibiting economic development. In order to be successful, emerging economies everywhere need cultural transformations that result in spiritual capital growth.

Building Spiritual Capital: The Transforming Power of the Gospel

Spiritual capital is the foundation for successful commerce, and Kingdom business professionals must equip the nations with the life-changing means of growing their spiritual capital account. We short-change a nation if we introduce laws that facilitate commerce and teach principles of accounting and yet fail to equip the nation with the means to establish a spiritual capital base on which to build its economy. Without the integrity, morality and love that comes from the Spirit of God transforming the hearts of men and women, nations will fall short of God's ultimate blessing.

Not all Christian-based groups involved in economic development see the connection between their work and the development of spiritual capital. Some are engaged in economic development (primarily through microenterprise development) yet do not present the gospel in the process. In some locations, these organizations offer funding to aspiring microenterprises, but they have few or no Christians on staff. Any rules and codes they impart do nothing to alter a person's inner constitution. They are not transformational. This lack of transformational change to an entrepreneur's core spiritual DNA tends to yield the amoral business practices described in the previous chapter. Unless written on the heart, rules and laws are not sufficient to act as a restraint. They are also insufficient to propel people to act in love.

Failure to bring the gospel is helpful neither to the individual nor to the nation. It may well lead the nation down the wrong path, one in which spiritual capital cannot accrue. If economic development is attempted without teaching both the gospel and the importance of developing spiritual capital, whether a person fails or succeeds economically, he or she will not improve or bless the nation. There will be no development of spiritual capital from that person's business dealings.

Say there is a villager who buys wheat by the sack and sells it by the quart, but he cheats his customer. If there is no alternate vendor, the customer may return, and the villager does well financially. However, the result is ill will and a loss of spiritual capital, and the nation fails to learn the value of honest weights and measures. There is an immediate economic penalty as well, since transactional costs are higher where there is low spiritual capital. For example, the other villagers may need to buy their own scales and conduct their own measurements in order to counter the cheating seller. In the long run, the lack of spiritual capital makes for an unhealthy and destructive business environment, and the nation, including the dishonest villager, will suffer. We see this today in many African states where a low level of trust has held back many economies.

Jesus' parable about the wise and foolish builders (see Matt. 7:24-27) is particularly instructive here. The wise man builds his house on the rock. The foolish man builds his house on sand. Business principles, technical training and start-up funding are just the walls, doors and roof of business. The transforming gospel of Jesus and the ultimate authority of God are the rock foundation. The businessperson must be committed to pleasing Jesus and doing what is right or his business will be built on sand. If these rock principles are not in place, they will not support the business structure in times of trouble. When the economic storms of life come, the uncommitted businessperson will revert back to what he fundamentally believes.

The gospel is an important component of developing an economy and blessing the nation through Kingdom business. Only the Holy Spirit has the power to transform the hearts of men and women. Only the gospel can work at the core level and alter the collective DNA of a society. Only the gospel can ingrain the biblical values that lead to spiritual capital accumulation and successful business. Only the gospel can bring a fundamentally changed life and eternal salvation. Business, the truth and the gospel are the basis for building Kingdom business in the developing world. New fundamental beliefs and a hope in Christ will allow the businessperson to stay the course in the face of adversity, which leads to the building of spiritual capital in a nation.

Conclusion

Developing nations are looking to the West to teach them principles and skills for successful business. The goals of Kingdom business include the development of a nation's economy and the creation of local jobs and financial resources. But we put the nation at a distinct disadvantage if we only teach principles of capitalism and fail to ingrain principles of the Bible. As my friend selling phone cards discovered, his competitors who practice dishonest business fail to build spiritual capital and ultimately suffer economically. More important than teaching business principles, we must equip the nations with the transforming power of the gospel, which leads to growth of their spiritual capital. Spiritual capital is the base on which successful businesses must be built. We cannot shortchange developing economies by exporting the capitalist system without the foundation that made it thrive in the West—the biblical values that permeated the culture and grew spiritual capital. Laws without morals are useless, like a house built on sand.

Transformed hearts lead to renewed minds in which a change in fundamental beliefs, values and attitudes has taken place. Eventually, the culture is transformed. But does a nation's culture really have any economic consequences? Yes. In fact, I believe the prevailing culture makes all the difference in economic development, which I will explain in the next chapter.

CHAPTER 6

GOVERNMENT, CULTURE AND KINGDOM BUSINESS

A couple of years ago, I invited a native evangelist from an Islamic country to have breakfast at my house. My wife was out of town, and although I am not a great cook, I was determined to be hospitable. So, testing the limits of my cooking skills, I offered him a simple American breakfast of bacon and eggs. My guest looked at his plate, mortified, though not for the reason I initially suspected. He was very polite, but it soon became apparent he was shocked that I would offer him bacon! After he explained to me that my interpretation of Acts 10 was wrong

and that it was unacceptable to eat pork, an unclean animal, I deferred to him and quickly changed the menu. But I learned that the cultural bonds of his Muslim country were strong. Even if many come to Christ, the people in his nation may never eat pork. Ideas, beliefs, values and attitudes that define a culture can have very deep roots.

Culture Is the Key

"Max Weber was right," concluded Harvard professor David Landes. "If we learn anything from the history of economic development, it is that culture makes almost all the difference."[1] Above all else, the evidence suggests that it is culture that drives the economic success and blessing of a nation. The most fundamental need of developing nations is not an infusion of capital, a higher level of education, a democratic government or even a more robust form of capitalism. The most fundamental need is cultural change that involves a transformation of core values, attitudes and practices. Economic, political and social improvements will occur as byproducts of that transformation.

For many, the term "culture" may evoke notions of specific foods, traditional clothing, language or even the racial composition of a society. (Indeed, my cultural experience above dealt with a specific food.) Those are important features that help define a group and make our created world beautiful and diverse, but they're not part of what we mean by culture in this context. The cultural aspects that David Landes says make all the difference in development have nothing to do with bacon or hamburgers, lederhosen or Swahili. Instead, they have to do with common mental dispositions such as ideas, beliefs, values and attitudes.

Richard Shweder of the University of Chicago defines culture as "community-specific *ideas* about what is true, good, beautiful, and efficient." He goes on to explain that "To be 'cultural,' those ideas about truth, goodness, beauty, and efficiency must be socially inherited and customary. . . . Alternatively stated, culture refers to . . . 'goals, values, and pictures of the world' that are made manifest in the speech, laws, and routine practices of some self-monitoring group."[2] Culture is the collective DNA of a society. It is the collection of beliefs, values and attitudes. Speech, laws and conventions reflect culture and are derived from it.

It is important to clarify that the lines drawn on a map outlining a country often comprises several people groups with distinct cultural belief systems. Throughout history, political boundaries have been drawn in ways that have split people groups or that have combined dissimilar people groups. For example, the Pashtus occupy a region that includes parts of Afghanistan and Pakistan, and the border between the two countries is virtually meaningless to them. Former countries like Yugoslavia, Czechoslovakia and the Soviet Union all contained distinct cultural people groups that later formed separate nations. In short, we cannot assume that every country has a single set of cultural values. These different belief systems can clash, sometimes violently. As Christians, we have the opportunity to support diversity of God's creation: "every nation, tribe, people, and language" (Rev. 7:9).

A country may maintain aspects of its tradition and diversity, but it is often the fundamental values and beliefs that keep a country from reaching its economic and political objectives. Thus, a cultural makeover grounded in the Bible is often needed for a nation to build its spiritual capital and its economy. The Bible is the bedrock of spiritual capital development and economic growth. A cultural makeover is also the basis from which a society will produce a more just, free and honest political system—a system that conforms to biblical values.

"The moral principles and precepts contained in the Scriptures ought to form the basis of all our civil constitutions and laws," said Noah Webster, an educator and legislator who promoted ratification of the United States Constitution in 1787.[3] While biblical principles form a solid foundation for the legal system, a nation that follows moral precepts with heartfelt conviction is compelled to respect the rule of law by a higher calling. "True religion affords the government its surest support," said George Washington, first President of the United States.[4] John Adams, who succeeded him firmly believed, "religion and virtue are the only foundations . . . of all free governments."[5] In other words, it is the morality and culture of faith—not the government—that is the primary foundation upon which a nation's future is built.

The Political System

As noted in the previous two chapters, a society is governed by three interrelated systems: the economic system, the political system and the moral-cultural system. The degree of a nation's commercial success depends on its culture and values. Successful broad-based capitalism is built on spiritual capital, which leads to moral capital as well as love for one's neighbor, trust of others, faith in the system, belief in the individual and hope for the future. All of these are based on biblical principles. The values, beliefs and practices of the moral-cultural system are the foundation for the commercial outcomes in the economic system. In short, the economic system is a reflection of the moral-cultural system.

Like the economic system, the political system comes out of the nation's culture. There is a commonly held belief that developing nations would succeed economically if only they adopted a democratic political system. Indeed, one can observe a correlation between wealth and democracy, but that does not indicate a causal relationship between open elections and growth. India is the largest and oldest democracy in the Third World, yet its democratic political system has not solved that nation's considerable problems.[6] Simply adopting a democratic political system will not effect economic transformation. Transformation efforts focused solely on a country's political system fail to address the cultural root issue. Both political and economic transformations must be built on the bedrock of moral-cultural transformation.

Though creating democracies is not the objective of Kingdom business, a nation's policies and political system do affect economic outcomes. "Without attention to political foundations, markets cannot flourish," concluded Stephen Haber, Douglass C. North and Barry R. Weingast, senior fellows at Stanford University's Hoover Institution.[7] Larry Diamond and Marc F. Plattner, in their book *Economic Reform and Democracy*, argue that democracy will not come without economic stability, and economic stability does not come without government stability.[8] Both business practices and political practices must be favorable for development. But the foundation of both is culture.

Governments Reflect Culture

Just as the economic system of a society can be marked by abuse, dishonesty, bribery, bureaucracy and greed, so too can its political system. Some nations are ruled by self-seeking dictators. Others are governed by a communist regime that limits freedoms. Still others are saddled by a corrupt or overly bureaucratic government. In most cases, the values and attitudes of the prevailing culture enable these political situations.

An adage says that in a democracy, people get the government they deserve. If democratic political leaders are dishonest, corrupt or self-seeking, it is only because the people either accept the practices or lack the will to force change. To a large degree, that appears to hold true under other political structures as well. The government reflects the moral strength and spiritual character of the nation. Like the economic system, the political system is a reflection of the moral-cultural system.

"The evidence suggests that culture plays a much more crucial role in democracy than the literature of the past two decades would indicate," concluded Ronald Inglehart of the University of Michigan. "In the long run, democracy is not attained simply by making institutional changes or through elite-level maneuvering. Its survival also depends on the values and beliefs of ordinary citizens."[9] For the most part, governments tend to reflect the views and attitudes of the people, which is why we witness some nations replacing one brutal dictator with another, one corrupt regime with another, one bureaucratic government with another. (This condition is not necessarily because the people are brutal, but because their tolerance for such brutality tends to be high.) For example, a nation with a culture that has fatalistic tendencies is inclined to allow dictators to take control. In some countries, the fatalism associated with Allah's will leads people away from action and toward resignation. Cultures that do not value the Golden Rule—do unto others as you would have them do unto you—end up with self-serving dictators who appear to care very little about their constituents. Countries in which individual accountability is not valued or in which there is no sense of hope tend to end up in the hands of capricious leaders. Societies in which the sanctity of human life is not respected tend to get leaders who sacrifice the lives of their people in pursuit of their ambitions.

Cultures that do not value the notion of absolute morality and accountability to a higher power also exhibit disregard for the rule of law. While recent history supports the general theory that strong economic development has been achieved in nations with Judeo-Christian institutions, it is also true that these institutions cannot develop fully without a strong adherence to the rule of law. According to Haber, North and Weingast, African nations make a great case in point:

> Over the years, the continent has been the site of large-scale experiments to reform its economies. But however ambitious, these projects have failed to generate sustained economic growth. Most African nations today are poorer than they were in 1980, sometimes by very wide margins . . . More shocking, two-thirds of the African countries have either stagnated or shrunk in real per capita terms since the onset of independence in the early 1960s.[10]

The failure in economic reform, they say, is attributable to a disregard for the concomitant need for political reform. Neither the government nor the people demonstrate a true commitment to the rule of law.

In some nations, the cultural value of human life is very different from what we experience in traditionally Judeo-Christian nations. In the United States, for example, there has been a raging debate over the number of arsenic parts per billion that is acceptable in our drinking water. How much should we spend to achieve a certain reduction? Reasonable citizens have differing views on this subject, but in many developing nations such debate does not even exist. In the West, there are laws around building codes that are intended to provide safety and protect life. As a result, far fewer lives are lost when natural disasters hit. There is some legitimacy to the argument that the difference in governance levels between developing nations and the West is also attributable to a difference in wealth. But countries that do have economic means demonstrate that a lack of resources cannot explain the difference. For example, Iran is an oil-rich nation, yet little attention is given to building codes that would prevent loss of life, at least in rural towns. An earthquake in 2003 measuring 6.6 on the Richter scale resulted in more than 30,000 deaths. By comparison, a 1989 earthquake in the densely populated San Francisco Bay Area measuring 7.0 on the Richter scale claimed only 63 lives, and buildings have been subjected to new codes and earthquake retrofitting ever since. The point here is that the political and legal system certainly reflects the prevailing culture, and differences in cultural values are evident in the governments and laws of nations.

The Culture of Development

"Attitudes, values, and beliefs that are sometimes collectively referred to as 'culture' play an unquestioned role in human behavior and progress. This is evident to me from working in nations, states, regions, inner cities, and companies at widely varying stages of development," concluded Harvard's Michael E. Porter, author of the classic *Competitive Strategy* and one of the world's most sought-after business gurus and strategists.[11] A nation's political and business environment tends to reflect its collective culture. Cultures in which biblical values are ingrained grow spiritual capital and establish the environment for successful commerce. Cultures that do not reflect biblical principles fail to grow spiritual capital. They may add some aspects of moral capital, which then are reflected in a code of laws and ethics, but these too come from tradition, acceptance and influence. Singapore and Hong Kong are case studies of acceptance of British moral law, property rights and respect for the individual without adopting on a wholesale basis the faith of Great Britain.

What are the specific features of some cultures that are roadblocks to development? Mariano Grondona, a professor of government, an author and a television host in Argentina, details a number of factors that are viewed very differently in cultures that favor development than in cultures that resist development. "These differences are intimately linked to the economic performance of the contrasting cultures," he concludes. Let's take a look at some of these beliefs and values that affect a nation's development.[12]

- *Religion.* As Weber noted, religions that exalt poverty promote values that are resistant to development while those that view wealth as a blessing promote values that are favorable to development.
- *Trust in the individual.* Societies that trust individuals are favorable to development. Distrust of the individual, demonstrated by oversight and control, typifies the society that resists development.
- *The moral imperative.* Cultures that resist development indicate a great divide between their official laws and everyday practice. In cultures that promote development, common morality is more closely aligned with the nation's laws.
- *Concepts of wealth.* In development-resistant societies, wealth is thought of in terms of what currently exists (land, natural resources). Development-favoring societies view wealth in terms of what does not yet exist (new ideas, technology).
- *Views of competition.* Societies favorable to development view competition as necessary and good for the creation of wealth and excellence. It is what drives capitalism and democracy. Societies resistant to development have negative views of competition, often under the pretense of fostering equality.
- *Notions of justice.* Cultures that emphasize justice for the current population over future generations focus on the present and are resistant to development. Those that consider the interests of future generations in their concept of justice are favorable to development. Thus, the former focuses on the right to current consumption, while the latter values the benefit of long-term investment.
- *Value of work.* Progress-resistant cultures do not value work. Often the contemplative life is glorified. Progress-favorable cultures emphasize a strong work ethic.

- *Role of heresy.* Societies ruled by dogmatic orthodoxy that demands unquestioned loyalty are resistant to innovation and development. Those that are favorable to the open forum of ideas are prone to innovation and development.
- *The lesser virtues.* Development-favorable cultures that are more respectful of the needs of others value the lesser virtues of doing a job well, being punctual, showing courtesy and creating order. Development-resistant cultures focus on self-interest and place less value on these virtues.
- *Authority.* In societies less inclined to progress, power is held by rulers whose will is mutable and sometimes capricious. In societies favorable to progress, the power resides in the law, and governments are subservient to it.
- *Visions of democracy.* Progress-resistant cultures place no institutional controls or legal limitations on the power of the government. Progressive cultures limit the government's reach and distribute its power through constitutions, and the rule of law is controlling.
- *View of life and future.* Cultures that resist development view life as something that happens to a person; there is a degree of fatalism and resignation, and the future is beyond one's control. Cultures that favor development view life as something that is engaged; there is an ability to influence the future outcome.

The difference between the mental models described here is stark, and their influence on behavior cannot be underestimated. I am reminded of the story told by Rabbi Daniel Lapin of two American women who were out fishing on a boat in the Arabian Sea when the vessel's motor died. The two Arab sailors on board looked worried, but they just lay down on the deck. "What are you doing?" asked the women.

"We are doomed to die," they replied, resigned to their fate. "It is obviously Allah's will. Otherwise, he wouldn't have stranded us out here."

The women were shocked. Without any help from the boat's operators, they rigged a sail and forged some paddles, then worked feverishly to get the boat moving. Eventually, it entered a shipping channel where they were discovered and rescued.

Ingrained cultural attitudes and thought patterns can be difficult to overcome. In a famous experiment, a dog was confined to a small cage from birth. After several years, he was removed from the cage. While the dog stood up, turned around in place, and sat right back down, sadly, he didn't move from the spot. The dog was still being kept in place, but the bars that were limiting his movement were mental, not metal. Minds need to be transformed. There is a cultural gap that needs to be bridged.

Institutions Necessary for Development Require Cultural Changes

Developing nations are besieged by attitudes that are limiting their development, and these cultural values are reflected in their institutions. Institutions are the formal and informal rules that emerge from its values. Formal rules include constitutions, laws, regulations and agencies, while informal rules include conventions and social norms. Freedom, lack of corruption, basic fairness and adherence to the rule of law come out of the people rather than out of an imposed system. All of these institutions are derived from a society's culture. African scholar Daniel Etounga-Manguelle uses a simple illustration to depict the relationship: culture is the mother, and institutions are the children.[13]

Since institutions reflect the underlying culture, creation of the institutions necessary for successful development requires a cultural change. Concerned with curing the plagues of his continent, Etounga-Manguelle rightly noted that "more efficient and just African institutions depend on modifications to our culture."[14] Cultural change is needed for developing nations to build their institutions and spiritual capital.

But how is change effected? Is culture best reformed from the top through changed governments and laws or from the bottom through changed individual lives? There has been a lot of attention in the United States in recent years on nation-building, a top-down approach to transformation. It was a major topic of discussion during the Clinton Administration with respect to Haiti. In the Bush Administration, nation-building is a central topic with respect to Afghanistan and Iraq.

It is apparent to many who look at this issue that it will be difficult to build a nation by starting at the top and working down to the people unless there is a powerful single group that controls the country. This governing group must embody the transformed nation and must begin to implement changes that will be bought into by the people. Even then, in many countries fatalistic notions are so prevalent that people will accept the changes without ever changing their worldview, leaving those nations open to eventual control by various power factions. Unless the underlying culture is modified, nations will not see effective transformation through a change of leadership or even through another system of government.

Without fundamental and traditional values in place, few nations' attempts at democracy survive serious economic downturns. If a democratic political institution is not supported by the nation's values, economic hardship could lead to what Diamond and Plattner call "democratic backsliding." As case studies, they point to Brazil and Peru where prolonged economic distress resulted in authoritarian governments that limited freedoms. Though there were no formal regime changes, the constitutional institutions in Brazil and Peru were "drained of their democratic content" as a result of economic hardships.[15]

Cultures will not see effective transformation through a new political system or through legislation. That would be reversing the causal relationship. In general, the government and its rules and laws are a reflection of culture rather than the other way around. When the United States founders wrote the Declaration of Independence and the Constitution, they were not seeking to impose ideas that were foreign to the population; they were merely codifying beliefs that were already ingrained in the emerging nation's collective DNA. Even so, finalizing these documents was a major undertaking for the founders, involving years of discussion and development.

Sometimes rulers use their power to impose laws that go against the country's beliefs and attitudes. In those instances, legislation is pitted against culture, but it does not result in true transformation of the culture. New legislation, political change and proper economic incentives may not provide the cultural transformation that leads to economic blessing. Culture is the mother, and these institutions are the children.

It Starts in the Hearts of Men and Women

If cultural transformation cannot start with economic or political institutions, where does it start? It starts in the hearts of men and women. Transformation of culture really starts with the individual. Culture is the collective beliefs and values of many individuals, and it can only be modified at the level of the individual. Cultural change is not something that can be imposed at a macro level from the top. There are no shortcuts. Person by person, hearts and minds must be transformed, and thus the culture of a nation begins to change. Individuals generally do not live in isolation from other members of their society, and their individual beliefs, values and attitudes come to bear in their relationships. It takes two people to exchange goods and services; we call that commerce. It takes two people to exchange ideas on how they will live together; we call that politics. It takes two people to share their beliefs about God; we call that religion. A transformed individual will bring his new beliefs, values and attitudes to bear on the economic and political systems and will begin to influence the collective culture. Cultural transformation happens one individual at a time.

"Therefore, if anyone is in Christ, he is a new creation; the old has gone, the new has come" (2 Cor. 5:17). Christ through the Holy Spirit is the only agent who can effect the transformation of one's core. Paul says, "We were therefore buried with him through baptism into death in order that . . . we too may live a new life" (Rom. 6:4). Old things have passed away; *all* things have become new.

As individuals are transformed by the Holy Spirit, the people as a whole come into agreement on a new set of values. Over time, these values will become institutionalized, part of the system. It does not happen overnight. The population of South Korea is now more than one-third born-again evangelical Christian. Many of the former political and business leaders have been or are being sent to jail. Why is that? In part, because the society is no longer allowing past ways to continue, and it is dealing with the dishonesty and corruption that remain in the system. There has been a significant change in South Korea since the 1950s, spiritually, economically and politically. As a corollary to this example, think about Russia, where faith was outlawed under communism for 70 years. With the fall of communism, economic and religious freedoms now exist, but without a transformed culture, corruption is allowed to flourish. Before a nation can adopt robust institutionalized values of a transformed culture, individual hearts must be transformed by the Holy Spirit.

Just as I Am

Englishwoman Charlotte Elliott was 30 years old when she was struck by an illness that left her bedridden for the rest of her life. When she was 33, a Swiss evangelist visited her town of Brighton, and she decided to follow Jesus. "You must come as you are," the evangelist encouraged. Her illness didn't matter to God. He takes people regardless of their current situation. In 1834, still an invalid, Charlotte penned a song that has been the call for thousands. With the choir singing her famous chorus "Just as I Am," Billy Graham has invited people for decades to make the decision to follow Christ.

"But God demonstrates his own love for us in this: While we were still sinners, Christ died for us" (Rom. 5:8). A wonderful hallmark of God's loving grace is that He doesn't expect people to be perfect before calling them. (Indeed, there would be no Body of Christ if this were the case.) He takes them just as they are. Some, like Charlotte Elliott, come with serious physical limitations. All come with sin. There are values, beliefs and behaviors that run contrary to God's will. But God takes people just as they are. Likewise, we need to take individuals, people groups and nations just as they are.

Transformed by the Renewing of Your Minds

God is in the business of saving imperfect vessels and sanctifying them. Paul tells the believers in Philippi of his confidence "that he who began a good work in you will carry it on to completion until the day of Christ Jesus" (Phil. 1:6). Paul was confident that God would continue His work of sanctification by transforming values, beliefs and behaviors.

Theologian Louis Berkhoff defines sanctification as "that operation of God by which He especially, through the Spirit, works in man the subjective quality of holiness."[16] It is the process of becoming holy, dying to sin and living unto righteousness. It is the process of transformation so that "we too may live a new life" (Rom. 6:4).

Paul describes sanctification as a paradigm shift from following the values, beliefs and behaviors of the world to following those of God. "Do not conform any longer to the pattern of this world, but be transformed by the renewing of your mind. Then you will be able to test and approve what God's will is—his good, pleasing and perfect will" (Rom. 12:2). In short, it is the Holy Spirit working a cultural transformation from the pattern of this world to the pattern of God. The process starts with a spiritual transformation through a personal relationship with God. Then it expands to other parts our lives that need work. The fully transformed life must be conformed to the pattern of God in every area.

The Holy Spirit uses different approaches to effect an individual's conforming to the pattern of God. Sometimes God has to take people out of the control of their cultural surroundings in order to prepare them for a blessing. Following his dramatic conversion, Paul spent three years in Arabia and Damascus. God transformed him and revealed to him the gospel he was to preach. Separated from the culture of his upbringing, Paul's mind was renewed (see Gal. 1:11-24). We also see it in the account of Abram:

> The Lord had said to Abram, "Leave your country, your people and your father's household and go to the land I will show you. I will make you into a great nation and I will bless you; I will make your name great, and you will be a blessing. I will bless those who bless you and whoever curses you I will curse; and all peoples on earth will be blessed through you" (Gen. 12:1-3).

God had to take Abram out of his circumstances, which included his culture and his family. Culture and family are very powerful traditional ties, bonds that can keep one from thinking about things in a new way. In short, Abram had to take off one set of glasses so that he could see through another set. God had to get Abram off where He could talk to him, where there was no one to teach him differently.

While Abram and Paul were taken out of their existing cultural surroundings, often God transforms people right where they are. That is the model most often encountered in Kingdom business. God must send His people into cultures to transform their beliefs, values and attitudes. Individuals must be taught a new paradigm of life by word and by deed. We must deal with the whole person, with all aspects of his or her life. People who can model godly character in different areas, including business, are a tremendous help in that process.

The Church is most comfortable dealing with a renewing of the mind in regard to God, but it too often stops short of dealing with a renewing of the mind in regard to the rest of life. We don't usually talk about a new mind toward business, education, politics, healthcare, parenting and poverty. As a result, these areas that consume the majority of our energy often remain untransformed.

Cultural transformation does not happen overnight. We know that it took Abram many years as God changed him and worked on his understanding. Even though he was called away from his family, Abram retained vestiges of the old life. Many cultural norms get in the way of our own walk with Jesus. Sometimes unknown to us, we hold to views that affect our relationship with God. Recently a Christian friend of mine visited an African country where his hosts were local believers. When he ordered a beer to drink, his hosts were absolutely beside themselves, and for his sake they tried to talk him out of it. Desiring not to offend them, he deferred. But later in the evening, they asked if he would like some entertainment, and to his amazement, they offered him a woman to spend the night with him. He carefully turned down the invitation. Both parties were amazed at the other's tradition and view of the truth.

The evangelist from a Muslim country to whom I innocently served bacon for breakfast also clung to aspects of his cultural tradition. Food, of course, is not going to affect how a culture deals with government, but these examples do show the staying power of cultural traditions and what we know and perceive as truth, even for believers. There are other cultural norms that are insidious and pervasive and affect the way we think about every subject, including government. God calls us just as we are, with all our personal and cultural baggage. When the Lord begins to speak to our spirit and we accept Him as our Savior, we begin to see our lives change. Things we used to do, attitudes we used to have, beliefs we used to hold no longer seem acceptable before God. It is the Holy Spirit performing His act of transformation in our lives.

Kingdom Business: Transforming Nations Just as They Are

We, like our Lord, must accept people just as they are. We must recognize that we will have to deal with people in their existing condition. The implication for Kingdom business is that we cannot wait for a country to have achieved a certain level of "sanctification." We must not require a free or non-corrupt nation as a prerequisite for Kingdom business. We may not like the government and may not like what it stands for, but just as Christ accepts us just as we are and begins the process of change, we must accept a country just as it is. No matter the current condition of a country, we must enter to bless the nation, expecting that God will take the seed we sow and from it reap great rewards. We must expect that God will begin to renew minds. We must expect that as people begin to hunger and thirst for righteousness, God will work to effect the cultural change required for the transformation of the nation.

To see this change take place, Kingdom business professionals must preach and teach the gospel and its relevance to business as an integrated part of the effort to develop local business. Only the gospel of Christ can effect the radical core transformation that will enable people to remain rooted in their new core beliefs regardless of circumstances. "So I will always remind you of these things, even though you know them and are *firmly established* in *the truth you now have*" (2 Pet. 1:12, emphasis added). To establish means to set, as in the sense of curing or setting as cement. It is important that we be cured and therefore hard as cement in the truth we now have in Jesus Christ. Old values, beliefs and actions that differ from the truth in Christ must be discarded. An individual must be established in the new truth of Christ. Kingdom business professionals must mentor that individual in business from this new point of view so that he or she learns to see things from God's perspective.

If we fail to present a gospel that produces core transformation, we will create what Jesus described as "hired hands." These individuals lack faith and therefore run when things begin to get difficult. "I am the good shepherd. The good shepherd lays down His life for the sheep. The hired hand is not the shepherd who owns the sheep. So when he sees the wolf coming, he abandons the sheep and runs away. Then the wolf attacks the flock and scatters it" (John 10:11-12). When business gets tough and governments begin to change, those who become Christians and are building Kingdom businesses will not react as the hired hand but will stay the course.

Those who are not grounded by faith will be "like a wave of the sea, blown and tossed by the wind" (Jas. 1:6). They will be double-minded, doing business as taught but ducking for cover at the first sign of trouble. That kind of person is not a witness for Christ. But if they are sold out to Jesus, set like cement in their faith and sure of the direct relationship between God and good business practices, they will stand firm in the power of the Holy Spirit.

I am reminded of a powerful story recently recounted by the head of an organization involved in Kingdom business. A Russian Christian was part of a group of local business people who were assembled by a Russian mafia group and asked for protection money. "Sit down if you agree to our offer," they were ordered. Terrified, others around him took a seat, but he remained standing. "Sit down," he was instructed directly. "No I won't," was the response, "I have a higher authority protecting me." The Christian businessman stood firm. "In that case, you're free to go," they said, believing that he was referring to a more powerful criminal element. He was never approached by that organization again.

Conclusion

Corruption and self-seeking institutions are significant barriers to development, and many developing nations need reform on both the political and economic fronts. But focusing on the government and laws first is looking at the problem backward. The place to start is in changing the hearts of men. Even in those few nations where there is an iron grip by a few, transformation starts with one person at a time and spreads. A nation's moral-cultural system is the foundation for its political and economic systems, and the government ultimately will be a reflection of what the spiritual, economic and moral drivers demand it to be. Therefore, it is important that developing nations first modify beliefs, values and attitudes that are holding them back. A culture that is conformed to the pattern of God will see lasting economic and political reforms.

Though capitalism is most successful in an environment of political freedom, we must begin to bless a nation through Kingdom business just as it is. Democracy is not a prerequisite for Kingdom business; nor is the establishment of democracies the objective of Kingdom business— the objective is to bring the gospel of Christ and see lives radically transformed by the power of the Holy Spirit. We must simultaneously bring business and the truth of Christ in the Spirit of God. Only the power of the Holy Spirit can produce real change in individual lives and effect the cultural transformation that leads to blessing in a nation. Any program that fails to include real spiritual transformation is incomplete and tantamount to building on sand. Development efforts are best built on the rock of Christ (see Matt. 7:24-27). But we might expect that as hearts are changed and cultures are influenced, there will be greater yearning for political justice, freedom and integrity. In fact, the cultural transformation produced by the gospel will lay the foundation for effective political change and economic development.

It is apparent to me that Kingdom business has the potential to bless a nation through economic and spiritual transformation. That's the vision God had given me for ET, the call center venture in India. But was this a new opportunity, a new revelation from God, or did any missions-minded saints that went before me have similar visions for business as missions? I was determined to find out the answer to this question and learn from the experience of these individuals.

CHAPTER 7

HISTORICAL PERSPECTIVE OF BUSINESS IN MISSIONS

It is said that history is the best teacher, and I wanted to learn. God had given me a vision for advancing the Church in India through business. It was a vision for business as missions. But was this unique? Had God called others in the past to use their business skills to take the gospel to faraway lands? The answer to this inquiry would prove interesting, encouraging and instructive.

I discovered that starting with the first followers of Jesus, Church history is full of examples of missionary efforts that used business as a vehicle for spreading the gospel. In reviewing this history, I learned a

number of lessons. I saw that business and missions can go hand in hand, working toward a goal of advancing the Kingdom of God. I saw that there are a number of ways to create Kingdom business opportunities. I saw that Kingdom business efforts can be fruitful, leading to spiritual and financial success. But I also saw that with success comes the danger of losing sight of one's priorities. Kingdom business is doing business as a mission, and the reason for doing it must remain foremost in the minds of those involved.

New Testament Business in Missions

The use of business in the worldwide missions effort of the Church is as old as the Church itself. The apostle Paul is famous for his missionary journeys that brought the gospel to the Gentiles of the Roman Empire. Trained as a tentmaker, he took his business with him wherever he went. In Corinth, Paul worked with Aquila and Priscilla, Jewish tentmakers who had been forced to leave Rome (see Acts 18:1-3). Paul also worked in the tentmaking business during his three years in Ephesus, where his hands supplied his own needs (see Acts 20:33-35). In Thessalonica, Paul made sure he was not a burden on anyone (see 1 Thess. 2:9), and he worked day and night to be self-sufficient (see 2 Thess. 3:8). He also did this to be a model of diligent labor for the Thessalonians to follow (see 2 Thess. 3:9).

Paul did receive financial support from some of the churches to which he ministered. Some of the funds were earmarked for the destitute believers in Jerusalem (see Rom. 15:26). Other funds helped finance his stays in Corinth (see 2 Cor. 11:8) and Thessalonica (see Phil. 4:14-19). Yet it seems that Paul took pride in adapting to each situation. To the Jews he became a Jew, to the Greeks he became a Greek, and to the Romans he became a Roman. Paul also became a businessman to the businessmen.

Priscilla and Aquila accompanied Paul on part of his missionary journey, taking their business with them as well. "Aquila was an accomplished tradesman," noted Heinz Suter and Marco Gmür. "His skill was in leather, and he made saddles, belts, and tents, [hence] a soldiering people like the Romans, so enamored of horses, provided him enough business. His choice of settlement was limited to places where he might again find something of the culture of Rome, as well as enough Roman knights and soldiers to provide him again with a living."[1] Priscilla and Aquila's business allowed them to travel throughout the area, from Rome to Corinth and Ephesus. A church met in the home of these faithful business people (see 1 Cor. 16:19), and they discipled the teacher Apollos for an effective preaching ministry (see Acts 18:24-28).

In Acts, we meet "Lydia, a dealer in purple cloth [or dye] from the city of Thyatira" (Acts 16:14). This woman responded to the gospel in Philippi, and her house served as the place where Paul and Silas met with their fellow believers after their freedom from prison. It seems Lydia had moved to Macedonia to promote the trade of purple cloth there. John later mentions her home town of Thyatira in Revelation 2:18-29 as one of the seven churches to whom messages are given, and it is quite possible that she took the gospel on business trips to her supply base.

Early Church Business in Missions

Merchant Missions

Christian traders were among the first to take the gospel to distant lands. Merchants from Asia Minor sold clothing and spices in Marseilles, Lyons, Alexandria and Carthage. The commercial cities of southern France were particularly popular destinations as they boasted ore mines, glass and ceramics production, and textile trade. Traders and settlers found their way there, and churches soon materialized in Marseilles, Arles, Vienne and Lyons.[2] Migrant Christian business people from Asia Minor kept close contact with their home churches, notes Norbert Brox.[3] In fact, the second-century bishop of the church in Lyons was Irenaeus of Asia Minor. Business between Asia Minor and ports all over the Mediterranean Sea took the first Christians to locations where the gospel needed to be heard.

Christianity spread to other parts of the world through business merchants. European traders were the first to bring the gospel to

Scandinavia. Arabia had Christians believers within a couple centuries after Christ. Located on the fringes of the Roman Empire, these Arabian believers were probably introduced to the gospel through commercial ventures. India also had Christian communities before the end of the third century. Since Indian trade routes were frequented by Greek merchants even before Christ, it is likely that businessmen played a part in introducing the faith to India.[4]

Nestorians

"There is very substantial evidence to support the fact that Christians who came to China did so in connection with the business and trade connections of Persian Christianity," stated Suter and Gmür.[5] Christian merchants followed the silk routes to China in the sixth and seventh centuries. It was these missionary merchants who introduced the silk trade to Europe.

The Nestorians, members of a Christian sect that developed in Persia, were particularly active in trade with Asia. There are historical accounts of churches and bishops in cities along the merchant route in Central Asia, including Merv, Herat and Samarkand. Not all of the Nestorian missionaries were traders; some were carpenters, blacksmiths, weavers and accountants. Arab and Mongol rulers employed Nestorians as assistants, secretaries, physicians and stewards.

The Nestorians were the most missions-focused church in history.[6] Together with the Antiochian church, they Christianized five tribes in Asia, the Keraiter, Naimaniter, Uyghers, Ongüts and Merkiter. About 200,000 Keraiter embraced Christianity at the beginning of the eleventh century, and the Uyghers of Eastern Turkestan also experienced great revival. Marco Polo reported that Nestorian chapels lined the trade route from Baghdad to Beijing. For centuries, Nestorian businessmen and professionals unleashed one of the most widespread missions movements the world has ever seen, and all of this was done through business as a funding and operating model.[7]

Post-Reformation Business in Missions

Dutch East Indies Company

In 1595, the Dutch East Indies Company (Vereenigde Oost-Indische Compagnie) sent its first trade ships to Asia. A major center of the company was in Maluku, formerly known as the Spice Islands, in present-day eastern Indonesia. The company established the spice trade, importing clove and nutmeg to Europe. In fact, for hundreds of years, the Spice Islands accounted for the world's entire production of these two valuable spices. Protestant missionaries soon followed the traders to settlements that the company had established.

There was a symbiotic and supportive relationship between the Dutch East Indies Company and the missionaries who were seeking to spread the gospel. It is true that there were business reasons for wanting to see the natives follow the Christian faith, but some company managers had more noble intentions for desiring the establishment of a local church. In fact, a director of the Company was the first to translate parts of the Bible into Malay. His translation of Matthew introduced the gospel to the locals in their own language.

Commenting on the history of missions efforts, William Carey, considered the father of modern missions, wrote that the Dutch East Indies Company had extended its commerce and built the city of Batavia (present-day Jakarta) where a church was opened in 1621. The Company sent additional ministers to Amboyna, where the ministers were quite successful. In the Dutch city of Leiden, a seminary was established to educate ministers and assistants, and the Dutch East Indies Company deployed many of the seminary's graduates to the East Indies. Carey noted:

> Some years a great number were sent to the East, at the Company's expense, so that in a little time many thousands at Formosa [present-day Taiwan], Malabar, Ternate, Jaffanapatnam, in the town of Columba, at Amboyna, Java, Banda, Macassar, and Malabar, embraced the religion of our Lord Jesus Christ. The work has decayed in some places, but they now have churches in Ceylon, Sumatra, Java, Amboyna, and some other of the Spice

Islands, and at the Cape of Good Hope, in Africa.[8]

Carey viewed the Dutch East Indies Company as a strong proponent of the gospel wherever it went. When the British took over the Spice Islands in the early nineteenth century, a total of 230 Dutch Protestant ministers were active in the area.[9]

Moravian Missions

The Moravians sent out more than half of all Protestant missionaries of the eighteenth century, declared Paul Pierson.[10] Not only were they great missionaries, but also they embraced business as their primary missions vehicle.

Who are the Moravians, and what drove their missionary zeal? Their spiritual roots date to the Church of the Brotherhood, founded by the Bohemian priest Jan Hus, and to the Waldensians, another sect that rejected the exercise of power and wealth in the official Church. In 1467, half a century before Luther nailed his theses to the Wittenburg church door, these two groups joined to become the United Brethren. Their emphasis was on the daily personal practice of Christianity. From Bohemia, the Brethren spread to neighboring Moravia.

The Reformation and Counter-Reformation virtually decimated the United Brethren, and those who remained migrated to Saxony. There, Count Niklaus Ludwig von Zinzendorf, an heir to a leading royal family in Europe, opened up Herrnhut, one of his estates, to these refugees and established a Christian community there in 1722. This society of pious believers maintained a continuous prayer chain that lasted more than one hundred years, and Herrnhut was the source of the largest missions movement of the century.

On a visit to Copenhagen, Zinzendorf met Anthony, a slave from the West Indies, and two Eskimos from Greenland. They all pleaded for missionaries to be sent to their people. Anthony was brought to Herrnhut, where he described the miserable physical and spiritual conditions of slaves in the West Indies. The community responded and resolved to send missionaries. In 1732, missionaries David Nitschmann and Leonard Dober were sent to St. Thomas in the West Indies. Others were sent to Greenland, St. Croix, Surinam, South Africa, North America, Jamaica and Antigua. Between 1732 and 1760, 226 Moravians settled in 10 foreign locations. Over a two-decade period, the Moravian missionary movement started more missions than all Protestant and Anglican efforts had in the preceding two centuries![11]

The Moravian model combined its missions reach with the establishment of business enterprises. Every member of the group was expected to have a trade, and once in a distant land, he was to work alongside the locals, witnessing by word and by deed in the daily marketplace. The group's work ethic was a prominent component of modeling the gospel of Christ. "In 1759 at the Moravian colony in Bethlehem, Pennsylvania, 36 percent of the male workforce were missionaries on assignment," noted Dwight P. Baker.[12] The itinerant preachers (*reisebrüder*) who roamed Europe also adopted the Pauline model. As craftsmen or teachers, they were able to finance their work wherever they went. The Moravians viewed their economic activity as virtuous service to their neighbors.[13]

In 1740, a third group of Moravian missionaries arrived in Paramaribo, Suriname. Among those settling there were a carpenter and a shoemaker. Other marketplace missionaries soon followed. In 1759, Christoph Kersten, who was trained as a tailor by his uncle in Germany, "got the assignment of working as a tailor and besides to carry out missionary work in Suriname."[14] In 1768, the Moravian missionaries established C. Kersten and Co., a tailoring business to which was attached a draper's business. Within four years, the company had earned 242,000 talers (old German currency). In 1777, a successful bakery that complied with European standards was added. C. Kersten and Co. was a trading company that demonstrated the intersection between business and missions and served as a support base for the missionaries. The slaves of Suriname were given employment, business training and the gospel. By 1926, the Paramaribo body was the largest Moravian congregation in the world, with 13,000 members in 7 church buildings.[15]

Today, 45 percent of Surinamese identify themselves as Christian, and 3 out of 4 Protestants are Moravians.[16] This small country in South

America is still considered a developing economy. Nearly 250 years after it was founded, C. Kersten and Co., N.V. provides employment to some 1,000 people in diverse production, trading and service businesses. Moravian missionaries no longer operate the company, having passed leadership to Surinamese locals. However, it is still owned by the Mission Foundation of the Moravian Brethren, and it continues to maintain its vision for Kingdom business. Today, the company states that it tries to realize its mission statement by:

- maintaining and expanding the fundamental operating activities of the company;
- producing and delivering high-quality products and services and the service policy connected to that;
- generating a reasonable return which in any case should be higher than the investment in normal, sound investments;
- offering equal development opportunities to all employees;
- acquiring and maintaining an important position in the national economy of Suriname; and
- supporting global activities of the Moravian Church.[17]

William Carey, Father of Modern Missions

William Carey was a shoemaker who set sail for India in 1793. Before his departure, he wrote *An Enquiry into the Obligations of Christians*, intending to rebuff the common arguments of his day against missionary endeavors to faraway, uncivilized and dangerous peoples. The first issue he addressed was the means of transportation. Carey appealed to the advances of the trading companies in preparing the way for missions efforts: "Men can now sail with as much certainty through the Great South Sea as they can through the Mediterranean or any lesser sea. Yea, and providence seems in a manner to invite us to the trial, as there are to our knowledge trading companies, whose commerce lies in many of the places where these barbarians dwell."[18]

Carey also reflected on a verse in Isaiah as a prophecy that the vehicles of trade and commerce would bring the gospel to faraway lands: "Surely the islands look to me; in the lead are the ships of

Tarshish, bringing your sons from afar, with their silver and gold, *to the honor of the Lord your God*, the Holy One of Israel, for He has endowed you with splendor" (Isa. 60:9, emphasis added). Business would be an instrument to promote the spread of the gospel, he concluded from this verse:

> This seems to imply that in the time of the glorious increase of the church, in the latter days (of which the whole chapter is undoubtedly a prophecy), commerce shall subserve the spread of the gospel. The ships of Tarshish were trading vessels, which made voyages for traffic to various parts; thus much therefore must be meant by it, that navigation, especially that which is commercial, shall be one great mean of carrying on the work of God; and perhaps it may imply that there shall be a very considerable appropriation of wealth to that purpose.[19]

Carey certainly saw an important role for commercial ventures in taking the gospel to every corner of the world.

David Livingstone, Missionary Pioneer

"A prospect is now before us of opening Africa for commerce and the gospel." These were the words of Dr. David Livingstone in 1857 at a Cambridge University speech recounting his missionary and exploration journeys.

> In going back to that country, my object is to open up traffic along the banks of the Zambesi, and also to preach the gospel. The natives of Central Africa are very desirous of trading, but their only traffic is at present in slaves, of which the poorer people have an unmitigated horror: it is therefore most desirable to encourage the former principle, and thus open a way for the consumption of free productions, and the introduction of Christianity and commerce. By encouraging the native propensity for trade, the advantages that might be derived in a commercial point of view are incalculable; nor should we lose sight of the inestimable blessings it is in our

power to bestow upon the unenlightened African, by giving him the light of Christianity. Those two pioneers of civilization—Christianity and commerce—should ever be inseparable.[20]

There can be no doubt that Livingstone, perhaps the most famous missionary of modern missions, was a firm believer in the linking of business and missions. His objective was to bless the Africans through spiritual and economic transformation. It would be difficult to present the idea of Kingdom business in a clearer manner than Livingstone did in his speech at Cambridge.

African Lakes Company

In 1859, Livingstone returned to Africa and explored Nyasaland (present-day Malawi). Pre-colonial Malawi was in turmoil as Arab and Portuguese slave traders, warlike tribes from the South, and ivory traders from the coast threatened the area. It was into that upheaval that Livingstone sought to inject the blessing of virtuous business activities. Other British missionaries followed Livingstone, most notably those sent by Scottish Presbyterian churches and the Free Church of Scotland Mission, beginning in 1875.

These missionaries concluded that legitimate business options were needed to combat and end the rampant slave trade. In 1877, Christian businessmen John and Frederick Moir from Glasgow founded the Livingstonia Central Africa Company, later renamed the African Lakes Company. Mandala was the Nyasaland branch of the company, located near the shores of Lake Nyasa (Malawi). Dr. James Stewart led the African Lakes Company's operations at Livingstonia where he introduced industrial skills and training in commerce. Operating steamers that transported and shipped products along rivers and lakes, the African Lakes Company began by transporting goods from ports in the Indian Ocean to trading stations in present-day Tanzania, Malawi, Zambia and Mozambique. Later, it diversified into general trading business.

The company served to promote virtuous trade, combat slave trade, establish transportation routes and transfer business and spiritual knowledge to locals. Those were the objectives of the African Lakes

Company's evangelical founders, and it was successful in fulfilling Livingstone's vision for bringing commerce and Christianity to the area.

Hawaiian Missions

There is a saying in Hawaii that "the missionaries came here to do good and did well." Certainly not every missions endeavor involving business has been successful. Sometimes the business venture fails. Sometimes spiritual objectives are sacrificed. The story of early missions efforts in Hawaii is a case of the latter.

Missionaries first arrived in Hawaii aboard the *Thaddeus* in 1820. Some of these missionaries and their children soon became active in commerce. The foreigners on the islands introduced the rulers to the idea of land ownership, an unknown concept to the native people. The Hawaiian Constitution of 1840 granted all land to the king, but just 8 years later, King Kamehameha III issued the Great Mahele, which divided the kingdom's real estate among the king (24 percent), the chiefs (39 percent), the government (36 percent), and the commoners (1 percent). Importantly, this division of Hawaii's land ownership allowed foreigners with business interests to purchase and control land. Indeed, private ownership rights were critical to the safe investment of capital in real estate and the formation of major sugar plantations. Hawaii proved to be extremely well suited for sugar cane, and ambitious businessmen built elaborate irrigation systems to supply water to their fields. They built sophisticated waterways over valleys, created tunnels through mountains, and revolutionized the sugar industry. The labor was cheap, much of it supplied by immigrant workers from Japan and China.

A handful of foreigners controlled both the politics and economics of the islands, and they did so through the "Big Five."[21] These five major companies included Castle and Cooke, which was founded as a general store in 1851 by Samuel Northrup Castle, a missionary teacher, and Amos Starr Cooke, the finance and purchasing director for the missions companies. It originally engaged in sales of farm tools, sewing machines and medicine but later invested in sugar plantations and shifted toward the sugar industry. Today, Castle and Cooke, Inc. is involved in real estate ownership and development and in several other industries. The company owns two of the world's highest-rated resorts and 98 percent of the Hawaiian island of Lanai.

Alexander and Baldwin, another of the Big Five, was started with 12 acres of sugar cane land by missionary sons Samuel Alexander and Henry Baldwin in 1869. The next year they added several hundred acres. In 1876, their 3,000-acre Haiku plantation in central Maui lacked water, so they built an ambitious 17-mile irrigation system from the slopes of the dormant volcano Haleakala. Alexander and Baldwin became the biggest sugar company in Hawaii. Today, it is a diversified corporation worth $1.2 billion with interests in property development and management, ocean transportation and sugar and coffee production.

Unfortunately, these missionaries and their descendants in Hawaii who engaged in very profitable business ventures were driven more by self-interest than by a desire to serve the locals. There is also no evidence that company profits were deployed in missions efforts. The powerful foreigners favored annexation of the islands to the United States in order to protect their economic interests. The Treaty of Reciprocity was signed in 1876. It removed trade barriers between the Kingdom of Hawaii and the United States, effectively tied the Hawaiian economy to the mainland, and eliminated the possibility of new economic powers from developing in the islands. Within 10 years, over 90 percent of Hawaii's trade was with the United States, and it was business rather than politics that eventually drove it to become a territory of the nation. The missionaries and their descendants "did well" economically but unfortunately lost their vision to "do good" spiritually.

Basel Mission

About the time the *Thaddeus* transported the first missionaries to Hawaii, war was ravaging Europe. The French General Barbanege threatened to destroy the city of Basel in 1815. Clergy and laymen from the Reformed Church of Basel and the Lutheran Church of Wurtenberg prayed for the safety of their city and pledged to start a missionary training school if Basel survived. Later that year, the French were defeated, and six Christian men founded the Evangelical Missionary Society of

Basel. In August 1816, the school opened with seven students, with the reverend C. C. Blumhardt as the director. The first Swiss mission school was initially designed to supply missionaries to the established British and Dutch Mission Societies; but within several years, the Basel Mission Society founded mission centers of its own in western Russia and in the Gold Coast (present-day Ghana). A revision to the British East India Company's charter in 1833 also opened up India to the non-British missionaries trained in Basel.

From the beginning, the Basel Misson believed that missionaries should receive both theological and business training. "Blumhardt's ideal was 'the craftsman-theologian,' an integrated model of human life in all its aspects," according to Suter and Gmür.[22] As an outsider, a missionary's life is his strongest witness, carrying more weight and influencing more powerfully than his words. "The Basel missionaries . . . saw the day-to-day activities of conducting businesses as themselves missional," noted Dwight P. Baker. "They were means through which industrial and commercial missionaries could give living demonstration of Christian character, diligence, thrift, honesty, faith, and compassion in action."[23]

Those sent by the Basel Mission were mostly businessmen. In India, the first missionaries arrived in Mangalore in 1834 and were soon involved in the economic sector. In 1840, a piece of land near Mangalore was given to the Mission, and the missionaries made unsuccessful attempts at coffee and sugar plantations. A subsequent farming venture was a partial failure as well. After abandoning agriculture efforts, the Basel missionaries determined that industrial business was more suited to the critical need of job creation.[24]

The Basel Mission's Joseph Josenhans visited Mangalore and concluded that more economic development was needed to give the Indian converts economic opportunities. He and Senators Sarasin and Christ, two other prominent Basel citizens with strong business connections, started an industrial commission in 1852 with the objectives of aiding new believers and modeling Christian virtues in the workplace. In 1853, the Basel Mission sent the missionary-merchant Gottlob Pfleiderer to India. In Mangalore, Pfleiderer opened a small trading business that imported goods for the missionaries and others in the area. The following year, Ludwig Rottmann, a German missionary-merchant, was sent to the Gold Coast. Rottmann established a small shop in Christiansborg, importing food, paper products, appliances, medicines and tools for the missionaries in the Gold Coast, who had founded a coffee plantation in Akropong.[25]

The Basel Mission Trading Company was formed in 1859 as a joint stock company with 100 shares and 200,000 Swiss Francs in capital. "Commercial activity," said the offering material, "is an effective helpmate in order to prepare the way for Christianity. The useful activity of labor will be a strong influence in preparing to win people over to the truth of the gospel, especially prepared by the new ethical standards presented herein."[26] The shareholders were prominent members of industry and business who were friendly to the objectives of the Basel Mission.

In 1862, another trading post (not located on a missionary base) opened in Ado Fa, Gold Coast. It was to be a "light in the darkness." Basel missionaries in the Gold Coast brought a number of cash crops to the region, including oil seeds, cotton, coffee and cocoa. A slave whose freedom was purchased by the Basel Mission brought cocoa beans from the territories of Fernando Po and San Thome on the African coast in 1879. A decade later, a missionary imported cocoa pods from Cameroon. The Gold Coast cocoa industry was born. The first cocoa shipment from the Gold Coast reached Europe in 1891, and 20 years later, the country was the world's leading exporter of cocoa. By this time in 1911, there were 34 European missionaries and 566 African coworkers in the Gold Coast mission factories.[27]

In India, the Basel missionaries started a weaving business in 1844 to provide employment. When they discovered that local looms were unable to compete with Western mills, they asked for help. In 1851, the European weaver John Haller was commissioned to India where he erected both a factory with 21 European handlooms and a dye house.[28] The Basel Mission's Mangalore weaving industry was a success, providing employment to hundreds. Haller, for his part, was credited with inventing the color khaki, first manufactured in Mangalore.[29] The factory's

Indian Christian workers were "so skillful that its products, known as 'mission-cloth,' became a synonym for quality."[30] The khaki material was designed to withstand the effects of intense sun and repeated washing. The Managlore police chief immediately equipped his men in "mission-cloth," soon followed by Lord Roberts whose British soldiers also donned the sturdy material.

A mechanical workshop founded in 1874 trained Indian apprentices as carpenters, blacksmiths and watchmakers. The Basel Mission Trading Company also started a tile-manufacturing factory in 1865 to produce roofing materials capable of protecting against India's heavy monsoon rains. It proved successful, and second and third factories were built in 1877 and 1880. By 1913, some 2,000 employees, both men and women, worked at the tile factories, producing 60,000 tiles a day.[31] The entire Basel Mission Trading Company operation in India employed 3,636 people that year. The company remained true to its objective of advancing the gospel and changing people's lives. Factories and trading posts retained their missionary distinction as centers of Christian education. Between its founding in 1859 and 1913, nearly ten million Swiss francs of company profits were invested in missions projects in India, China and the Gold Coast.[32] At today's conversion rate, this amounts to about $8 million, a considerable sum for Christian missions at the time.

World War I caused the organizational divorce of the Trading Company and the Mission. Great Britain and Germany were on opposite sides in the war. The Gold Coast and India were both British colonies, and the Basel Mission Trading Company, with its high-ranking German personnel, fell into disfavor. All European employees were sent back to their countries, and the Basel Mission sold its 40 percent share in the Trading Company in 1917. After the war, Many of the deported Gold Coast missionaries returned to operate the Union Trading Company, which assumed both operation of the Basel Mission Trading Company businesses and financial support for local missions work.[33]

In India, the industrial concerns of the Basel Mission Trading Company, considered to be a German organization, were confiscated by the British government. Looking for jobs, Indian blacksmiths and carpenters who had been trained in the Basel Mission factories migrated to Bombay. Once settled there, they formed the Basel Mission Canarese Church.

In the end, the Basel Mission achieved the objectives of Kingdom business. It achieved economic development in underdeveloped regions. It provided employment and training for Christians and non-Christians. It ran profitable enterprises that served their communities with useful products. It supported missions work through the proceeds of its commercial ventures. And it took the gospel in word and in deed to people who needed to hear the life-changing message of Jesus.

Lessons Learned

Business as missions experienced success in the past, and it can again. In light of what we have learned about culture, government and spiritual capital, how should we evaluate these Kingdom business efforts? What are the lessons we can learn from this survey of business as a missions vehicle throughout history? There are several worth highlighting:

- There are many ways to create opportunities that combine business ventures and missions efforts. A number of models and structures have been and can be employed.
- Missions efforts using business can be fruitful, leading to the growth of the Church. People all over the world came to Christ through Kingdom business.
- Business conducted with a missions or Kingdom-building objective can be profitable and effective. Companies founded by missionary business people provided the missionaries with a livelihood and sometimes grew well beyond that to create significant financial resources.
- With success comes the danger of losing sight of the priorities that were established when the business was first started. This led to some companies and business people abandoning the motivation for being located on the mission field, which much

be recognized and prevented.

- There is a need for technical and business skills as well as financial resources. The Basel Mission Trading Company showed us that successful Kingdom business efforts require both personal talent and investment money to make an impact. Of the two, investment is the least critical.

- Private property rights are critical to developing individual businesses and personal responsibility. As the history of Hawaii illustrates, business can only flourish once private property laws are established and enforced.

- Long-term success depends on building local ownership and supporting the business with a church that provides a strong spiritual base to which the business and its owners are accountable. It is more helpful to a nation to impart business skills and biblical values to local entrepreneurs and managers.

- Kingdom business companies that are leaders in their markets can be megaphones to the nation through which the gospel is proclaimed and business practices are reformed.

- In order to achieve a more lasting transformation, business development must focus both on building spiritual capital and on removing negative cultural barriers.

- Past missions-minded business efforts may have missed the fundamental link between developing biblical principles and enabling successful business. Many of these business as missions efforts, it appears, did not make building the nation's spiritual capital an explicit objective. The renewing of minds to the pattern of God must be a deliberate and significant objective of Kingdom business; it is the cultural foundation required for business to flourish.

We have not specifically mentioned the London Livery Companies in this chapter (see chapter 4) since they are not related to foreign missions efforts. However, there is also an important lesson from their story we can incorporate in Kingdom business. The London Livery Companies started with just a couple of business people who desired to follow God. So too can Kingdom businesses change nations with a small, committed Gideon band of dedicated business folks.

For all the successes illustrated in this historical overview, unfortunately sustainable transformation remained an elusive goal of past Kingdom business approaches. Perhaps partly due to their limited scope and partly due to their lack of understanding the importance of widespread cultural change, missions-minded business efforts failed to achieve sustainable transformation in a nation. Those engaged in Kingdom business must consider themselves agents of transformation rather than agents of individual salvation or business development. The difference might seem subtle, but I believe it is significant. As agents of economic and spiritual transformation, we should seek to develop spiritual capital in a nation.

Conclusion

Throughout history, God has used businessmen and women to take His Word to the ends of the earth, and some of the greatest missions movements were founded on the idea of the lay missionary using his or her business trade in the marketplace. Industry was established, jobs were created, missionary efforts were funded and the gospel was preached in word and in deed.

Kingdom business is not just a missions strategy of the past—it is a concept that the Church must rediscover today. Fortunately, a growing number of Kingdom-focused business people have done just that. They are seeking to achieve sustainable spiritual and economic transformation. Kingdom businesses are located in every part of the world and range in size from one person to many hundreds of employees. But what are the objectives that lead to sustainable transformation, and is there a way to categorize the various approaches? Armed with what we know about past business as missions efforts, what should we focus on as we take Kingdom business to the field?

CHAPTER 8

KINGDOM BUSINESS OBJECTIVES AND APPROACHES

Vili and his brothers own and operate Trim Line Bakery, a successful Kingdom business in western Romania that employs some 150 people.[1] The bakery specializes in confectionery items, such as cookies, cakes and pastries. Vili has a refreshing view of the integration of his faith and his business. When asked about his motivation for running the company, he stated, "First, to help my family; then to help my friends; then to help my church; and then to help my community." Vili's focus on helping others is a central component of the objectives of Kingdom business. Without negating personal profitability and financial shareholder value,

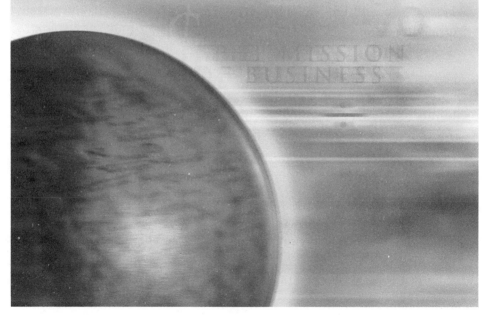

those engaged in Kingdom business have goals that transcend personal financial gain. Seeking to make their Kingdom business a vehicle for sustainable transformation in their community, they have more than one bottom line.

If sustainable spiritual and economic transformation is the ultimate goal, what particular objectives should we focus on? This chapter will delve much deeper into the three objectives of Kingdom business. It will also describe the three approaches of Kingdom business and present a framework for categorizing, evaluating and prioritizing the many diverse efforts in this emerging Church movement.

Objectives of Kingdom Business:
The Triple Bottom Line

A growing trend in secular philanthropy and economic development is the emergence of social value funds that invest in companies or organizations committed to a "double bottom line." Not only must a business provide strong financial returns, but it must also provide significant social or environmental returns. For example, the EcoEnterprise fund has $10 million in committed capital earmarked for ventures that affect environmental conservation in Latin America and the Caribbean. The Solstice Capital II fund invests $60 million in companies that offer solutions to major social and environmental challenges. And the focus of the $130 million ICV Partners fund is on businesses that improve inner city and ethnic minority areas in the United States. There is recognition that more than the single bottom line of profitability should be considered—that additional objective is some aspect of "social value."

A number of secular companies are known for their commitments to multiple bottom lines. Johnson and Johnson's longtime CEO Robert Wood Johnson captured his organization's objectives in a document called "Our Credo." It sums up Johnson and Johnson's responsibilities to the four important groups it serves: customers, employees, communities and stockholders. "The deliberate ordering of these groups—

customers first, stockholders last—proclaims a bold business philosophy: If we meet our first three responsibilities, the fourth will take care of itself."[2] Likewise, Hewlett-Packard's founders outlined their corporation's culture and commitment to multiple constituents in *The HP Way*. Ice cream makers Ben Cohen and Jerry Greenfield built their company on a "values-led" business philosophy. For many years, Ben and Jerry's donated 7.5 percent of its pre-tax profits to charitable causes.

Kingdom business rests on a similar recognition that our objectives should go beyond financial returns. For the Christian, however, there is an additional concern that is not captured in the examples above—that of spiritual transformation. Effective transformation involves addressing spiritual, social and economic conditions. That is the comprehensive ministry that Jesus modeled and the one to which Kingdom business is committed. And in order to achieve a lasting impact, the vehicle for transformation should be sustainable.

Stated succinctly, the overall objective of Kingdom business is *sustainable spiritual and economic transformation*. Sustainability implies the need for profitability of the business venture or economic development program; it also implies that a useful quality product or service is being offered. Spiritual transformation means pointing people to Jesus, developing them in their faith, teaching biblical values, and supporting the local church numerically and financially. Economic transformation means imparting a culture that develops spiritual capital, teaches business principles, creates jobs and builds local wealth.

So then, sustainability, economic transformation and spiritual transformation leave us with a three-fold objective for Kingdom business, a "triple bottom line" that may be outlined as follows: (1) profitability and sustainability, (2) local job and wealth creation, and (3) advancing the local church and building spiritual capital.

Each of these objectives is important, and they should be pursued simultaneously. None should be sacrificed. Failure to pursue profitability leads to outcomes that require a continual flow of donations; the organizations will not sustainable. Failure to pursue local job and wealth creation leads to outcomes that are no different from the funding of traditional missions efforts by profitable ventures in the First

FIGURE 2

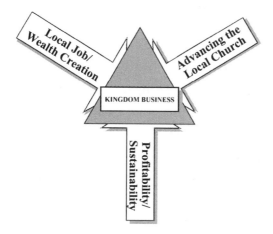

World; economic development will not be achieved. Failure to pursue advancement of the local church and the development of spiritual capital will lead to outcomes that are indistinguishable from those achieved by the social value funds mentioned previously; there will be no spiritual transformation component.

It is very important to measure results in light of the triple bottom line as the Kingdom business operates. Each of the three objectives should have some specific measure designed to evaluate the degree to which a Kingdom business effort has succeeded in achieving that objective. These measures must be appropriate to the situation, and they must be established in advance. The following sections detail the reasons why each of these three objectives is important, caution against ways of misapplying the objectives, and suggest some potential measures of success vis-à-vis each goal.

1. Profitability and Sustainability

Vili's stated objectives are to help others. But that doesn't mean he considers making a profit unimportant. On the contrary, helping others from his family to his church to his community requires that Trim Line Bakery be profitable. The quality of the company's products and the honesty it displays have earned Trim Line Bakery a substantial share of

the bakery business in its region. The company is profitable and growing. It now distributes baked goods throughout the country from its
facility in western Romania, and the company is planning to establish
additional bakeries.

Three of Vili's brothers are equity partners in Trim Line Bakery. The
dividends from the profits of this Kingdom business allow them to work
primarily in non-business ministries. In addition to working in the bakery, one brother is a youth pastor, another runs English-language outreach camps, and the third has planted a church. Profitability is the
source of Trim Line Bakery's ongoing operation and ability to help
others.

Importance. Profit is the lifeblood of a company, and without it, the
venture dies. Long-term sustainability depends on profitability. If a
Kingdom business helps others by providing useful goods or services,
but fails to achieve that in a sustainable manner, it cannot continue to
serve. Likewise, employment levels depend on profitability. A healthy
company can grow and enable more individuals to use the gifts and talents God has bestowed. An unprofitable company will contract or even
cease to exist, thus eliminating employment for those in need. And profit objectives provide an important discipline on those leading and managing companies.

Profit is also a reflection of the value of the good or service. It is the
sign that a company is effectively serving others. The more a customer
values a product or service relative to its cost, the more there is room for
profit. Companies that prove to be poor stewards of their resources will
experience high costs. Companies that fail to offer something others
find helpful or desirable will experience low sales. In either case, little or
no value is created, and little or no profit will result. Profit is the sign
that others are being served in a cost-effective manner.

From a business operation standpoint, profitability serves a number
of critical functions. Profit is the oil that keeps a company operating. It
provides additional funds for business expansion. It allows inventories
and receivables to grow, and it provides a cushion against market fluc-
tuations that affect cash flow. With the periodic ups and downs of sales,
profits protect against bankruptcy during a downturn.

Profits also have significant implications for wealth creation. Employees and investors/owners of a business benefit financially from profitability. Employees receive raises and promotions and participate in profit-sharing plans. Investors/owners experience a return on their investments. Profits result in significantly increased company valuations, enabling investors to raise more capital or receive a payback of their investment. These funds may then be deployed for future Kingdom business ventures. Both sets of stakeholders are thus increasingly capable of supporting financially the efforts of the local church.

It's not about . . . Though company profits are sometimes used to fund the church, in some cases that is not appropriate. When there are business owners or employees who are not explicitly committed to the Kingdom objectives of the company, profits from operations should be treated with more sensitivity to all stakeholders. Christians in business may be tempted to use corporate profits to support their favorite missions efforts. They may call it their company's "tithe" or ascribe some other spiritual term to it. However, as noble as the intentions, such unilateral practice is actually doing an injustice to co-owners who do not subscribe to the same belief. If the business includes nonbelieving shareholders, it is wrong to appropriate funds for causes that are not aligned with their interests.

At Inmac, I had partners and employees who were not Christians and who had no desire to see their company supporting some of the efforts that were of interest to me. As the CEO, I simply could not take from the common pool to fund causes that would seem rather objectionable to many others in the organization. (The only cause Inmac directly supported was charity that benefited the community in which the company was located.) I decided to let each shareholder determine what to do with his or her share of the earnings. Profits were shared with employees, and dividends were paid to shareholders. Each of us had the freedom to deploy the proceeds of profitability as we wished. Some supported giving and others did not.

Potential measures of success. The first measure of success is rather obvious—net profits from the business activity. However, there are a number of other measures that could indicate how well a Kingdom business is achieving the goal of profitability and sustainability:

- Net profitability of the venture
- Long-term increases in business profitability
- Overall revenue growth
- Increase in company valuation
- Successful liquidity events (sale of part or all of the company)
- Good risk-adjusted return to investors
- Growth in capital base for future deployment in Kingdom businesses

Profit is essential to the sustainability of Kingdom business efforts. We cannot fall into the trap of justifying unprofitable business by calling it "ministry." That is not a valid excuse. Once the profitability objective is sacrificed, it fails to meet the criteria of Kingdom business. Profit is the oxygen that allows Kingdom businesses to thrive and fulfill the other objectives of providing employment, improving standards of living, and furthering the mission of the Church.

2. Local Job and Wealth Creation

Vili's Trim Line Bakery provides meaningful employment to scores of Romanians. But it goes even further by making a concerted effort to hire people who face challenges to employment. The Life Center, an orphanage in Vili's region, is dedicated to training orphans in social and business skills through an employability program. Vili provides jobs for the orphans who graduate from this program.

Profits from Vili's Kingdom business have also allowed him to invest in a café and small bakery in a town close to Serbia that provides employment for "unemployable" women in the village. Jobs are being created, talents are being deployed, wealth is being developed and the standard of living is improving.

Importance. Kingdom businesses that experience rapid, profitable growth should lead to the creation of local jobs and wealth. Growth means significant job creation. A decent income becomes available to employees, and they are given a venue for exercising their talents.

Upward mobility becomes a possibility. Individuals in developing nations rise above the standard of basic subsistence living.

It is important that this Kingdom business objective be kept in mind and pursued actively. Failure to make local job and wealth creation a goal means failure to produce economic transformation. When the Americans and British withdrew their proposed assistance in building Egypt's Aswan Dam, the Egyptians turned to the Soviet Union for expertise in the project. The giant dam, built where Lake Nasser flows into the Nile, would provide hydroelectric power for much of the country. But very few Egyptians were involved in its design and construction. Russian engineers, developers and operators got the contracts and jobs, and all the profits flowed back into the Russian economy. The dam was completed in the 1960s at an enormous cost, and the Egyptians were forced to borrow heavily from the Russians. Egypt will be repaying those loans for a long time, and it is doubtful if the project helped the country develop. Likewise, Kingdom businesses that fail to create local jobs and wealth fail to bless the nation in which they are located.

It is through the creation of jobs that developing nations are most effectively helped. Programs that simply distribute handouts may meet immediate needs in the short term, but they fail to provide long-term solutions. Remember the maxim "Give a man a fish, and you have fed him for a day. Teach a man to fish, and you have fed him for a lifetime." Provide a man with capital and skills to build a successful fishing business, and you have enabled personal wealth, provided dozens of jobs, and fed many for generations.

Local wealth creation can originate from two sources: a Kingdom business's current profits and the potential for future profits. The latter is the basis for ascribing an economic value to the company. The prospect of future profits will lead to the value of a business exceeding its assets. In fact, for a profitable ongoing venture, the promise of future earnings is much more valuable than its current earnings. For example, the U.S. stock market has historically valued companies at an average of roughly 15 times their earnings. Using that ratio, if a business earns $100,000 per year after tax, the owner could sell the company for $1.5 million. In essence, many years of future profits can be captured in a single liquidity event—the sale of the enterprise. And therein lies the potential for significant wealth creation. Of course, a Kingdom business owner could turn around and deploy the proceeds of the company sale in starting another venture. If successful, more local jobs and more local wealth will result. A good entrepreneur can repeat this cycle over and over. Every company created improves the situation of everyone related to the business.

Wealth is the accumulation of assets to improve the economic viability of those around us. Wealth can provide for those who are in need. Those with financial means can provide investment funds for others, and they have the power to effect change through their influence.

A short anecdote in Ecclesiastes illustrates the point that lack of financial resources often means limited influence for change. "Now there lived in that city a man poor but wise, and he saved the city by his wisdom. But nobody remembered that poor man. . . . The poor man's wisdom is despised, and his words are no longer heeded" (Eccles. 9:15-16). Though wise, the man did not have lasting influence because he was poor. Wealth provides Christians a platform for sharing the gospel and effecting change. Perhaps most importantly, the creation of wealth changes the dynamics of a nation, launching it out of the cycle of poverty and despair and into the cycle of success and hope.

It's not about . . . The goal of local job and wealth creation is not to make a society fabulously rich. Rather than luxurious living, the objective of Kingdom business is an improvement in the employment situation and an overall increase in the standard of living. While some individuals in a developing nation may accumulate significant personal assets in the process, the focus is on poverty reduction and economic well-being of the region or country. Kingdom business is an opportunity to bless a nation in the name of the Lord Jesus Christ, and a migration toward the basic living standards of First World nations is the objective.

Potential measures of success. Employment and financial resources are desperately lacking in many parts of the developing world. For better results in meeting these needs, anyone who is funding Kingdom business efforts should set measures to define success. Several criteria relating to economic development could be used to evaluate effectiveness toward meeting these needs:

- Number of jobs created and sustained directly
- Number of secondary jobs developed
- Change in local unemployment rate
- Average salary level for jobs created versus local average salary or GDP
- Growth in company valuation
- Value of businesses sold
- Economic impact on the community as noted by local papers
- New institutions established or influenced

As Christians in the Third World earn incomes and run successful businesses, they become empowered to support the efforts of the local church. Rather than relying on funding from missions-sending nations, local believers can take more financial ownership in the ministries in their communities.

3. Advancing the Local Church and Building Spiritual Capital

As previously noted, Trim Line Bakery provides the means for Vili's brothers to serve in local church ministries. Vili and his brothers also demonstrate the love of Christ to employees and customers in their everyday business conduct at the bakery. By treating others with dignity and respect, by providing quality products, and by dealing honestly in their work, they are a living gospel to those around them. Serving others and sharing Christ through Trim Line Bakery is Vili's ministry.

Vili's new venture near Serbia also has explicit objectives to advance the local church. The café provides a Christian outreach, and one of Vili's brothers has planted a church in the village. The company's business practices have certainly managed to earn respect for the local Christian church. Impressed with the desire to hire "unemployable" women and serve the community, local authorities are providing the bakery and café facility at a greatly reduced rent.

Importance. Kingdom business can lead to advancement of the Church in a number of ways. Kingdom-focused management acts as a megaphone for the gospel instead of being a difficult intermediary. As role models of a comprehensive gospel, those in Kingdom business can introduce employees, partners and suppliers to the transforming message of Jesus in the setting of everyday life—the marketplace. As minds are transformed by word and by deed, spiritual capital can be developed. A more honest and caring business climate results in economic improvement, a blessing to the entire nation. Furthermore, as Kingdom businesses achieve success, management can utilize the platform that accompanies success. The gospel and the church enjoy increased respect among local community leaders, and the gospel is proclaimed in the community.

The church may achieve greater economic means and influence as well. The creation of new jobs could primarily benefit believers. At ET, we started to recruit employees for our call center from local Christian universities in India. After finding them to be excellent performers, we continued to hire from that source. In a society in which Christians often face economic challenges due to their social standing, the opportunities provided to these graduates were significant. Eventually, Christian groups got excited and agreed to prescreen candidates for us. Today, about 60 percent of ET's 1,000 employees are professing Christians.

The local church also benefits from the increased ability of its members to tithe. As Christian business owners and employees accumulate wealth, they are able to deploy it in local ministry. Local economic development results in a potential shift in the source of ministry support. No longer must local ministries rely on heavy support from foreign interests; the local church can now assume much more of the economic burden and therefore leadership of local ministries. Taking stewardship seriously, the owner of a successful Kingdom business in Croatia helped pay for significant renovations at his church. "And we did it with no Western money," he proudly announced.

"Local people everywhere deserve the blessing that goes with giving to their own churches," states Glenn Schwartz, Executive Director of World Mission Associates. "It is as simple as that—otherwise someone far away takes away their blessing and their self-respect."[3] He tells the story of a black South African church leader who regularly visited the United States to ask for money for his poor church. On one visit, this pastor sensed God instructing him to return home and raise the funds from his own people— a daunting prospect given that his church consisted of unemployed women and children! God spoke again and directed him to teach the women in the church four things: how to care for their families, how to bring their husbands to the Lord, how to make something marketable with their hands, and how to appreciate the importance of giving some of their earnings back to God. The women of that church began to participate in local commerce, and they accumulated financial resources. They also started to gather annually for a weekend conference at Thaba Nchu in South Africa. In 1994, the tithe collected from these women at the conference amounted to nearly $1 million! A needy South African church had broken Western dependency through successful local business.[4]

It's not about . . . Advancing the Church does not mean that only Christians should be employed in a Kingdom business. The company itself can be a mission field. It is where Christians can present the gospel by word and by deed. A manager of a Kingdom business in Slovakia partnered with a government drug rehab center and hired recovering addicts in order to share the love of Jesus and to get them on their feet. A Bulgarian Kingdom business brought several orphans on board for the same reason. As a result, in Kingdom businesses all over the world, everyday people are becoming followers of Jesus. Within the company itself, the mission of the Church can be advanced.

Potential measures of success. The local church may be advanced by adding to its numbers, by improving its standing in the community, and by increasing its economic resources. The following measures speak to these means of furthering the local church:

- Number of Christians hired
- Number of employees exposed to the gospel or coming to Christ
- Share of management in mentoring, discipling or accountability relationships
- Participation by management in local evangelistic activities
- Numeric growth of local churches
- Growth in community giving to local churches
- Growth in local and national respect for company and management (such as public or government recognition, positive press, regional or national awards)

Concluding Thoughts on Kingdom Business Objectives

There is much truth to the saying "You get what you measure!" We must recognize that measurement and accountability relative to these Kingdom business objectives is required. Failure to monitor and evaluate progress on all three goals will virtually guarantee failure to achieve one or more of these objectives. We may fail to achieve profitability and thus be left with projects and ventures that are unsustainable. We may fail to create local jobs and wealth and thus be left with efforts that achieve no economic development or poverty reduction. We may fail to advance the local church and thus be left with programs that produce no spiritual capital or worldwide missions benefits.

One experienced entrepreneur who has established a number of Kingdom businesses in Asia fosters accountability to the different objectives in an innovative way. Every Kingdom business professional in his companies reports to a corporate manager for business objectives *and* to a missions agency for Great Commission objectives. He is responsible for economic and spiritual results, and both the corporate manager and the missions overseers can fire him for failing to perform.

The triple bottom line of Kingdom business is critical. Neither profitability and sustainability, local job and wealth creation, nor advancement of the local church may be sacrificed at the altar of the other two. It is this three-fold objective that sets Kingdom business apart from secular social work, traditional missions and conventional business.

Approaches to Kingdom Business: The Three Segments

First World efforts to cure the problems of the developing Third World are increasingly focusing on economic development. At one end of the spectrum, the World Bank and other multinational organizations are extending many millions of dollars in loans to developing nations in order to support their economies. These funds are often earmarked for infrastructure improvements such as the building of roads. At the other end, organizations such as the Grameen Bank in Bangladesh are extending loans that average less than $200 to individuals in order to enable them to start or expand very small and basic businesses.

Within this wide spectrum, Christians have found three segments of economic development efforts suitable for Kingdom business: microenterprise development (MED), small and medium enterprises (SME), and overseas private equity (OPE). (The subset of MED conducted by Christian organizations is often termed Christian microenterprise development [CMED]; there is no similar acronym to describe Christian efforts to assist SMEs or promote larger OPE ventures.) These three segments can be categorized on the basis of the typical investment amount that supports a business:

FIGURE 3

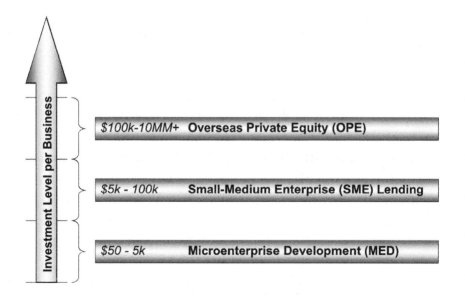

One important caveat to these broad investment ranges for each of the three approaches must be noted: Different local economic situations will affect the actual dollar amounts that are deployed for an approach.

For example, one Christian MED organization lends an average of $120 per microenterprise in East Asia, while its loans to microenterprises in Eastern Europe average $1,300. The reason the figure for loans to Eastern Europe is more than 10 times the amount of the loans to East Asia is due to the healthier economy in Eastern Europe where GDP per person is significantly higher. A more rigorous method for assigning financial investment figures to each Kingdom business approach might account for differences in local GDP per person situations.

Later chapters will explain and analyze thoroughly each of the three approaches to Kingdom business. But a short explanation of the overall framework and examples of each approach may be helpful at this point.

1. Microenterprise Development (MED)

With loans as small as $50, Christian microenterprise development organizations are making a difference in the lives of individuals who use the funds to start, expand or improve their microenterprises. One such person is Lola Tasuna, who lives with five other people as a squatter in Manila in the Philippines. Their home is nothing more than a shelter constructed from scrap materials. At age 72, retirement is not an option. In order to eat, she must work every day.

Lola's business is creating kerosene lamps. Prior to becoming a client of a Christian MED known as Opportunity International, she had to search through garbage dumps to find jars from which she could make lamps, cleaning them with her fingernails in a bucket of cold water. However, with the funds she received from a microloan from Opportunity International, Lola now has the resources to buy clean jars at 5 cents a piece. She no longer has to spend her mornings searching for discarded jars, and her production is not limited by the number she can locate. Employing family members to help her paint the lids, add wicks, and attach metal handles, Lola can make up to 300 lamps a day, netting $30 daily in gross profit from her business.[5]

Though individual microloans affect the employment of a couple of people at a time, the low financial investment of each loan means that MED organizations can impact thousands of individuals with fairly modest loan portfolios. And as each loan is repaid, the funds can be recycled to improve the life of another family. In short, Christian MED is Kingdom business with the power to transform cultures at the individual and family level.

2. Small and Medium Enterprises (SME)

With financial commitments typically ranging from \$5,000 to \$100,000, some Christian development organizations are seeking to assist small and medium enterprises. Maria is a sportswear designer in Bulgaria. When she met representatives of the Christian SME lending organization Integra Ventures in 1999, Maria's business was housed in a single room with six employees and four sewing machines. In order to display her product line, Maria also ran a retail shop in her neighborhood. The business was doing well, but she lacked the confidence and funding to expand.

Integra provided both the strategic plan and financial resources that Maria needed. She was encouraged to expand her production into a larger facility and to increase her marketing effort. The market was ripe for her casual clothing in larger sizes—Maria just needed to reach it. With a \$10,000 loan, training and support from Integra Ventures, she renovated a new production facility and bought new machines and raw materials. Within months, Maria's Kingdom business had increased production by 50 percent. She now employs more than a dozen people, including some who might otherwise have little opportunity for work. Maria donates clothing with minor defects to local orphanages and gives large discounts to Christians who purchase apparel for the orphanage. And she is ready to move her business forward.[6]

Even in the developed world, it has been recognized that small businesses account most significantly for job growth. SME lending targets this segment with financial and training resources that allow Kingdom business owners to grow their companies and expand their influence. As loans are repaid, additional SMEs can be assisted and other communities impacted. Christian SME development is Kingdom business with the power to transform cultures at the organization and community level.

3. Overseas Private Equity (OPE)

Some Kingdom businesses represent either a sufficient current size or a significant growth potential to warrant major investments of $100,000 or more in the form of private equity transactions. Often, but certainly not always, these companies are managed by Christians from the developed world.

One such Kingdom business entrepreneur is Ken Crowell, an American who developed a passion for blessing the nation of Israel. An engineer by training, Ken pursued an offer from Motorola in 1968 to conduct research and development in Israel. During his three-year stint, God gave Ken a vision for Kingdom business. Upon returning to the United States and with the agreement of his employer, Motorola, he proceeded to launch Galtronics, a company that produced UHF-VHF antennas. His first employees were Christians who shared his desire to bless Israel.

After resigning from Motorola, Ken moved Galtronics to Tiberias, Israel. The city needed industry and the government was eager to help—despite Ken's openness about his Christian motivations. "I am not so concerned about your Christian involvement as I am about our need to strengthen our economy by establishing new businesses within Israel," assured a consulate director. "We will welcome and assist you in Israel." At its Israeli founding in 1978, Galtronics stated that its purposes included establishing a witness, supporting the building of the local church, providing work for believers, blessing the nation of Israel, and strengthening the local economy. "We fully understood from the beginning," said Ken, "that the business must be self-supporting and profitable."

Galtronics grew to become the largest employer in its city, exporting antennas "Made in Israel" to one-third of the cell phone manufacturers in the world, including Motorola and Nokia. The company received the nation's highest industrial award, the Praz Kaplan. Additional businesses were added over the years, and Ken's ventures now range from messianic music to fix-tuned radios. Customer concern about the stability in Israel led to additional factories being built in Scotland and China and the employment of more than 700 people worldwide. By 1998, Galtronics was worth $70 million.

Alongside the company, a local church called Peniel Fellowship sprouted. Initially comprised of seven people, Peniel Fellowship is now a thriving church of more than 250 believers. The company has also sponsored a summer volunteer program to expose engineering and business students from several U.S. Christian universities to the practice of Kingdom business. After sharing their talents and faith for a summer at Galtronics, some of these business students have returned to settle in Israel and bless the nation.[7]

Though OPE requires higher levels of capital investments, the potential to influence a nation is significantly greater as well. Christian OPE seeks to build sizeable corporations that impact hundreds or thousands of people economically and spiritually. A successful venture yields an increased capital base from which additional Kingdom-focused companies can be funded. Christian OPE is Kingdom business with the power to transform cultures at the industry and even national level.

Conclusion

Kingdom business must be committed to achieving a triple bottom line that speaks to sustainable economic and spiritual transformation. Specifically, the three objectives of Kingdom business are profitability and sustainability, local job and wealth creation and advancement of the local church, and the three approaches to Kingdom business are microenterprise development (MED), small and medium enterprises (SME) and overseas private equity (OPE).

When and where is each of these approaches most appropriate, and how well has each approach succeeded in achieving the three objectives? Those are important questions for anyone intending to pursue Kingdom business. I did some more digging for answers.

CHAPTER 9

ROLE OF EACH KINGDOM BUSINESS APPROACH

A Filipino woman turns jars into simple kerosene lamps. A small Bulgarian textile business designs and manufactures clothing. An Israeli company produces cell phone antennas and has become the largest employer in its city. As we have seen, all are the result of Kingdom business efforts to achieve sustainable economic and spiritual transformation.

Even though modern technologies like television and the Internet seem to make the world a smaller place, there is one truth that is amplified by these examples from other nations: the world is not homogenous. There are cultural differences that are expressed in various attitudes, beliefs, attires and relationships. There are economic differences that

yield a wide array of standards of living and economic infrastructures. There are political differences that affect freedoms, rules and levels of enforcement. There are educational differences that result in a significant variance of literacy rates and technical know-how.

Just how do we implement Kingdom business in a world that is so disparate? As I have outlined briefly, Kingdom business professionals are pursuing economic and spiritual objectives using three approaches: microenterprise development (MED), small and medium enterprises (SME), and overseas private equity (OPE). But is there one that might be considered the best, to which the Church should devote its resources? Do certain approaches work better in some places than in others? What is the role of each Kingdom business approach?

A Kingdom Business Framework

These are the questions that prompted the development of a basic Kingdom business framework. There must be recognition that conditions around the world vary and that a single approach is not optimal in every situation. For example, a call center business like ET in India would stand little to no chance of succeeding in parts of Africa, because basic infrastructure requirements simply do not exist. Likewise, it would make little sense to help individuals establish small roadside vegetable stands in the United States, since microenterprises do not provide sufficient economic value by Western standards. Every region or nation is at a different stage in the migration toward successful capitalism, and the specific way of assisting a country depends on the prevailing conditions there. As a nation increases its capacity for more advanced forms of capitalism, the options expand to allow more sophisticated Kingdom business efforts.

Criteria to Consider
Evaluating a particular region's suitability for different Kingdom business approaches requires a careful look at local conditions. What is the current business climate? Does the workforce have proper education? Is

the legal infrastructure friendly to business ventures? The following criteria should be considered when evaluating Kingdom business options:

- *Pervasiveness of poverty.* Only very basic economic activities can be undertaken in situations of widespread poverty. Poverty creates hopelessness, lack of confidence and a narrow way of thinking about opportunity. More sophisticated business ventures can be undertaken in wealthier countries; the cycle of success often yields more confidence.
- *Degree of industrialization.* A nation that is more industrialized can participate in advanced forms of commerce. One that is more less developed is likely to be confined to simple cottage industry activities.
- *Size of domestic economy.* The larger the local economy, the greater the domestic resources and markets for products, and thus, the greater the potential for more significant enterprises.
- *Level of spiritual capital.* A culture that embraces successful business qualities such as integrity, excellence and hard work is better suited to more complex ventures than one that does not value them. Where spiritual capital is not present, trust is eroded and dreams are limited. A few might develop great wealth, but the nation as a whole does not prosper; businesses remain simple and small.
- *Level of education in the workforce.* Some developing nations have a very high education level while others have not yet overcome basic illiteracy problems (e.g., Bulgaria has a higher literacy rate than the United States, while only one in five Nepalis can read). This affects the type of industry that can be sustained.
- *Economic infrastructure.* Sophisticated businesses require an economic infrastructure that boasts established potential suppliers, partners and customers. Advanced commerce also requires an environment in which goods, services and money are allowed to move freely, safely and rapidly and in which companies are free to operate without excessive governmental burdens.

- *Physical infrastructure.* Significant business enterprises can only thrive in areas that have the necessary physical infrastructure they need to operate, communicate, transport and trade. Thus, adequate roads, reliable utilities (e.g., power, communications) and stable banks are important.
- *Legal infrastructure.* Regions are far more attractive for larger ventures where property rights are protected, the rule of law prevails and corruption is curtailed. Investors shy away from areas that do not offer the protection of a proper legal infrastructure.
- *Currency strength.* Investors also pay close attention to the strength of a local currency. Where the risk of a country-wide economic collapse is real, significant investment in local businesses is limited. If inflation is excessive, economic opportunity and development is limited.
- *Degree of freedom.* Kingdom business is particularly attractive in locations that offer certain basic freedoms, especially religious freedoms that permit Christians to worship and discuss their faith in public. Kingdom business efforts do better in nations that are less restrictive of foreigners owning assets such as bank accounts, stock, companies or land.
- *Degree of political stability.* Uncertainty about the longevity of the current political climate also impacts the attractiveness of a region for larger ventures. If there exists a significant threat of a government overthrow and subsequent decline in the business climate, companies will seek alternative locations. The key is predictability. A stable political environment with some freedoms is more important than an unstable free environment.

Conditions vary widely in the Third World, and local infrastructures and environments affect which Kingdom business approaches are best suited. Taking these criteria into account, we can segment the developing world into three broad categories: poorest regions (e.g., Botswana, Haiti), developing regions (e.g., Bulgaria, Guatemala), and industrializing regions (e.g., India, China). (Appendix C provides a list of developing nations that fit each of these categories.) While this segmentation is a general rule, it is difficult to paint it with such a broad brush—there are many exceptions to the rule. It is important to look at specific countries and have a sense for what types of businesses those countries can sustain before embarking on a program of economic development.

Categories of Developing Regions

Poorest Regions. Some of the poorest areas of the world have minimal socioeconomic and legal infrastructures, negative or unstable macroeconomic environments and major cultural barriers to overcome. Not only is there little spiritual capital, but prevailing cultural values do not lend themselves to growing the account. The rule of law is not respected, authorities are often corrupt, and the legal infrastructure is inadequate. These regions usually impose tight restrictions on foreign currency exchange and stock ownership.

Poorest regions have a very small domestic market and very few trade agreements with other nations. These regions lack basic infrastructure such as reliable electricity, roads and banks. They most often have a high illiteracy rate that precludes the local population from participating in higher-level business roles. As a result, much of the economic activity is classified as basic cottage industry. Countries like Bangladesh and Ghana fit this classification.

Poorest regions are best assisted through MED to build simple microenterprises that generally operate in the informal sector, largely unaffected by tax laws, government regulations, exchange rates or the state of the economy. Indeed, in some locations, conditions are such that MED is the only option—often the infrastructure and local economy simply cannot support larger, more advanced companies. OPE, in particular, is often unrealizable due to restrictions in many locations on issuing or owning stock outside the country.

That is not to say that the other approaches cannot work in all poorest regions. The trading model developed by early Christian-motivated trading companies can still work, but it tends to involve cottage industries brought together by outsiders to create a supply for foreign markets. For example, one Kingdom business professional is running a 700-

person clothing company in Central Asia, and another has established a 450-person picture-frame manufacturing company in Haiti. It is important to note that larger ventures like these are operated and managed by Western Christian business people. The businesses still rely on cottage industry work (sewing and woodcarving) while lending structure and standards to the design, quality and distribution of products. But in general, MED will be most effective in poor regions when it creates a base structure of business and starts people on a new way of thinking.

Developing Regions. Some developing regions have limited legal and socioeconomic infrastructures, somewhat unstable macroeconomic environments, and real cultural obstacles to overcome. While there is some spiritual capital, many prevailing cultural values are not aligned with successful business and growth of the spiritual capital account. There is corruption in the political and economic system that is harmful to commerce. These regions usually impose currency controls, and even when available, stock markets are underdeveloped.

Developing regions often have small domestic markets and limited trade agreements to facilitate exports. Currency instability and inflation represent real risks in these regions, and the physical infrastructure needed for business is lacking. These regions may have an educated workforce, but they often represent smaller economies with significant barriers to successful capitalism, such as inexperienced workers, corruption or political risk. Somewhat more sophisticated businesses can be sustained, but the poor infrastructure often precludes large ventures. Macedonia and Colombia fit this classification.

In these regions, SME development seems best suited to the local conditions. SME development helps to build sustainable SME businesses, create jobs and foster a somewhat skilled labor force. However, since these regions will likely have some aspects that appear more like poor regions or industrializing regions, SME assistance should not be the only approach. In particular, there is likely to be a role for MED among the poor in developing regions. Although there are certainly some developing regions whose start in commerce will best be pursued in simple cottage industry activities, in general, SME lending and mentoring does seem to be the most appropriate approach for creating jobs, increasing financial resources and growing spiritual capital in these regions.

Industrializing Regions. Industrializing regions are characterized by basic socioeconomic and legal infrastructures; stable, export-friendly macroeconomic environments; and fewer cultural barriers to successful capitalism. There will be some history of economic growth in the region and, most likely, venture activity will already exist. Although more spiritual capital has amassed in these regions than in other Third World regions, there is still a need for cultural change in order to really grow the account. Immoral and corrupt practices can be a problem.

These regions may be part of a large domestic economy. Though not yet First-World, they have an established economy with a number of stable exporting companies. Often cash can be moved freely in and out of the country, and a sizeable portion of the population is educated. Industrializing regions may be found in India, China and Northern Mexico.

Industrializing regions are poised to sustain larger enterprises built through OPE investments, but as in all developing nations, there will be subsets of the population for whom MED or SME development would be most beneficial. In short, all three approaches have a place in industrializing regions. However, the potential for OPE Kingdom businesses to create jobs and wealth, impact the region and industry for Christ and achieve sustainability makes that approach particularly appealing.

Kingdom Business Framework Diagram

The particular Kingdom business approach that is most appropriate depends on local conditions for successful capitalism. As noted, these include the socioeconomic, legal and cultural infrastructures. Where these are minimal, MED is most needed. Where these are limited, SME development is most helpful. Where these are basic, OPE can succeed.

The following diagram indicates the *potential* of each Kingdom business approach given the local conditions and infrastructures in a nation. In the United States, a nation that has a high level of socioeconomic, legal and cultural infrastructure, there is a lot of investment in small businesses and large ventures but very little in microenterprises. By contrast, a nation like Bhutan, with a low level of socioeconomic, legal and

FIGURE 4

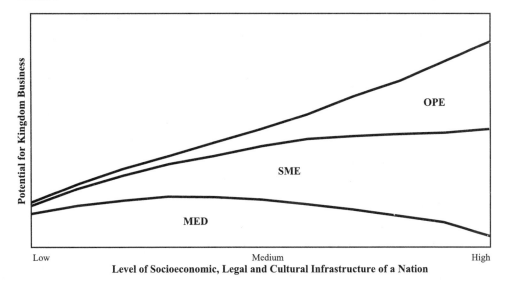

cultural infrastructure, provides an environment that is less conducive for medium to large businesses. In that country, microenterprise development makes a lot of sense.

Observations on the Framework

It would be a generalization to claim that every country falls into a single segment or that a single Kingdom business approach should be pursued in each country. In a large and economically diverse nation such as China, regions around Hong Kong are thriving economic zones where OPE might be most suitable, while in poorer regions near Kyrgyzstan and Kazakhstan, MED or SME development might be most appropriate. Likewise, Northern Mexico's economy is much more developed than that of Southern Mexico. Different approaches within that country are needed.

Even developing nations that have less regional variability within their borders may merit multiple approaches. India is a case in point. Its infrastructure, economy and population stratification are such that all three approaches have value. In the Philippines, some segments of the society are prime for basic MED while others are suitable for SME assistance.

As the "Potential for Kingdom Business" diagram illustrates, there can be a role—albeit sometimes limited—for all three Kingdom business approaches in each region. Every developing nation has poor people who are best served through MED. Growing SMEs can be found all around the world. And even some of the poorest and least-developed regions like Haiti and Central Asia have Kingdom businesses with hundreds of employees.

Using the Framework

There are two ways to use the Kingdom business framework presented here. The first is to consider it as a snapshot analysis tool. At any given point in time, the current conditions in a region can affect which of the Kingdom business approaches is most appropriate. A snapshot shows different regions ripe for different approaches.

Second, the Kingdom business framework can be used as a roadmap for development. This involves looking at a particular region and its prevailing conditions over time. A region that is underdeveloped and lacking in basic infrastructure may be a good candidate for MED programs today, but there is an expectation that it will improve its condition over time and become suitable for more advanced approaches to Kingdom business. As the nation's infrastructure and conditions for successful capitalism improve, more Kingdom business resources may be devoted to SME and even OPE economic development efforts.

Developing Spiritual Capital

Kingdom business that presents the gospel can grow a nation's spiritual capital at several levels of development. That development process can be likened to the building of a house: some nations are at the stage in which they are manufacturing individual bricks (MED); other nations are building walls (SME); still others are building complete houses (OPE). But whatever the nation's current stage of development, the gospel is critical for spiritual capital growth, the foundation on which all houses of business must be built.

Many emerging economies are at the very beginning of that process. As they take their first baby steps in MED, the basic unit or building block of spiritual capital is also promoted. The values acquired by microentrepreneurs are then shared with the family. But in order to lay the building blocks of spiritual capital, faith must be added to MED training. This is a necessary first step so that nations can begin to develop. The gospel is important in MED efforts, because spiritual capital grown through MED is necessary for a nation to graduate to more advanced economies that feature successful medium-size enterprises.

Once some spiritual capital is in place, more complex organizations can be created. This is the basis of successful SME development. In SMEs, these spiritual building blocks work together to create the culture of a company. SMEs bring together individual spiritual capital building blocks to create small pieces of a structure. Values are shared within the business, and they are also shared with suppliers and associates. The spiritual capital created by SMEs results in the first joining of bricks.

Akin to an entire section of a wall, OPE ventures represent even larger structures that share values and grow spiritual capital. With the advent of OPE companies, the size of the group effecting spiritual capital will grow to include industries, associations and related suppliers. These in turn establish the various institutions that are necessary for the regional and national success of spiritual capital and therefore for the blessing of a nation. This is the economy's infrastructure—the whole house. Cultural values and spiritual capital developed and evidenced at the economy's macro level set a nation on a path to success and blessing. Without the fundamental spiritual capital reserve and cultural values in place, a nation will more likely resemble the failed capitalism of Russia where a few achieve great wealth but the nation is not blessed.

Kingdom business professionals are best equipped to bring the transforming gospel that leads to spiritual capital. Commenting about his charity, Samaritan's Purse, Franklin Graham recently said, "Our focus is the gospel. We are an evangelistic organization that happens to do relief."[1] Likewise, Kingdom business organizations must be first evangelistic organizations that happen to do MED, SME or OPE development—not the reverse. The development of spiritual capital through the transforming power of the gospel is the heritage that will make the country successful. It is what truly provides the blessing to the nation.

Governments and Kingdom Business

In developing nations, governments can be a cause for serious concern to Kingdom business professionals. Some business people believe that Kingdom business must not be attempted in countries characterized by graft and corruption or where stable governments do not already exist, pointing out that these problems prevent business from developing with integrity. Certainly, Kingdom businesses should not be involved with bribery or support corruption in a country. Furthermore, what happens in an unstable country where property rights are not respected as they are in Judeo-Christian nations and where investments can be confiscated by the government at a moment's notice? In countries with unfavorable governments, some have avoided business development efforts altogether.

These are all valid concerns. So, where does that leave Kingdom business in the face of such problems? Kingdom business professionals must begin to work with each country "just as it is." Kingdom business can begin to achieve spiritual and economic transformation even in the most challenging political situations.

In countries where corruption exists, property rights are not respected, and governments are unstable, the most appropriate Kingdom business option is Christian microenterprise development (CMED). The seeds of faith and good business can be planted through CMED, which can lay the fundamental building blocks required to build the spiritual capital that blesses a nation. Most individual CMED investments are small and represent small asset values. As such, they fall below the radar of corrupt officials, and they are too small to warrant bribery attempts. Protection rackets focused on the poorest do exist in some countries, but the return generally tends to be too low to make this official practice. (However, CMED funds might be targets of corruption and if possible should be located beyond the reach of corrupt governments.)

The development of CMED in these countries provides important values. It brings the gospel and with it the opportunity for individuals to experience a renewing of their minds, allowing them to conform to the pattern of God rather than to the pattern of their world. As they gain an understanding of God's values, one by one, gradually the culture of their families, communities, and eventually the views and culture of their nation can be changed. CMED can establish a spiritual beachhead in a nation.

In a national environment characterized by bribery, corruption and a lack of respect for property rights, investment in SMEs is more apt to attract the interest of corrupt officials and organized crime. More than likely, SME activity will not be appropriate in situations of serious government corruption. Involvement in larger ventures through OPE investment is simply out of the question. Large investments attract corruption like flies to honey, and OPE investors will stay away. Such a nation may not be ready for these two types of investment. Even so, an opportunity may exist to begin softening the hearts of country leaders armed with the secular knowledge of what blesses nations.

Common Sense Risk Assessment

Even (or perhaps especially) in Kingdom business, risk is an important topic. It is like gravity. If you jump off a tall building, the risk is that you will be killed or injured. We have examined a number of the criteria that produce significant business risk, such as the level of spiritual capital, the pervasiveness of poverty and the legal infrastructure. Jumping into an environment that is not suited for the particular business approach defies the laws of business. For example, attempting an OPE activity in the poorest regions is cause for serious risk analysis. There is simply insufficient cultural, legal and economic infrastructure to expect success.

While we look to God for direction, we must also employ common sense. We cannot assume that our Kingdom business efforts will necessarily succeed because we are doing them for God. More than likely, they will fail if they defy basic laws. Jesus refused to put His Father to the test of defying gravity (see Matt. 4:5-7). We should do likewise and take care not to defy the laws of business. To ensure that a Kingdom business approach is appropriate, conduct a careful evaluation of the local conditions in light of the criteria described in this chapter.

Conclusion

FIGURE 5

Approach	Investment Size	Objective	Type of Jobs Created	Suited Environment	Example Countries
Microenterprise	$100–$5K	basic subsistence	lowest level, very low pay	poorest regions; limited legal and economic infrastructure	Botswana, Bangladesh, Haiti, Sudan
Small and Medium Enterprises (SME)	$5K–$100K	small business growth	somewhat skilled, low pay	developing regions; minimal legal and economic infrastructure	Macedonia, Colombia, Belarus, Guatemala
Overseas Private Equite (OPE)	$100K+	significant economic expansion/ wealth creation	more skilled, higher pay	industrializing regions; basic legal and economic infrastructure	India, Poland, Brazil, China

This table summarizes the Kingdom business framework in chart form, noting the three Kingdom business approaches and the environment for which each is best suited. MED, SME and OPE all have pros and cons. No single approach may be termed "best" in every situation. Each has its place, and each plays a role in the economic development path of a region. MED promotes the basic building blocks of economic activity and infrastructure, SME development assembles those blocks to grow small companies, and OPE extends that concept in the form of sophisticated businesses that transform industries.

Of the three Kingdom business approaches, there is one that has been applied in even the most difficult environment. It seeks to bless people with precious few resources and empower those individuals to function as successful entrepreneurs. For as little as $30, it helps people like Marawa Rosina become economically sustainable. How is that possible? We'll find out in the next chapter.

CHAPTER 10

MICROENTERPRISE DEVELOPMENT (MED)

What is the power of $200 in the business world? Well, in many parts of the world it's quite a lot. That is the average amount lent to microentrepreneurs by the largest CMED organization. On average, each loan is credited with sustaining one job and creating another half job. That's 1.5 jobs directly impacted by a $200 loan! Even more, the funds are repaid and re-loaned in such a way that $200 in capital could impact six jobs a year.[1] "Microfinance has proven that it helps people help themselves," said Citigroup vice chairman Stanley Fischer.[2]

Marawa Rosina spends long days designing and manufacturing traditional African clothing in Harare, Zimbabwe. Due to a shattered local economy, she embarks on two-day trips to neighboring Botswana to sell

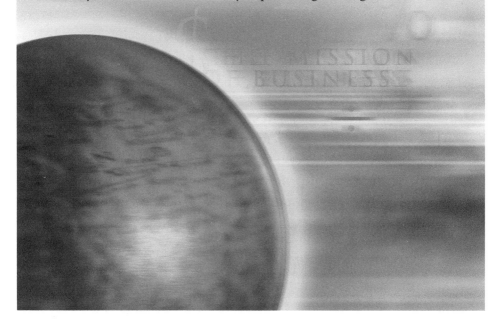

her merchandise. The resulting sale of a considerable amount of clothing makes the grueling bus trips worth the effort. But she did not always produce enough volume to justify the expeditions to Botswana. For microentrepreneurs like Marawa, it was almost impossible to obtain the necessary credit to boost her fabric inventory. Fortunately, MicroKing, the Zimbabwe affiliate of the large secular MED organization called ACCION, offered her a $30 loan. This wasn't a large amount by Western standards, but with that money she increased her production substantially—enough to enable her to sell in Botswana. Now on a fourth loan in the amount of $130, she has been able to save enough in a single year to cover tuition and uniforms for her grandchildren's schooling.[3]

Kingdom business professionals involved in CMED provide financial and business assistance to microentrepreneurs like Marawa. But they go even further by addressing people's eternal state through the gospel and by developing in them biblical values that come from personal faith. CMED Kingdom business professionals manage CMED lending programs, teach spiritual truth and business concepts to microentrepreneurs, cast a vision for loan recipients, and identify which ones have the potential to be future SME or OPE leaders.

MED Organizations

The vision shared by secular and Christian MED organizations is to assist the world's economically disadvantaged by providing two important services: financing and education/training. Although attention has been focused on MED since the 1990s, microenterprise development has actually been practiced for several decades. For example, the Ecumenical Church Loan Fund located in Geneva, Switzerland, has been involved in MED for about 40 years. With a rich history of experience and study, even the largest and most successful MED organizations are still learning lessons.

Who Are the "Economically Disadvantaged?"
MED organizations service the masses, typically poorer people who are considered "unbankable." Certainly these people lack resources that

could be used as collateral, but even worse, they often fall into social classes that are outside the comfort zone of the local banks. They lack the connections that would allow them access to capital from traditional sources. MED recipients are more typically women or members of a lower caste (the CMED organization Opportunity International reports that 86 percent of its loan recipients are women).[4] MED programs have found that women are often more responsible borrowers than men and that they are more inclined to spend their microenterprise earnings on the welfare of their families. "Loan default rates for female borrowers are three percent compared with ten percent for men in the same programs," noted a United Nations report.[5]

"MED programs often promote that they work with the 'poor' or the 'poorest of the poor.' But this is almost never realized in the field," CMED experts Bussau and Mask noted.[6] The "poorest of the poor" often suffer from homelessness, mental problems, malnutrition and disease, which usually prevents them from participating in the economy. MED typically serves the economic class right above that category. To be sure, MED clients are certainly considered poor by any Western standard. These individuals are usually sole proprietors engaged in relatively simple economic activity: for example, vendors who buy fruit to resell on the street or women who sew garments at home. In these cases, the loan funds would be used to purchase an initial supply of fruit or to acquire a sewing machine. An estimated 500 million microentrepreneurs are potential clients for microfinance; in 2003, 57 million borrowers worldwide earned less than one dollar a day. The number of borrowers is expected to reach 100 million by the end of 2005, according to the Microcredit Summit.[7]

What Is "Microfinance?"

Though often used interchangeably, the terms "microfinance" and "microeconomic development" refer to different functions. Microeconomic development involves activities such as funding, training and mentoring to promote the development of business among the economically disadvantaged. Microfinance is a subset of Microeconomic development and is comprised of three financial services functions:

microcredit, microsavings and microinsurance. Today, there are some 7,000 microfinance programs worldwide.

Microcredit was the initial thrust of MED efforts, since access to capital is such a critical component of successful economic development. Indeed, this has resulted in millions of MED borrowers worldwide, with outstanding balances totalling in the billions of dollars. Though the average loan size is around $400, there is significant variation across geographies, from $45 loans in Thailand to $5,000 loans in Eastern Europe. To account for economic differences, academics often define a microloan in terms of local gross national product (GNP) levels.[8] For purposes of this book, I, like most practitioners, define MED as dealing with loans below $5,000.

MED organizations view lending as their primary function, but there is a growing realization that other financial services are important for the success of this segment of the population. In particular, *microsavings* is a much-needed service in many developing nations. Since the poor are not serviced by traditional banks, MED programs are starting to fill the gap. The poor will save when possible, and many are doing so. The level of inflation in many developing nations is so high that those who stuff their money under their mattresses suffer severe economic detriment. Furthermore, money kept in a home is susceptible to the very tangible threat of theft. Microsavings is found mainly in Asia and East Africa.

The third and least-developed component of microfinance is *microinsurance*. Microentrepreneurs have insurance needs like any other business owner, yet they find it nearly impossible to obtain these services. Microinsurance is a recognized need that is still in a nascent phase of development.

MED Lending

Interest Rates

By Western standards, MED loans are not cheap. With a pretty sizeable variation in interest rates, a typical microloan borrower pays interest at a 36 percent annual real flat rate. (It can be higher in countries where inflation is a serious problem. "Flat rate" means the amount of interest owed is calculated on the initial loan size and does not decrease as the principal balance declines.) However, before lobbing accusations of usury at these rates, which compare unfavorably even to the highest consumer credit rates of the West, it is important to note several points of context.

First, MED clients are all too happy to accept these lending conditions, and there is no shortage of potential borrowers. Banks refuse to lend to them at any interest rate. Where available, street lenders offer far less desirable terms. Street interest rates can run up to 10 percent per day, and the means of enforcing repayment are much less attractive. Usually, MED organizations are the only feasible source of funding for the poor, as evidenced by their continued popularity. Second, the cost of servicing these microloans is very high compared to the average loan size. Even the most efficient MED operations experience annual field costs of 12 to 25 percent of their loan portfolios. Some organizations expend more in costs than the amount they lend.

Lending Structures

To be successful, a MED organization must solve the problem of loan repayment. What will influence the borrowers to fulfill their obligations under the loan agreement? Getting the risk management scheme right is perhaps the most important step in the establishment of a MED lending program.

No single solution can be universally applied in all locations and situations, and lending officers have used a number of tools. Do borrowers have any assets that can be used as collateral against the loan? Can collection of this collateral be enforced? Is a person's standing in the community a strong motivating factor? Could peer pressure act as a means for ensuring loan repayment? Does the community have natural or established groups? Would these groups be able to make individual lending decisions or provide some loan guarantee through group savings? Is the ethic and imperative for personal responsibility high enough through teaching the gospel to stimulate repayment responsibility? And not insignificantly, which solutions allow for the effective teaching of business and spiritual principles? In considering these, MED organizations have developed and employed three basic lending structures.

1. *Individual lending.* This structure is akin to lending relationships encountered in the Western world. Loans are made to individuals—or more specifically, to individual businesses. Clients served through the individual lending structure are not the very poor. Loans are guaranteed by collateral assets or by the assurances of cosigners, and loan officers perform careful analyses before making individual lending decisions. Often, loans are individually tailored to the needs of borrowers. A close relationship between the lending officer and the MED loan recipient typically continues throughout the loan. However, the lending officer often calls in partner organization professionals when clients require business training services, and the cost of these education and mentoring services is usually covered by the microentrepreneur receiving the assistance.

2. *Solidarity group lending.* This method has been made most famous by the Grameen Bank in South Asia, but it is also popular in other areas of the world. It is better suited for people who have no means of securing a loan through personal assets. A small, self-selected group of perhaps a half-dozen individuals is formed. The group selects its membership and makes decisions on individual loans within the group, which often frees credit officers to be more hands-off. The Grameen Bank has been able to increase the number of loans serviced per officer by delegating many responsibilities to the group.

   The key to solidarity group lending is that the entire group guarantees each loan. If a group member defaults, that person has both forced the rest of the group to cover his or her loan and incurred the wrath of other group members. A very popular version of the solidarity group lending method adds to the repayment peer pressure by providing rotating access to the funds. Each member of the group gets a turn at a loan, but the successful repayment by one member is the condition for subsequent group members to receive loans.

Often, attendance is required at regular meetings. Rather than providing business training and gospel teaching, these meetings typically provide information about the microfinance program and reinforce the obligation to repay loans.

3. *Village banking.* This structure delegates even more authority to the local community. MED organizations lend funds to larger groups of several dozen people who exercise a significant amount of independent control over the use of those funds. These groups employ democratic means to establish their own policies and rules. The group makes individual lending decisions and handles all transactions to and from the borrower. Individual loans are not guaranteed, but peer pressure within the group serves as the means of protecting against default. Often, group savings are used as a means for providing some guarantee for the loan made to the group. MED loan officers deal with the group as a whole rather than with individual borrowers and therefore are further removed from the ultimate loan recipient.

MED Education and Training

The level of education and training provided by microlenders varies significantly and is driven by different philosophies about the value of these services. Every MED organization lays claim to an emphasis on business training services in its promotional materials, but reality reveals a broad range of practices. The perceived economic value of this training to the MED organization often drives the degree to which it is offered.

At the one end, some MED programs attempt to keep costs low by providing only what is required to service the loan. Borrowers are taught the basics of the lending structure and the repayment schedule, and the importance of not defaulting is emphasized. A careful eye is kept on overhead and loan-servicing costs, and there is relatively little contact between the borrower and the lending officer.

At the other end are those MED organizations that view business mentoring and training as a vital component of their MED programs.

Indeed, these organizations consider these services to be an important investment in the repayment probability of their clients. Training can vary from basic classroom instruction on personal finances to individual business consultations with the loan officer.

When asked what the top three issues for MED success are, the head of the Tanzania program of the Christian Reformed World Relief Committee (CRWRC) responded, "Training, training, and training." CRWRC has a program called MICRO-MBA Business Training, an intense and basic weeklong training course. The topics of the course include: investigating the market, using a calculator, buying, costing and pricing, selling, working out a business plan, weekly money management and controlling stock. Rather than provide the training itself, the CRWRC trains the trainers who receive a fee for each successful graduate they instruct. The trainers must recruit training clients who each pay the program a fee to attend. The MICRO-MBA program is graduating some 700 entrepreneurs per year.[9]

In addition to business training, Christian MED organizations must consider an additional aspect of transformation—that of spiritual transformation and the adaptation of biblical principles. Not only is it an important component of the triple-bottom-line objective of Kingdom business, it is absolutely critical to the development of spiritual capital, the key to blessing a nation. Realizing that the goal of spiritual transformation has sometimes proven to be a challenge for CMED organizations, partly due to the same economic forces that also shortchange other aspects of mentoring and partly due to other forces that hinder evangelism. (These challenges will be explored in detail later in this chapter.)

The gospel and biblical principles must be a central part of CMED programs if the nation is to be blessed and set on a firm foundation for successful capitalism. The CMED organization Christian Enterprise Trust of Zambia (CETZAM) explicitly included this component in its vision and mission statement when it was founded in 1995:

> The Christian Enterprise Trust of Zambia exists as a voluntary trust of Christians in business committed to empower potential or existing business people in small and medium sized business-

es through the provision of:
  - small capital loans for business start up or expansion,
  - training in business skills,
  - sound business counsel in the planning and operations of a business;

and *through the promotion of Christian principles in business* by:
  - discipling business people in the Christian faith,
  - networking within the business and Christian communities to build relationships,
  - and upholding a biblical standard of right moral and ethical conduct in business;

in order that:
  - individual spiritual, social, and economic needs are met,
  - righteousness, justice, peace, and stability prevail in the community,
  - *and the kingdom of God is established, extended, and exalted in the nation of Zambia.*[10]

Evaluation of Christian Microenterprise Development

CMED's Profitability and Sustainability

To date, the goal of profitability and sustainability has been a major challenge for CMED organizations. Sustainability is not only a concern to Christian MED efforts; secular MED organizations have struggled in this area as well. MED analysts have devised a number of levels of sustainability, but the levels most commonly discussed lie at either end of the spectrum: operational sustainability and financial sustainability.

Operational sustainability is a measure of whether a MED program can cover its current costs through its revenues. In other words, the MED program takes in more in the form of interest and fees than it spends in overhead to run the operation. In accounting terms, it is essentially a cash-flow measurement. The operational sustainability measure is a ratio and is expressed in percentage terms. An operational sustainability value of less than 100 percent means that revenues do not cover costs, while a value of greater than 100 percent, or "operationally self-sustainable," means that revenues exceed costs.

Operational Sustainability = (Reported Operating Income ÷ Reported Operating Expense) x 100%

Financial Sustainability is a measure of whether a MED program would be profitable if all combined costs were considered. In other words, the program would still show a profit if it took into consideration various economic benefits it receives. For example, most MED organizations receive subsidies and in-kind donations. Moreover, they are not responsible for paying any rate of return on donated funds, a cost they would incur if they obtained funding from the financial market rather than from donations. Also, the financial cost of inflation and reserving for loan losses must be considered. And many multinational organizations do not include an accounting of their centralized headquarters overhead in the calculation of sustainability for each country-specific implementing program.

If operational sustainability is likened to an accounting measure of cash flow, financial sustainability is likened to a financial measure of true unsubsidized profitability. Financial sustainability is also a ratio expressed in percentage terms. A Financial sustainability value of less than 100 percent means that the operation is currently unsustainable without subsidies, while a value of greater than 100 percent, or "financially self-sustainable," means that the program can survive on a stand-alone basis without any donations or subsidies.

Financial Sustainability = (True Operating Income ÷ True Operating Expense) x 100%

The reason for analyzing the laborious technical details of these sustainability measures is because they are important to understanding the profitability and sustainability of MED programs. Those MED programs that are operationally self-sustainable are able to continue operating under current conditions with the understanding that donations and subsidies contribute to that ability. The ultimate MED profitability measure is financial sustainability, and it is the goal of MED programs to become financially self-sustainable.

Observations About MED Sustainability

The MicroBanking Bulletin collects self-reported financial data from 135 microfinance programs. They represent a cross-section of predominantly secular MED organizations, and most programs in the group are focused on financial performance. Results taken from 2002 are shown in the figure below:

FIGURE 6

Size of Portfolio	Avg. Loan Port. (SMM)	Avg. No. Borrowers	Avg. Loan Size	Avg. Loan/ GDP per. cap.	Loans per Officer	Lending Rate	Tot. Admin. Expense
Small MEDs	0.6	3,886	$303	35%	314	47%	53%
Medium MEDs	3.6	13,069	$685	61%	310	39%	29%
Large MEDs	67.2	322,501	$993	96%	333	31%	18%

The world of MED programs can be divided into three subsets according to the size of the loan portfolio. Though exact definitions in dollar terms vary by continent due to economic differences, small MEDs tend to have portfolios under $1 million. The loan portfolios of medium MEDs generally fall in the $1–$10 million range, and large MEDs often have portfolios in excess of $10 million. This segregation allows us to make several important observations about MED sustainability.

Few MEDs are financially self-sustainable. The self-selected participants in the MicroBanking Bulletin are some of the most financially focused MED organizations. Yet only about one-third of the organizations included in these results have achieved a level of profitability, and those tend to be larger programs. The financially self-sustainable MED programs have a much larger average portfolio size than those that are not financially self-sustainable.

Scale drives sustainability. A quick glance reveals that there is a strong positive correlation between the size of the MED program and its sustainability measure. In general, the larger the loan program, the more sustainable the program. That is true both for operational sustainability and for financial sustainability. Small MEDs have average operational sustainability and financial sustainability values of 90 percent 79 percent, respectively, while large MEDs have average operational sustainability and financial sustainability values of 114 percent and 105 percent, respectively.

Large MEDs spend a lower percentage on administrative costs than small MEDs. Why is scale so important to sustainability? First, we must note that MED profitability, like that of any business, is determined by the difference between revenues and expenses. In lending, revenues are generally the interest payments and fees from the borrower, while expenses are generally the costs of obtaining funds and administrative and overhead costs associated with making and servicing the loan. These expenses include the cost of any training or other services provided to clients.

- Across the board, the average loan officer load is just over 300 loans. Considering that the average loan lasts only three months, the average officer has 1,200 loans per year! That is an enormous number of clients, but we have seen that many MED programs have structures that delegate individual lending decisions to the receiving community. What *does* vary by program size is the average size of the loan extended. Large MEDs lend more than three times as much to each client as small MEDs do, and therefore, a loan officer in a large MED services three times the loan portfolio in dollar terms.
- In relation to the portfolio size, administrative costs are significantly higher for small MEDs. While in absolute terms we would expect small MEDs to run lower costs, their much smaller portfolio sizes mean that administrative costs per dollar

loaned are higher. For small MEDs, administrative costs are 53 cents for every dollar outstanding, while for large MEDs those costs are 18 cents per dollar outstanding. That is a very significant difference.

• To make up for this, small MEDs tend to charge a higher average interest rate. While large MEDs lend at an average rate of 31 percent, loans from small MEDs carry an average rate of 47 percent.

• Even so, small MEDs find it very difficult to cover the huge burden of administrative costs. Simply put, large MEDs are able to spread fixed expenses over a much larger book of loans.

Scale is important to sustainability in the Christian MED world as well. As the following graph indicates, an analysis of 40 CMED programs worldwide shows that larger programs are more likely to reach self-sustainability.[11]

FIGURE 7

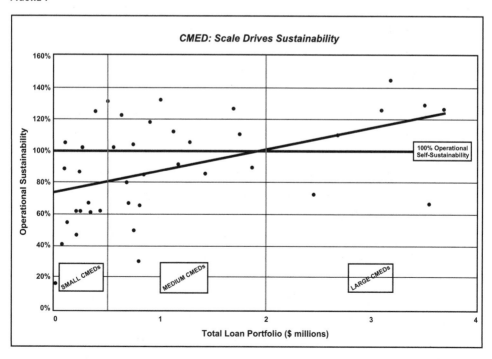

Only 27 percent of CMED programs that have total loan portfolios under $0.5 million (small CMEDs) are operationally self-sustainable; 50 percent of CMED programs that have total loan portfolios of $0.5–2.0 million (medium CMEDs) are operationally self-sustainable; while 71 percent of CMED programs that have total loan portfolios over $2.0 million (large CMEDs) are operationally self-sustainable. In other words, large CMED programs are almost three times as likely to be operationally self-sustainable as small CMED programs. As a result, many Christian MED organizations are racing to achieve scale. Larger size is seen as the key to profitability and sustainability of the program.

Unfortunately, most Christian MED organizations fall short of the sustainability objective. While most fail to achieve operational self-sustainability, precious few (if any) are currently operating at a level of financial self-sustainability. To be fair, there are some factors that contribute to this, and these are worth discussing.

- Christian MED programs tend to serve poorer populations and seek to reach a larger number of people. Therefore, they carry a lower average loan size. While Opportunity International's secular counterparts that are running similar-sized programs would be expected to have an average loan size of over $400, Opportunity International lends an average of only $200 per client.
- CMEDs also allow more loan officer time per client. As we have noted, the industry average is over 300 loans per MED officer. In contrast, even the largest CMED organization has fewer than 200 loans per officer.
- Christian MED programs have not yet achieved the level of scale found in the largest secular programs. Opportunity International is a giant by CMED standards, yet two-thirds of its lending programs are small MEDs while one-third consists of medium MEDs. Other CMEDs operate at an even smaller scale.

Sustainability is an important objective for Christian MED programs. If financial sustainability can be achieved, the doors to significant growth will be thrown open. Profitability means that lending and training programs can be increased through profits. CMED organizations will also be ripe for significantly higher levels of funding. CMED efforts currently rely on donor funds, but profitability opens the possibility of large amounts of investment money, propelling the programs to greater magnitudes. The objective of sustainability for CMED programs is also important in that it imposes on loan officers and program directors the same business pressures experienced by their clients. Loan recipients are faced with the discipline of operating profitably and so should the CMED organizations that advise and mentor them.

CMED's Impact on Local Job and Wealth Creation

The great strength of MED is in the effect a small amount of capital can have on individual lives. As mentioned, the largest CMED organization in the world has estimated that 1.5 jobs are impacted per loan—one job sustained and another half job created. This CMED organization operates in very poor countries, and the average loan size is about $200. So on average, one job is impacted per $133 loaned and one job is created per $400 loaned. Another CMED program run by Integra Ventures in Eastern Europe reports one job created or sustained per $400 it loans.

Other MED organizations have conducted similar analyses, and the results are in line with the above findings that every two loans create one job. For example, a study of a MED operation in Peru, where the average loan size is quite a bit higher than $200, concluded that a new job was created for every $1,348 loaned. Another study by the MED organization Fundusz in Poland found that every $3,571 loaned resulted in the creation of a job.

While these job creation numbers are encouraging, anecdotally it appears that small MED loans are better designed to sustain jobs than to create jobs. This is especially true at the lower end of the loan-size range. David Bussau, described as the father of CMED, noted that $50 loans typically do not create jobs; instead, they are used to ensure the recipient's economic and physical survival.[12] Larger MED loans do sometimes enable microentrepreneurs to expand their business by bringing in another family member or friend as a partner or employee. MED efforts certainly do result in new employment, but they are often more effective at sustaining existing employment. And where employment is sustained through MED programs, it usually becomes better, more effective employment.

Anita Bebe and her seven children live in the South Pacific nation of Vanuatu. Comprising more than 80 small islands, Vanuatu is a poor country with an annual GDP per person of only $2,900. Times were tough for Anita and her family. She worked as domestic help in the capital of Port Vila while her husband could only find work on another island. Her children were unable to attend school regularly. With a $150 MED loan, Anita made improvements to her home and built a small shop in order to start a retail business. She demonstrated leadership skills and soon became the MED borrower group leader, overseeing 30 other borrowers. A second loan of $300 helped to expand the business. Anita's store now brings in revenues of $60 and profits of $10 per day (after covering salaries and all other expenses), and it has allowed her husband to return to help with the business. Her children attend school, and she even has aspirations to send her oldest to university. Anita credits the MED program with providing better, more effective employment for her and her husband.[13]

MED is also a vehicle for wealth creation. Enterprises funded by MED programs are small—a handful of people at most—and are often strongly tied to the microentrepreneur. But even with a $500 loan and a cottage industry business, MED can create wealth in a nation that is many times the amount of the loan. For example, Anita Bebe's retail shop in Vanuatu earns $10 per day in profits. In a year, it makes more than $2,500. Based in its income, her business may be worth $10,000 or more, which means that approximately $10,000 in wealth has been created for Anita and for her nation.

Though typically contained to the profits of the business, wealth can and does accrue through MED efforts. Analysis by the Polish MED program Fundusz found that its loan recipients saw an increase in average total income of 20 percent over a nine-month study period, which includes the cost of repaying the loan.[14] Of course, not everyone puts the funds to profitable use. One individual with a long involvement in CMED observed that the level of entrepreneurship and innovation is often lacking at the MED level. People are sometimes worse off after receiving the loan because they can't figure out anything good to do with it. It is true that some MED programs delegate the individual lending decisions to the target community and therefore may not verify sensible business uses for the funds prior to the loan. However, a MED program that has both a strong training and mentoring component and a close relationship with its clients should be able to mitigate that risk significantly.

CMED's Impact on Advancement of the Local Church

CMED programs attract a multitude of clients from the general population, and they are therefore well designed as vehicles for evangelism. Borrowers who apply for much-needed loans and training can be presented with the gospel in group meetings or other interactions with Christian lending officers. Extending the helping hand of the church, local staff of CMED organizations can share the love of Christ and the transforming message of the gospel with their clients. Due to its wide reach, CMED constitutes an evangelism vehicle through which people can come to Christ in significant numbers.

If a relationship between scale and sustainability is observable, there is an analogous relationship between scale and advancement of the local church. However, here the relationship is reversed. Smaller Christian MEDs seem to have a stronger focus on spiritual results than many of their larger counterparts, whose focus is more often on financial results. In order to explore why various CMED programs might emphasize different objectives, it is helpful to discuss the structures of the organizations themselves.

There are two basic models for CMED organizations: the multinational model and the stand-alone model (see Figure 8 on next page). The largest representatives of CMED are multinational organizations that are located in the developed world. These are the institutions that interface with potential donors, raising funds and advancing the cause of CMED. Funds are then allocated to a portfolio of implementing programs in specific countries around the world. For example, Opportunity International has made over $85 million in loans to more than 400,000 microentrepreneurs through some 40 partner implementing organizations located in countries such as Zambia, Ghana and the Philippines. Other leading CMED organizations such as World Vision, World Relief, Mennonite Economic Development Associates (MEDA), Food for the Hungry and Christian Reformed World Relief Committee (CRWRC) follow a similar multinational model.

FIGURE 8

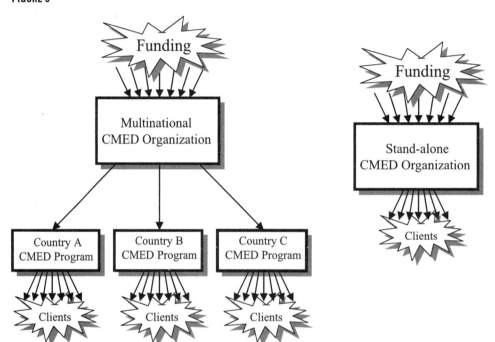

The implementing organizations in developing countries are considered affiliates or network members of the multi-national CMED organizations. Often, the names of the local implementing organizations have no relation to their parent multinational. For example, Cambodia Community Building is actually World Relief's affiliate in Cambodia. The degree of independence these implementing organizations enjoy varies, but they are accountable to their multinational umbrella organizations, and their performance is closely monitored.

In addition to providing the necessary funding to start and usually sustain local CMED programs, multinational organizations often supply the infrastructure needed by implementing organizations. This includes provision of financial record-keeping and portfolio analysis software, training for loan officers, production of educational materials for loan recipients, and the establishment of performance metrics.

The second model that is encountered in the CMED world is the stand-alone model. As the name implies, these organizations exist in isolation and are responsible both for the raising of the required capital and for the administration of individual loans. Standalone CMED programs are often the result of economic development efforts by individual missionaries, missions organizations or churches. For example, in 1996, a Youth With a Mission missionary started Project Love in Family Environment (Project L.I.F.E.), a stand-alone CMED effort in Thailand.

However, the difference between multinational CMED organizations and stand-alone CMED organizations does not stop with their structure. It may come as no surprise that these stand-alone CMED organizations are typically smaller than those associated with the multinationals. Project L.I.F.E. has about $15,000 in loans to about 100 clients, while the World Relief-affiliated Cambodia Community Building portfolio has over $600,000 in loans to about 13,000 clients. The level of financial sophistication and discipline is also typically lower in stand-alone CMED programs.

FIGURE 9

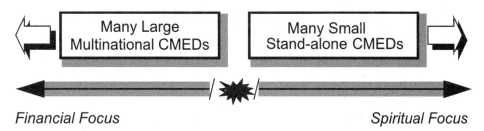

Many large, multinational Christian MED organizations have a financial focus. Thus, they emphasize sustainability, profitability, larger scale, and financial metrics of success (e.g., number of loans per officer, borrower repayment rate). Spiritual metrics of success are sometimes marginalized. For example, one multinational CMED organization evaluates its affiliate programs on six major performance standards. Four of these pertain to loan portfolio performance, one evaluates the program's governance, and the final one rates the program's transformational focus. Only one of four criteria that affect that final transformation rating deals with spiritual objectives.

The degree to which larger Christian MED organizations have turned to secular sources for funds (e.g., government sources, multinational sources) often influences their ability to speak about their faith. CMED organizations are finding in government funds an important mechanism for achieving scale, but unfortunately the money comes with some strings attached. Given these limitations, some Christian MED organizations have decided against pursuing funds from secular institutions.

Many smaller, stand-alone CMED programs are affiliated with a specific church, missionary or missions organization. Thus, they are characterized by a missions mind-set, a heavy reliance on donor subsidies, smaller scale and spiritual metrics of success (e.g., changed lives, local church growth). They exhibit more of a spiritual focus.

FIGURE 10

Financial Focus	Spiritual Focus
Sustainability	Missions mind-set
Profitability	Donor support
Larger scale	Smaller scale
Financial metrics	Spiritual metrics
Loans per officer	Changed lives
Repayment rate	Church growth

Even within a multinational CMED organization, the degree of spiritual influence can vary widely from country to country. There are CMED implementing programs with a definite evangelical focus and others where Christians constitute a minority of the staff. CETZAM, the Zambian CMED effort whose mission statement we examined earlier, is an organization in which Christian principles and spiritual objectives are emphasized. CETZAM explicitly includes Bible teaching, prayer cells, mentoring and Christian networking in its program plan, and it also provides a host of business skills training and counseling services. The program has nearly 18,000 active clients and $1 million in loans outstanding. Unfortunately, CETZAM also falls far short of self-sustainability goals.

Some CMED programs are far less effective at furthering the local church. Indeed, several microfinance efforts that fall under a multinational Christian MED umbrella have a minority of Christian employees, and some are reported to have no Christian staff at all! The only MED personnel that most clients see is that of the lending officer. Obviously, if the lending officer with whom one is dealing is Muslim, the gospel of Jesus will encounter significant barriers.

What drives some multinational CMED organizations to allow a few network members to staff their programs with a significant number of non-Christians? Two lines of reasoning lead to this outcome. Some argue that any assistance to the poor is a laudable pursuit, whether supplied by Christians or not. Therefore, presenting the gospel is a nice goal, but ultimately not essential. The conclusion is that MED efforts by non-Christians, though perhaps not preferable, should be supported. A second argument is that it might be necessary to build MED programs without Christians in areas where an insufficient Christian presence currently exists. The ultimate goal would be to migrate the program to Christian leadership, but the start-up phase requires a minority Christian presence.

It seems that CMED efforts are caught in a perceived tension between scale and sustainability on the one hand and advancement of the Church on the other hand. Clearly, however, this perception is short-sighted. It focuses too narrowly on individual financial transactions than on the infrastructure and environment needed for successful commerce. Many of these groups do not understand the importance of spiritual capital development, which blesses the entire nation rather than a few individuals. It is the development of spiritual capital that will lead to real economic development in a nation.

A case in point is the experience in Bangladesh of the Grameen Bank, a secular MED pioneer. Since 1976, the Grameen Bank has embarked on the world's most famous MED program, loaning $3.7 billion to 2.4 million borrowers in Bangladesh. The total MED effort in the country has reached about 10 million borrowers. Bangladesh was one of the poorest nations in the world when it was first targeted for MED, but even though billions of dollars have been invested, the country remains in the bottom quartile in GDP per capita. Poverty is still pervasive, and the economy hasn't developed much. It is also worth noting that Bangladesh has the highest perceived corruption in the world.[15] There is no doubt that the lack of spiritual capital has inhibited economic development, yet this is an issue the Grameen Bank and other MED programs do not address. The provision of loans without the development of spiritual capital ultimately fails to bless the nation.

Issues and Opportunities in Christian MED

The Inherent Tension

CMED organizations have been straining to achieve financial and spiritual goals simultaneously, and there appears to be a fundamental, continuing tension between profitability and sustainability and advancement of the local church. Not all CMED organizations operate with this tension, but this typically stems from their inclination toward one of these two goals and neglect of the other. I believe this tension can and will be solved as CMED efforts grow and mature.

Dave Larson of HOPE International notes that CMED has taken on four different faces in the way it emphasizes or relates economic development and spiritual objectives:

1. Some MED organizations may have had Christian origins, but they are now truly *secular in nature*. As the Young Men's Christian Association (YMCA) in the United States has drifted from its Christian roots to become a secular institution, these MED organizations no longer have any Christian connections. They are secular in nature.

2. CMED programs can have Christian motivations but are *secular in practice*. The CMED organizations staffed with very few Christians fall into this category. They believe in the value of MED, but there is no fundamental commitment to cultural change. Faith is the motivation for assisting the poor, but spiritual objectives will give way to economic development or sustainability objectives when push comes to shove. However, as noted in previous chapters, successful capitalism is rooted in deeply held moral convictions, and these thinkers clearly do not understand the strong connection between the two.

3. Some CMED efforts are used as *a means to an end*. If the first two are described as approaches that overemphasize economic development objectives, this one falls at the other end of the spectrum and overemphasizes spiritual objectives. The MED program is simply a means for gaining access to a region and is a cover for evangelism. In that respect, it is no different from the tactics of missionaries who operate pseudo-businesses or enter countries on student visas. For example, one CMED operation has allocated only $10,000 of its $700,000 in capital to economic development. The rest is set aside for evangelism.

4. A fourth approach might be termed *truly holistic Christian MED*. Organizations that are fully committed to the sustainable development of both local economies and local churches fit this description. This approach practices a comprehensive ministry that recognizes that economic, social and spiritual needs must be met. Because it does not sacrifice any objectives, this is also the approach that experiences the greatest

tension between economic, social and spiritual development objectives.[16]

There is no reason the goals of sustainable economic development and advancement of the Church are mutually exclusive. Many organizations see their spiritual development efforts yielding financial benefits as the repayment rates of their borrowers increase. Already, a number of CMED programs are operationally self-sustainable, and individual lives are being touched. As Larson puts it, Christian MED organizations need the heart of a pastor and the head of a banker.[17]

Donation or Investment?

The distinction between a donation and an investment is that the former involves no financial payback while the latter comes with the expectation of a positive return. To date, CMED efforts have been funded largely by donation dollars. Individuals, churches and foundations pour their tax-deductible contributions into programs, and many people around the world are helped. These monies are not simply distributed in the form of handouts, and there is significant leverage of the funds. As we have seen, a repaid loan can be recycled many times over. However, when the enterprise is operating at an overall loss, there is a net drain of capital and additional donations are needed to sustain it. And until CMED programs are able to generate enough cash not only to grow their own efforts but also to establish funds in new locations, there will be a need for start-up capital to come in the form of donations.

While CMED has struggled to date to reach the goal of self-sustainability, it is not inherently unprofitable. A number of programs have reached the point of operational self-sustainability, and these could be in a position to raise additional funds through investment vehicles. Indeed, Opportunity International is offering a return of zero to three percent to investors through the Calvert Foundation's Community Investment Notes. Several other CMED organizations are already heading down the road to profitability, and it constitutes welcome progress and maturing of this Kingdom business approach. We have seen that scale (size of portfolio) is an important factor in the creation of sustainable MED programs. Significant investment dollars could provide a means for CMED organizations to grow, and this in turn will help to improve profitability.

If the critical change from donor-funded CMED to investor-funded CMED is going to materialize, there must be a push toward financial profitability. This is possible. Bank Rakyat Indonesia (BRI) earned $140 million in profits during the first half of 2003. At its initial public offering later that year, the bank was valued at $1.2 billion. Still largely owned by the Indonesian government, BRI is the fourth largest lender in the country by assets. Microloans account for 30 percent of BRI's lending and 68 percent of its net interest income. Only 2.5 percent of the microloan portfolio is nonperforming or more than 90 days past due—less than half the bank's overall rate. BRI has 3,931 branches throughout Indonesia, each treated as a profit center responsible both for managing its own balance sheet and for sourcing its own funds through deposits. In 1998, when the Asian crisis was at its height, BRI's microlending unit earned a pretax profit of $89 million while its corporate-banking and retail-banking divisions lost $3.4 billion.[18] If MED can be profitable in Indonesia during such challenging economic times, there is reason for optimism that CMED programs can achieve financial profitability.

The prospect of financial sustainability is a prerequisite for investment-based funding. The goal of the large secular MED operation ACCION is to create microfinance institutions that are fully sustainable. Its affiliate programs around the world are providing over $600 million a year in funding to more than one million loan recipients. ACCION offers guarantees that allow its affiliate microfinance institutions to obtain commercial sources of credit, and some of its most successful affiliates in Latin America and the Caribbean are receiving equity investments through ProFund Internacional. Based in San Jose, Costa Rica, ProFund calls itself "the world's first private equity fund solely dedicated to microfinance investment." A total of over $20 million has been invested in 13 microlenders, which are regulated, for-profit institutions. The fund is dedicated to earning a high rate of return for its shareholders, which indicates that MED institutions can be investment-grade operations.

Making the transition from donor-based funding to investment-based funding will be a major challenge for Christian MED organizations. Few are in a position where this seems attainable at the moment, but the pursuit is imperative. If the Kingdom business of CMED is to be self-sustainable, it must achieve broad profitability; potential investors will take note. But the prospect of significant CMED program growth through investment-based funding is predicated on financial self-sustainability. That is when the doors of opportunity swing wide open.

The First Step in Economic Development

Millions of people have benefited from MED efforts and have been able to build their microenterprises with the help of loan funds. Many of these individuals have shown real business acumen and are ready to take the next step—to grow their businesses beyond the microenterprise level. But too often, there is no avenue for follow-on funding.

CMED programs are established with the commendable objective of meeting the needs of the poor, and they seek to touch as many as possible. Thus, the level of funding they provide is small. But rarely does a CMED institution reserve some of its funds for those who graduate from the micro program. Indeed, the issues faced by SMEs are so distinct from those of simple microenterprises that a different entity with different staff is needed to assist those entrepreneurs who have grown to that level. If a CMED organization does make the decision to serve only microenterprise clients, it could and must eventually partner with an SME lending group that serves the successful entrepreneur who discovers an opportunity for further business growth.

Conclusion

When presenting the Kingdom business framework, it is important to note that a developing nation will be ready for increasingly advanced approaches to Kingdom business as its infrastructure and economy improve. CMED must be viewed as the first step in that economic development process, not as a standalone structure. To be sure, it is a very critical first step: It builds a base structure of business and starts people on a new way of thinking with a set of heartfelt, spiritually based, internalized values. CMED builds spiritual capital in a nation at the level of individuals and families. The poor are enabled to engage in productive commerce, and new jobs are created. They learn basic business skills and biblical principles that lead to successful commerce. They take ownership in their work. As clients, they are served and treated with the dignity of those created in the image of God. The good news is presented, and many decide to follow Jesus.

Without the spiritual base, the nations will not be blessed. CMED is Kingdom business that serves the poor by opening new opportunities, both economic and spiritual. It is the building block upon which more significant and complex business can be built. It lays the foundation for other Kingdom business approaches, which we will look at next.

CHAPTER 11

SMALL AND MEDIUM ENTERPRISES (SME)

In the United States, small and medium enterprises (SMEs) added more than 75 percent of all new jobs in the U.S. economy from 1990 to 1997.[1] SMEs are recognized more and more as a critical part of economic growth. In developing nations, SMEs may be even more important to economic advancement. They create local employment and wealth, and their success and growth have a trickle-down effect on suppliers, partners, distributors and customers. In small- and medium-size businesses, the more complex aspects of spiritual capital are built—those aspects that affect organizations and communities. As Kingdom businesses, SMEs also further the mission of the local church, generating financial resources and serving as the vehicle through which the gospel is preached by word and by deed.

Horvat Limited

The son of a Baptist pastor, Ivica Horvat sensed that the marketplace was to be his venue for serving God. In 1993, Ivica founded Horvat Limited, Inc., a company that manufactures work clothing and uniforms in his hometown in Croatia. Two years later, Ivica met Bob Fulton, founder and former CEO of a multimillion-dollar U.S. manufacturing company. Bob had helped establish Integra Ventures, a Christian SME development organization, and he recognized the challenges Ivica was facing. A major obstacle to growth and success was the fact that small Croatian businesses the size of Horvat Limited cannot obtain bank loans. Integra not only provided two helpful loans but also offered the business training and mentoring in financial management that Ivica needed to succeed.

But success was not without its protraction. The mid '90s brought added challenges as the Balkan War affected the Croatian economy. When the owner of a building Ivica was renting went bankrupt, the police seized the building. In the process, Ivica lost the entire inventory he had stored there. Other economic influences threatened his business as well. But through all the difficulties, Ivica has remained committed to being "salt and light" to his employees, suppliers and customers as his Christian values drive his actions in the workplace. He is a shining light of integrity in a climate in which corruption is the norm. Instead of paying bribes, Ivica conducts business by emphasizing the quality of relationships and products and the importance of meeting obligations, thus promoting spiritual capital. Many business colleagues have inquired about the reason for his integrity.

Despite difficult economic and political conditions since its inception, Horvat Limited has grown. Today, the original uniform manufacturing business has been complemented with the wholesale distribution of specialty work clothing and safety equipment. It now supports the families of 40 employees at Horvat Limited and additional workers at subcontracted organizations.

In addition to those who earn a living from his company, Ivica's business provides clothing and other humanitarian aid to the poor in his community. He has also sponsored local sports teams and events. Ivica organized a group for Christian business people, and he leads a Bible study with other business people that focuses on faithful Christian living in the marketplace. He even finds time to serve his local church. As a deacon, he preaches, teaches and ministers to the youth. Thanks to the profitability of Horvat Limited, Ivica was able to offer significant funding for the needed renovation of the church building. "We did it with no western money," he proudly announces.[2]

The Nature of SMEs

Although some think of SMEs as microenterprises that have grown to a larger size, there are a number of fundamental differences between the two segments. While microenterprises typically operate in the informal business sector, SMEs have crossed the line into the formal business sector. They are legal entities, which require greater knowledge and understanding of the legal system. They have an organizational structure and management requirements. SMEs also have reason to interact more with local government officials on matters ranging from permits to taxes to leases.

Those involved in economic development efforts are growing in their appreciation of the fact that not everyone is an entrepreneur. Not everyone has the self-motivation toward sole proprietorship, the ingenuity, or the initiative to benefit from MED efforts. "Perhaps ten percent of people are entrepreneurs," observes Business Professional Network's John Warton. "SMEs provide employment for the rest."[3] A leader of a Christian organization active in both MED and SME development notes that about half the MED applicants will not finish the loan application process. Many discover through the process of writing a business plan that they aren't entrepreneurs and will likely fail.

The issues facing SME owner-operators are more complex than those encountered by a microentrepreneur. Interpersonal dealings are more prominent. Indeed, those who work with SMEs identify corporate structure and management issues as the most important keys to success.

While MED training might focus on learning to use a calculator or to identify cash flow problems, SME leaders must deal with contracts, hiring and firing, business strategy, exports, and the more complex dimension of spiritual capital and the resulting company culture. Company cultures build their own and the nation's spiritual capital when they reflect the biblical attitudes of respect for authority, responsibility to others, obedience and building community.

If MED is the building block for developing a nation's spiritual capital, SMEs represent the spiritual capital building blocks being molded into company culture that reflects biblical values. Company culture is defined by the business actions and attitudes of its leaders. Every organization has a culture—even the Mafia! Likewise, SMEs develop a culture. Although company cultures should reflect the faith of the believers who manage the businesses, ingrained local culture often directs their actions. In Guatemala, for example, almost half the population claims to be born again, yet this has made no significant impact on the country's culture and spiritual capital. Kingdom business professionals can play a significant role as they establish mentoring relationships with SME owner-operators, through whom company cultures will be defined. As SME leaders adopt the biblical values of the Kingdom business professionals, their businesses become breeding grounds for the development of spiritual capital within the company, the local business network and the nation.

SME Lending Organizations

SME-Focused Organizations

Some Christian organizations working with SMEs have been established with the specific purpose of assisting SMEs and their owners. The model of these SME-focused organizations generally involves a deeper level of mentoring, and the majority of clients are already followers of Jesus. Promising Christian SME owners are usually identified through churches and Christian networks within the region. Training, mentoring and discipleship relationships are formed. In fact, training is the important first step for prospective clients. Some SME managers are then mentored and discipled. The final step is a financial investment in the business.

Integra Ventures, the organization that helped Ivica, is one of a small but growing number of Christian organizations that were founded with the explicit purpose of assisting SMEs in the developing world. More than 60 SMEs throughout Eastern Europe have received Integra's business support in the form of financial investment, training and discipleship. In 1993, the Swiss ministry Christian East Mission established ROMCOM, a program to help SMEs in Romania. It has provided loans and training for over 330 businesses that have created more than 3,000 jobs. In Kyrgyzstan, Business Professional Network (BPN) is replicating the Romanian model. Each year, 15 to 25 worthy businesses are selected for funding and training. In 2002, the Kyrgyz SMEs that participate in BPN's program created nearly 300 jobs. That's a real blessing to a country with a 65 percent unemployment rate.

CMED Outgrowth Programs

While the organizations mentioned above were founded with the explicit objective to help SMEs, other Kingdom-focused SME programs are the result of an expanded Christian MED mission. The approach of CMED outgrowth programs toward SMEs is similar to the one used with microentrepreneurs. Often applicants are sourced through a wider channel and loan officers handle a greater portfolio. Fewer clients are believers, and the program is seen more as an opportunity to share the love of Jesus with an additional set of people, owners of businesses too large for microloans.

Large CMED organizations like Opportunity International and World Vision are reaching beyond microenterprises and have started to make larger loans to SMEs. Partners for Christian Development also added financing and education for SMEs to its CMED effort in Kenya. "The whole boat is moving in that direction," observed former Opportunity International CEO Charles Dokmo, "but Christian MED groups have been slower to embrace the trend."[4]

The foray of CMED organizations into SME lending is being driven by several factors. First, some MED institutions see SMEs as a potential solution in their quest to reach financial sustainability. Since loans to small- and medium-size businesses are larger than MED loans, the economics for the lender are more attractive. A loan officer can service a larger loan portfolio while shepherding fewer recipients. Second, by expanding the size of an organization's total loan portfolio through the addition of an SME program, fixed costs are spread over a larger capital base. And third, many MED programs are discovering that successful graduates from the program whose businesses have grown beyond the microenterprise stage have nowhere to turn for further help. One Christian professional involved in those segments of Kingdom business estimated that perhaps 10 to 15 percent of microenterprises become SMEs. Thus, a few organizations have consciously linked their MED and SME lending activities to provide a clear path for progression. In Kenya, Partners for Christian Development's MED program, Ambassadors Development Agency, has been complemented by two SME programs into which successful members can grow: Christian Entrepreneurial Society and Kenya Investment Trust.

SME Funding

Christian SME development organizations see their mission as providing two desperately needed services: funding and training. While credit systems in the West have developed to the point where most people carry several personal credit cards, this is certainly not the case in the developing world. Businesses often find insurmountable obstacles in their quest for capital. "Banks don't bank in these countries," observed emerging markets expert Roger Leeds of Johns Hopkins University. Lending is short term, it requires heavy collateral, and it is only extended to the top companies. "Most of the private sector is shut out from financing," he concluded.[5] Christian SME lending organizations have stepped into this void to show faith in businesses that banks refuse to serve.

The specific amount of funding extended to businesses can vary based on the company's location and size. In Eastern Europe, Integra Ventures' loans typically range from $5,000 to $100,000 per business. Kenya

Investment Trust's average SME loan amounts to $6,000. Business Professional Network's SME lending program in Kyrgyzstan averages $12,000 per company, though there are a number of recipients of $20,000. There are certainly examples that fall outside this range, but for purposes of this book the level of SME lending is defined as $5,000 to $100,000.

Compared to MED loans, those loans extended to SMEs carry much lower interest rates. We have noted that a large amount of microfinance carries 36 percent or more annual interest rates. By contrast, Christian SME funding often falls in the 5 to 15 percent range, partly due to the lower cost of servicing the loan. Oiko Credit, an ecumenical SME financing organization headquartered in the Netherlands, offers its loans at 9 percent. Kenya Investment Trust's loans are at 12 percent interest, and the cost of financing through BPN in Kyrgyzstan is expected to rise from 5 to 10 percent. Clients are extremely grateful, given that they operate in an environment in which funding from other less-friendly sources, if available at all, might carry 24 to 27 percent interest rates.

While MED loans typically have a short payback period of six months or less, SME funding is usually extended over several years. Most SME loans have a two- to five-year life. Some organizations offer an initial grace period before payments are due. The Kyrgyzstan SME participants in BPN's program, for example, have no installments due for the first year.

Most often, funding is in the form of cash loans, but local conditions or regulations sometimes require alternate arrangements. Due to conditions specific to Kyrgyzstan, BPN's program in that country does not offer its funding in the form of cash payments to the recipient SME. (It also does not permit loans to go toward the cost of a building; BPN expects entrepreneurs to have some a vest interest in the venture by investing in their facilities.) Instead of loaning money, BPN buys needed equipment and allows the SME to "borrow" it while the cost is repaid over four or five years. Not only does this ensure that the funds are put to proper use, but BPN's legal ownership of the equipment also provides some protection against default. At the end of the borrowing period, and upon successful repayment of the original cost plus interest, the SME assumes ownership of the equipment.

SME Education and Training

In addition to providing funding, programs that assist SMEs offer training and mentoring. Christian training efforts focus on both business and spiritual education, and many SME development organizations believe this actually meets the greater need of businesses in developing nations. Where the lack of spiritual capital is impeding economic growth, Christian training and mentoring of SME managers instills values that are necessary for success. As leaders set the company's culture, these biblical principles then permeate the rest of the business.

In countries where very few entrepreneurs have been taught the basics of business due to either a lack of formal education or a recent economic transition from socialism, SME managers are clamoring for basic business training. The instruction required by SME owners is more complex than that offered by MED programs. Issues of business strategy, organizational structures, contract negotiation and leadership are important to those who manage SMEs. Believers are also taught how to integrate their faith in the business. SME education typically happens in two ways: formal training and informal mentoring and discipleship.

Formal Training

The group setting in a classroom environment is an effective venue for formal training, using curricula developed specifically for the challenges and issues faced by SMEs in a specific location. As part of the emerging Integra "Management Center," Integra is developing a program that will address issues critical to business development. Integra has found that some of its clients are clamoring for the type of instruction found in MBA programs, and it intends to provide similar training while ensuring it is practical. The approach Integra will use is to integrate biblical principles with every business question that is addressed (for example, with the topic of marketing, one could ask, "How does being a Christian impact how I market or advertise my business?"). Therefore, although Integra will not offer separate courses in the Bible, the Bible will be applied to the business and leadership training topics that are covered.

ROMCOM and BPN offer training seminars from SERVUS, a Swiss business development organization led by Christians. In Romania, ROMCOM presents four-year training courses to business leaders in its SME program. In fact, its business management seminars are considered a vital part of the ROMCOM project. Four blocks of seminars present the basics of professional management: creating a simple business plan, creating a simple marketing concept, the basics of cost estimation and accounting, and employee management and negotiation techniques. Concurrently, program participants receive individual consulting and assistance. ROMCOM is also quite clear on the value it ascribes to spiritual capital development. Potential applicants are told that apart from economic topics, emphasis is placed on training in Christian business ethics.

Informal Mentoring and Discipleship

The relationship Bob Fulton developed with Ivica in Croatia goes well beyond issues of business. It has become a vehicle for informal mentoring and discipleship. "SME staff are mature leaders," noted Integra's Terry Williams. "They get to know the businessperson's families. They are let into their lives, and in that context the discussion will turn to church and spiritual growth."[6] In these informal settings, SME managers are shown how they can integrate their faith and their work in the business. Seeking to establish close mentoring relationships, Integra assigns no more than 12 SMEs to each of its business advisors, North American Christians with business experience and, increasingly, national staff who have been trained and developed during their time with Integra. Their goal is to impart successful business practices and biblical business principles to managers in the developing world in order to transform local corrupt or dysfunctional economic environments and grow spiritual capital.

Daniel is a Christian businessman who operates a Romanian graphic services business. He is also involved in Christian ministry outside the company. Daniel has received loans from Integra Ventures and others that have helped grow his business. He first opened his shop in two rooms—now he operates in nine rooms with 14 employees. In the past two years, his revenue and profits have more than tripled. Every six to eight weeks, Daniel meets with a Kingdom business professional from Integra for business mentoring and discipleship. Those familiar with the situation state that this informal yet regular education, training, consulting and fellowship with the "client advisor" are key to the entire SME program.[7]

Evaluation of SME Lending

SME Lending's Profitability and Sustainability

Though there is room for optimism, overall profitability of SME lending has been elusive. To be fair, assistance to small businesses is a relatively novel component of economic development. This is especially the case for Christian efforts, and it is expected that the economics of SME lending programs will improve over time.

Several groups are moving toward sustainability. World Relief's economic development effort in Kosovo extends loans of up to $15,000, though the average is a more modest $1,500. With over 1,000 clients, this program has reached operational sustainability and is now aiming for financial sustainability. Integra Ventures has far fewer, albeit larger, clients. It relies on donor support and has received additional funding from Citigroup and USAID. The North American expatriates who serve as business advisors to Integra's SME clients receive financial support from their home countries in a manner similar to that of traditional missionaries.

Secular SME lending programs that have achieved significant scale are beginning to reach financial sustainability. *The MicroBanking Bulletin* collates financial results self-reported by predominately secular lending institutions in the developing world. It has defined SME lending programs as those with average loan balances greater than 2.5 times the local annual GDP per person. (Those below that threshold are considered MED programs.) The financially focused SME lending programs that participated in its survey are operating at a 111 percent operational and 102 percent financial sustainability level. Figure 11 from *The Microbanking Bulletin* summarizes the results of this survey.[8]

FIGURE 11

Target Market	Avg. Loan Port. (SMM)	Avg. No. Borrowers	Avg. Loan Size	Avg. Loan/GDP per. cap.	Loans per Officer	Lending Rate	Tot. Admin. Expense	Sustainability Operational	Financial
SME Lending	10.5	3,669	$2,792	353%	93	27%	14%	111%	102%
[MED]	12.2	42,414	$523	47%	351	41%	36%	104%	91%

SME Lending: Avg. loan balance > 250% of GNP per capita   **Source:**   MicroBanking Bulletin
MED: Avg. loan balance < 250% of GNP per capita

A couple of observations about these results must be considered. First, the average portfolio size of the group reporting to *The MicroBanking Bulletin* is more than $10 million, which is much larger than the average Christian SME program. Second, the average reported lending rate of 27 percent interest is considerably higher than the 5 to 15 percent often found in most Christian SME lending programs. Third, the surveyed group also assigns far more loans to each lending officer. Perhaps extending the model for financial success in microfinance, these programs have an average of nearly 100 loans per officer. In many ways, these organizations might be considered "micro-plus" lenders.

The results posted by this group of secular lenders bodes well for Christian programs, but the challenge of profitability still exists. Christian SME assistance organizations will need to find ways to improve on the model. Local talent usually costs a fraction of Western salaries. More local native support and intense "train the trainer" programs may improve the overall economics of SME programs.

SME Lending's Impact on Local Job and Wealth Creation

Rose is the owner of a Kenyan SME that manufactures and sells detergents. Her small business employed four people when she obtained a loan of $4,375 from Partners for Christian Development's Kenya Investment Trust. Among other benefits, the funding allowed Rose to take on additional credit sales. One year later, Rose's detergent venture had grown to nine employees and her sales and profits had increased dramatically.

Job creation is a strength of small business support. As noted previously, small businesses in the United States account for the vast majority of job growth.[9] While MED loans more often sustain than create jobs,

SME loans typically lead to business expansion and job creation. Several studies by SME lending organizations have sought to quantify the effectiveness of this Kingdom business approach for job creation. The World Bank estimates that its SME program in Bosnia and Herzegovina creates one new job per $3,430 loaned. In Eastern Europe, Integra Ventures calculates one SME job created or sustained per $2,762 loaned. A BPN program in Central America conducted in partnership with the Latin America Mission found that $500 resulted in one new job. This added employment addresses a serious problem in many developing nations.

Though the funding required to create an SME job is higher than MED programs, there are important differences that need to be appreciated. The findings above for the investment per new SME job generally correlate with each country's annual GDP per person, or the total market values of goods and services produced per worker each year. In other words, while the creation of SME employment requires more capital, each new job also represents greater production in terms of goods and services.

Employment by an SME more often involves training and the acquisition of a skill or trade. SME employees are generally more upwardly mobile, are exposed to more technology, and receive more skill-based training. Thus, the local jobs created are generally higher paying, more sustainable, and provide a more transferable skill set. Furthermore, SME employment produces a greater trickle-down effect on job creation in the economy as SMEs in the formal sector deal with suppliers, partners, distributors and customers.

SMEs can create wealth in several ways. First, wealth accrues to employees engaged in meaningful work. Most of the population is better suited to job-taking than to entrepreneurship. For this majority, SME provides means for an income. These are usually more than the subsistence jobs that often result from MED. Many employees can start to think in terms of careers rather than jobs, and in the long run, more pay and more wealth accrues to those receiving employment.

Second, SME owners are finding that current earnings from operations provide a financial resource that can be deployed in a number of ways—both inside and outside the business. Many are using their share of the profits to further the mission of the local church. For example, it was through Ivica's share of Horvat Limited's earnings that he was able to fund his church's building renovation.

Third, in some cases, the company itself has a long-term value. (See the discussion in appendix A on business, which describes how aggregate wealth is created through business.) Unlike microbusinesses that are most often sole proprietorships tied to an individual, some SMEs can be sold. Though certainly not trivial or even commonplace, there does exist the potential for a sale of part or all of the business.

Fourth, SMEs create wealth by promoting the nation's infrastructure. Growing SMEs play a valuable role in creating an environment for successful business that benefits the entire economy, and they begin to fund the means through which the country can compete in the world market. SMEs are part of a business network of partners, suppliers and customers, and they require institutions and infrastructures that foster business relationships and trade. As the country's economic and physical infrastructure matures, GDP per person increases and the level of the nation's wealth rises. This sets the stage for significant international trade, a condition for the greatest economic growth.

SME Lending's Impact on Advancement of the Local Church

If CMED programs are well designed for evangelism efforts, Christian SME programs are well designed for evangelism, discipleship and the support of the local church. Christian SME programs typically identify attractive candidates through local churches and Christian networks and assist Kingdom businesses whose owners are committed to returning to God the blessings He bestows. Much more than microenterprises, SMEs empower owners and employees with greater financial resources to support the local church.

The relationship between SME managers and business advisors is often heavy on training, mentoring and discipleship. Believing SME owners are taught how to integrate their faith and their daily work, and the business and local marketplace are venues for the gospel to be proclaimed by word and by deed. Employees, customers and suppliers witness God's sanctification at work. Furthermore, the platform of success provides Kingdom business leaders a vehicle for influence in the wider community. Christian SME owners, mentored and trained in biblical business principles, infuse their sphere of influence with virtuous business practices. In this manner, a nation's culture is transformed and its spiritual capital is grown. Nations will benefit from a middle class of Christian managers who operate biblically in their businesses and advance Christian values in their cultures.

Not all SME clients are Christians, and therein lies an opportunity for evangelism. BPN's effort in Kyrgyzstan intentionally sets a program limit of 85 percent Christian. The organization is thus able to pursue evangelistic objectives by sharing the gospel, teaching biblical business principles and extending the blessing to non-Christians. SME owners who are not yet believers can also build the nation's spiritual capital by running their businesses with integrity.

As Ivica demonstrates through his management of Horvat Limited in Croatia, a Kingdom-focused SME owner can have a significant Kingdom impact in his local church, in his business community, and in his company. In his church, Ivica's business success has allowed him to provide significant financial support. In the business community, he belongs to a group of Croatian Christian business managers who are seeking to transform the local economic environment from corruption, dishonesty and distrust to one in which biblical principles prevail. In his company, Ivica is a shining example of Christ's love to employees and business associates in his everyday work. So caring is his attitude toward others that a non-Christian single mother in his employ stated, "Ivica is my pastor."

Issues and Opportunities in SME Lending

Challenge of Sustainability

Like CMED organizations, Kingdom business in the SME sector is still working to achieve sustainability. While the benefits to businesses in developing nations in terms of job and wealth creation and the benefits to the local church in terms of furthering its mission are apparent, sustainability will unlock the potential for much larger impact. As in other Kingdom business segments, profitability and sustainability of SME lending programs is the prerequisite for the transition from funding through donor dollars to funding through investment dollars, which would unleash resources for significant expansion of SME development in the emerging economies. There is room for optimism given the growth of Christian SME lending organizations and the sustainability successes achieved by some secular programs.

Scale and Mentoring

We have noted that the large number of loans per loan officer is a factor contributing to the sustainability of some secular efforts. Taking a page from MED practices, these programs see scale as the key to success. Some Christian organizations engaged in SME lending—especially those whose efforts are an outgrowth of an MED program—are also pursuing sustainability in this manner. In many cases, they are largely replicating the MED model. Unfortunately, the increased load per loan officer or advisor means that business and spiritual mentoring activities receive less attention, which results in less spiritual capital development.

A number of Christian SME programs, perhaps placing a higher emphasis on comprehensive training and mentoring, have resisted extending themselves to that degree. However, this also increases the challenge of reaching sustainability. The tension will continue to exist, and as financial metrics become more prominent, the pressure to improve overhead costs by loading business advisors with more clients will mount.

It appears that a new, more economical model for training and mentoring leaders of growing SME businesses must be found. The solution may involve the greater use of locals instead of (more expensive) Westerners. As SME programs mature, local advisors and instructors may assume the administrative and mentoring duties currently handled by relatively expensive Western business professionals. For example, BPN does much of its mentoring by bringing its loan recipients together to encourage and train each other. This creates a network for accountability and fellowship without significant involvement of BPN staff.

Though challenging, Christian SME lending programs must continue their commitment to both sustainability and transformation goals.

Risk Reduction

Accountability and mentoring are critical components of SME lending efforts, for in addition to providing entrepreneurs counsel in business and spiritual matters, they help to reduce the loan default risk. In 1992, the International Christian Chamber of Commerce (ICCC) established the Shalom Israel Foundation through which four businesses in Israel received loans. Though the loans were extended to Christians, all four defaulted. One ICCC member familiar with the experiment says that the program failed because it lacked accountability—the loans were not followed up with personal mentoring or relationships. Ongoing accountability serves to reduce the investment risk in SMEs.

Business failure is another significant risk in SME lending. Small businesses are particularly susceptible to economic storms and stagnation. One factor mitigating this risk is the tendency for competition to be less fierce in the early development stage of a business. Less competitive pressure means more room is left for profit, allowing small companies a greater chance to get established. But even so, business failure is usually a substantial risk with SMEs. Therefore, SME business advisors who can assist growth by opening doors in the First World are an invaluable asset. As small businesses in developing nations increase their access to overseas markets and partners, the potential for growth and success rises significantly. The risk of business failure and subsequent loan default decreases accordingly.

Graduate Programs

Under the leadership of particularly adept entrepreneurs, some microenterprises will thrive and grow to become SMEs. Therefore, the purposeful connection of MED and SME programs is an encouraging trend. Though relatively new, this model holds great promise for advancing nations beyond the infant stages of economic development.

The partnership between MED and SME programs is promising, but it also holds a danger of being instituted inappropriately. As noted,

SMEs represent far more complex organizations, and the challenges encountered by a business manager are different from those facing a microentrepreneur. As a result, those individuals mentoring SME leaders need a skill set that is very different from that needed to assist microenterprises. SMEs deal with organizational issues, company culture, management challenges, accounts receivable, contracts, permits and business strategy. By contrast, MED training focuses on basic skills that assist often-illiterate clients to account for their finances and keep to the loan repayment schedule. The danger is that those individuals accustomed to working with microloans will be employed to train and mentor SME owners. It is highly probable that they will be ill-equipped to assist SMEs properly.

Conclusion

Growing small and medium enterprises, such as those led by Rose and Ivica, is an important step in the advancement of local economies. Managers of SME Kingdom businesses influence their communities for Christ by transforming local business practices, and spiritual capital is grown at the business and community level. SME Kingdom businesses also provide needed employment and advance the mission of the local church. Just as some microenterprises grow to become SMEs, some SMEs in turn advance to the level of potential OPE investments. They constitute the breeding ground from which business leaders of larger ventures will emerge.

Some successful Kingdom business professionals will be afforded an incredible platform for promoting the gospel through OPE Kingdom businesses. The Kingdom-focused founder of a multibillion dollar company in a country officially closed to missionaries is one of those individuals. His amazing story is next.

CHAPTER 12

OVERSEAS PRIVATE EQUITY (OPE)

Since God first opened my eyes to the opportunities for the gospel through business, I have been encouraged by the stories of others who have pursued larger Kingdom business ventures, or overseas private equity (OPE) opportunities. One of those is the story of Richard Chang and some of his colleagues, who are Christians committed to using their business to advance the Church in China. Their business is a semiconductor fabricator with 3,100 employees, one of the most advanced in the country. And they have received government approval to open an "unofficial" church for their employees.

Richard Chang was born in Nanjing, China, but his parents, motivated by the communist takeover of the country, moved to Taiwan when

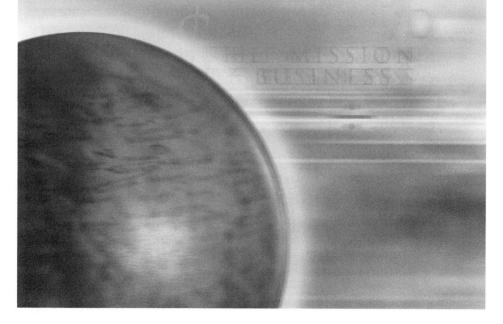

he was still an infant. After graduating from Taiwan's most prestigious university, Richard moved to the United States to pursue a masters degree in engineering. He then began a career at Texas Instruments that would last two decades. During that time, the company expanded globally, and Richard helped manage the establishment of six semiconductor chip factories in Asia and Europe. He retired early from Texas Instruments in 1997 and returned to Taiwan to found a custom chip manufacturing company. When that business was sold to another Taiwanese chip company for $515 million in 2000, his investors and customers encouraged him to start another business. He secured an astonishing $1.6 billion in funding and Semiconductor Manufacturing International Corp. (SMIC) was born in Shanghai, China.

While the location in Shanghai was attractive for many reasons, the primary reason in Richard's mind was its spiritual opportunity. "China is a good place in many aspects," he said, "but frankly, I was thinking about how I could share God's love with the Chinese more than how I could help the economy." Richard attracted a core management team with great technical expertise. Speaking at Chinese churches across North America, he shared his Kingdom objectives for the company.

As a result, many employees like Shou Gouping now share Richard's commitment to taking the gospel to China. Gouping had left Beijing for the United States after the 1989 uprising at Tienanmen Square and thought he would never return to his country. He earned graduate degrees in electrical engineering and worked for several Silicon Valley technology companies. Then Richard Chang came along. "I had a feeling that my life should be in China, serving people and God," Gouping said. With his wife, Gouping returned to his homeland, where he took a position as a technical manager in SMIC's design service department.

SMIC's employees are paid at prevailing Chinese rates. For senior executives, this is about 25 to 30 percent of salaries in the United States. Still, more than 20 percent of the employees come from outside mainland China, primarily from Taiwan. Richard has been able to attract world-class expertise from overseas, lured by opportunities for spiritual impact and economic growth. Some believe China is poised to become the major producer of semiconductor chips, replacing higher-cost venues like Taiwan. SMIC manufactures high-quality chips designed by leading technology companies in Japan, Europe and the United States. In March 2004, SMIC went public on the Hong Kong and New York Stock Exchanges. The company was valued at $6.4 billion, four times the initial investment. It is now the fifth largest contract chip maker in the world. "Every time we have done something successful, I openly mention that this is done with the Lord's blessing," Richard said. "At first, some people felt awkward about this. But as they realize we really practice our beliefs, they accept us."[1]

Because of the technical expertise and economic development his company brings to China, Richard has been granted permission to build a church for his 3,100 employees. "We come here as engineers to help build this industry in China, and the Chinese government supported us to have Sunday service as we share God's love through our work," Richard explained.[2] In fact, as an open congregation not affiliated with the official government-sanctioned church, SMIC's assembly of several hundred worshiping Chinese nationals and foreigners is highly unusual.

OPE Distinctives

OPE involves the development and promotion of companies like SMIC that can become large and established (or represent tremendous growth potential). OPE differs from MED and SME lending in several ways. First, the nature of OPE companies makes them much more attractive for equity investments. Loans are the appropriate vehicles for the micro-, small- and medium-size businesses promoted by MED and SME lending. For businesses in that size range, equity investments are too small, and the limited growth potential makes equity inappropriate. Furthermore, equity investing is simply not possible in many countries. However, the size, stability, or growth potential of OPE companies in some locations may merit participation in the ownership of the venture. OPE involves larger investments (generally over $100,000) in Kingdom businesses, and participation is in the form of equity investments in the companies.

A second distinction of the OPE approach is that Western Kingdom business professionals are more likely to hold a position in the company as board members, founders or managers. In the MED and SME approaches, Kingdom business professionals act as lenders, mentors and trainers to the businesses they serve, but very rarely are they employees of the Kingdom business themselves. By contrast, the OPE approach involves larger, more complex and technology-based ventures in which Western Kingdom business professionals sometimes participate directly as founders, managers or directors. Kingdom business mentors, investors and trainers are also needed.

This chapter is concerned with both aspects of OPE in which Kingdom business professionals may participate: as investors (outside the company) and as managers (inside the company). The discussion will focus first on the investor perspective and explore the experience to date in OPE investing (both secular and Christian) before turning to individual Kingdom businesses from the company perspective of the founders, board members and managers who are guiding these ventures.

Investing in OPE Kingdom Businesses

When my Indian friend approached me in 1999 with a business plan for ET, requesting my advice and investment in his fledgling venture, I had no idea that God was presenting to me an exciting way to build His Kingdom. Unlike Richard Chang, I am not involved in the day-to-day operation as a manager of the company. But I've discovered that outside board members and investors can have a major Kingdom impact through OPE ventures. Investors are as important to the development of OPE Kingdom businesses as water is vital to a seed, for they provide the capital that enables a venture to germinate and grow.

Why equity investing and not lending? Simply put, for such large projects, the risk is too great, and therefore loans are unavailable. Even in the West, banks rarely loan large sums for start-up ventures. While the return on a loan is limited to the predetermined interest rate, equity investments can yield a many-fold return commensurate with their risk as the company increases in value. The prospect of such a return is necessary to encourage investment of capital in higher-risk ventures.

What are the conditions that make equity investing particularly attractive? Professional investors who take an active role in the guidance, strategy and growth of a company look for two types of situations: the opportunity to grow a new venture or the opportunity to turn around and expand an established company. When we talk of OPE, we are referring to both of these opportunities to create value.

Focusing on the first opportunity, venture capitalists are in the business of investing in budding ventures that have a great idea, a compelling business plan and, above all, a good management team. The business must be in a growing market and show high potential for growth and profit. Venture capitalists work to reduce the risk and establish a strong business presence. They assist companies to move from the risky start-up phase to a position of stability and establishment. They work to reduce risk before substantial amounts are invested. Still, successful venture capitalists play the odds. If they invest in 30 businesses, 10 may fail, 10 may be passable and 10 may do well. Hopefully, 3 of those last 10 will be home runs. Many early-stage ventures fail, but those that succeed can yield a very high return on investment.

Focusing on the second opportunity, private equity investors are in the business of investing in established companies whose valuation can be increased significantly through a turnaround or market expansion. These investors often bring in a new management team, set corporate strategy and introduce new sales opportunities in order to improve the company's results. Business failure is less frequent than with the start-ups funded by venture capitalists, but the potential return on an individual investment is also lower.

Both venture capitalists and private equity investors normally invest a sufficient amount of capital to assume a controlling interest in the business. Professional investors usually maintain this controlling interest until there is a liquidity event, a way for investors to convert their equity back to cash. While loans have a built-in mechanism for returning cash to the lenders, equity investors need opportunities to sell their stock. In the United States, venture capitalists and private equity investors often look to the public stock markets to provide the exit strategy. A successful company that is economically sound "goes public" through an initial public offering (IPO), and the investor's stock can be sold to other investors. Venture capitalists and private equity investors exit at this point because the high risk has been mitigated and the prospective returns going forward are therefore lower.

In the Third World, public stock markets are far less developed and this option is very rarely available. Occasionally, as in the case of SMIC, a foreign company with significant ties to U. S. or European markets can seek an opportunity to trade on one of the Western stock exchanges. But often investors are left with another common exit strategy, a company buyout. The sale of a business to a company or investor provides owners with another means for converting their equity holdings to cash, and this has proven to be the more promising exit option in the developing world.

The Risk Factor

Every business contains a certain level of risk, some more than others. General Electric has a higher chance of being a thriving and profitable corporation two years from now than a start-up company trying to sell T-shirts on the Internet. This is not to say that large, established companies are immune to failure or that small, fledgling ventures cannot grow and thrive. Enron, one of the most highly valued companies in the United States, experienced a spectacular collapse, and eBay has made the transition from inception to dominant giant in less than 10 years. However, in general, early-stage ventures that lack a proven product, a proven market and a proven business model represent higher-risk propositions.

If early-stage ventures and turnaround candidates are risky in the First World, they are particularly risky in the developing world. In the First World, these companies are faced with the uncertainty of markets, products, competition, financing and the ability to deliver. The developing world brings added risks of inexperience in the local market, cultural misconceptions, underdeveloped economies, lacking infrastructures and volatile currency exchange rates—not to mention inexperienced management teams. In that environment, the complexities and challenges of guiding a company are multiplied. However, there are also some mitigating factors. The markets in the developing world tend to be less competitive and more protected, and there is a higher potential for capturing a market.

Business is all about managing risks, and value is created when risk is reduced. Thus, companies that can reduce the risk of failure by hiring experienced leaders, demonstrating demand for their products, attracting respected investors or earning major contracts will increase their value. As the probability of success rises, so does the company valuation. While the risks can be high in developing nations, so too can be the potential rewards.

Private Equity Funds

One way for investors to mitigate overall risk is to diversify and spread out their investment over a number of different companies. In the same way that mutual funds invest in many stocks and thus reduce exposure to any single company, venture capital and private equity funds invest in a number of companies to reduce risk. Many of the successful Silicon Valley ventures, such as Yahoo, eBay and Apple Computer, received early investment capital from these funds, which shared in the financial benefit of the companies' growth and success.

Though subject to business cycles that see years of plenty and years of drought, U.S. venture capital and private equity funds that invest in domestic businesses have experienced a very good overall return. For the 20-year period through 2002, U.S. venture capital funds returned an average of 16.6 percent per year while private equity funds returned 12.3 percent per year. By contrast, the U. S. public stock market, NASDAQ, returned an average annual rate of only 7.1 percent over that same period.[3]

OPE Funds: The International Finance Corporation. The success of private equity funds in the U.S. has prompted some to look for similar success overseas. The International Finance Corporation (IFC), a division of the World Bank, has been especially enthusiastic about the potential to assist developing nations through private equity investments. Ten years after starting its emerging markets private equity efforts, the IFC has over $1 billion in total capital invested in 142 different funds and select individual companies. More than half of the funds on its books are less than five years old.

New venture investors do not normally perform as well as the old hands. Most first funds are less successful than later funds. Thus, it may come as no surprise that the first round of private equity investing in the emerging markets has not been as profitable as the experience in the United States. The IFC estimates that about 15 percent of its funds "did well," about 40 percent of its funds had "a slightly positive return," and 45 percent of its funds had "a negative return."[4] Overall, the investment portfolio reports an aggregate real return of about six percent, though some insiders admit it has only broken even. The disappointing results are partly due to an untimely downturn in the emerging markets sector and partly due to mistakes that were made along the way.

Noted emerging markets private equity expert Roger Leeds of Johns Hopkins University analyzes the situation as follows:

> The most sweeping lesson learned from this disappointing experience is that the venture capital model that worked so successfully first in the U.S. and then to a lesser extent in Europe does not travel well to emerging markets. Virtually everyone involved in the early years assumed that a little tinkering around the edges was all that was needed to replicate the success achieved by private equity investors in a few industrialized nations. The development finance institutions (DFIs), as strong promoters of private sector development, encouraged investors to support identical fund structures and investment approaches even though the regulatory and legal frameworks did not provide adequate investor protection. Fund managers adopted similar processes for identifying, analyzing and valuing the target companies and structuring the deals despite the dramatic differences in accounting standards, corporate governance practices and exit possibilities. Investors also willingly jumped aboard the bandwagon. Faced with disappointing early results,

however, all stakeholders are being forced to rethink their approach. Although the rationale for private equity investing in emerging markets remains as compelling as ever, the original model must change on every level.[5]

The IFC, for one, remains optimistic about the future prospects of private equity in the developing world. As an early pioneer in and perhaps the largest contributor to emerging markets private equity funds, the IFC has gained significant experience in the field and has learned valuable lessons. This experience includes the critical importance of fund management (which requires both an expertise in the local culture and market and preferred access to investment opportunities), selection of the specific country, and the presence of a healthy mergers and acquisitions market or a healthy public stock market to offer investors an exit option.

Social Value OPE Funds: Small Enterprise Assistance Funds. A few secular OPE funds have a secondary objective that pertains to a social value. For example, the EcoEnterprises Fund invests venture capital and technical assistance in environmentally compatible businesses in Latin America and the Caribbean. The social concern of the EcoEnterprises Fund is protecting the environment, and it seeks to promote this concern through relevant business investments.

One OPE fund of particular interest is Small Enterprise Assistance Fund (SEAF), which seeks to achieve economic development through the promotion of growing businesses. With an average investment level of $380,000 per company, SEAF is committing fairly significant amounts of capital to each venture—enough to meet the definition given in this book of OPE. Investments in companies are made through a dozen region-specific funds all over the developing world, including Romania, Bolivia, Uzbekistan and China. The funds typically buy a 20 to 49 percent stake in a specific company. Only 5 to 10 percent of SEAF's funding is to start-ups; the rest is to established companies.

SEAF uses its social-value proposition to justify a slightly higher fee structure than the private equity industry norm. Since it is working in underdeveloped locations and is limited in the size of individual investments by the nature of its target companies, the fund charges 3.5 to 6.0 percent in annual management fees. Even so, SEAF has found profitability to be a challenge. It has received grants, primarily from government organizations, totaling about 10 percent of its portfolio. These donated funds are important to its continued operation.

SEAF has a dozen portfolios, each averaging about $10 million in assets. It estimates that profitability would require an average portfolio size of $15 to $20 million. To date, very few of its funds are more than three years old. SEAF believes that more time and additional experience in the field will yield dividends in terms of profitability. The next round of investing looks more promising as fund managers progress up the learning curve and internalize their experience.

Kingdom Business OPE Funds

Though there have been some attempts to create OPE funds that have Kingdom objectives, they have been both tentative and few in number. London-based Act Investments intended to establish two funds of $25 to $50 million in 2001 and 2002 that would have close ties to the International Christian Chamber of Commerce (ICCC). Act Investments was led primarily by investment banking professionals, and it was expected that investment opportunities would come to their attention through ICCC member companies. Profits from the fund would flow to a "storehouse" to support four primary Kingdom development efforts: MED, business education, aid (widows and orphans) and mentoring services. Though a worthy idea in its conception, the fund ultimately failed to materialize.

Strategic Frontiers Enterprise Fund was founded in 2000 in the United States with the intention of funding Kingdom business efforts around the world. It sought to raise $5 million and invest no less than 75 percent of its portfolio in businesses that met the Kingdom-building goals of the fund. The group had already identified some promising Kingdom businesses it intended to support through investment. But in the end, Strategic Frontiers Enterprise Fund was undone in its fundraising efforts by poor timing, a difficult business climate and an idea that was perhaps ahead of its time.

The virtuous cycle. Though no one has succeeded in establishing a Kingdom business OPE fund to date, this is clearly an idea whose time has come. Some individual investments in specific Kingdom businesses have yielded good returns, and a fund seems to be a welcome progression. A Kingdom business OPE fund can promote a number of large Kingdom businesses through financial and advisory investment, and if successful, a new follow-on fund can be established. It has the opportunity to be the ultimate "virtuous cycle," a positive feedback loop in which one good thing leads to another.

FIGURE 12

The Virtuous Circle

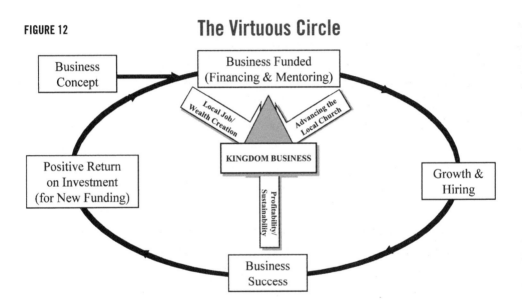

The graphic above illustrates how the virtuous cycle operates. Entrepreneurs with great business concepts need financial capital to act on their ideas. A Kingdom business OPE fund evaluates the people and the business plan. Fund managers must use standard criteria to determine the attractiveness of the potential investment. It is critical for them to resist the temptation to lower the bar simply because the venture has Kingdom objectives. (When evaluating Kingdom business opportunities it is important not to check our brains at the door and gloss over glaring deficiencies in the business case. The story of IPIC in chapter 3 should serve as a warning that we must not eschew the business sense God has given us.)

If the venture is deemed promising in terms of business and Kingdom-building objectives, the fund's managers provide the funding and mentoring required. The Kingdom business grows in number of employees and sales. Meaningful jobs are created for both Christians and non-Christians. The company develops a culture in keeping with biblical values that builds spiritual capital, both within the company and within the market. The business finds commercial success, and managers are given a platform for the gospel. Profitability means that the business continues to grow. Local employees and owners reap the financial rewards of profitability, and they become financially empowered to support the mission of the local church. Eventually, the sale of the business allows investors to earn a profit on their investment in the company. The financial resources of the Kingdom business fund grow, and new Kingdom businesses can be funded. The cycle continues.

This virtuous cycle—created by profitable and self-sustaining Kingdom business—yields a number of important benefits. Successful ventures are grown, desperately needed jobs are created, necessary goods and services are rendered, the gospel is preached by word and by deed, profits are generated, and positive investment returns are yielded. Rather than consuming funds, this missions concept creates funds for greater investment. Resources for the church and the worldwide missions effort are grown rather than expended.

Individuals, foundations and churches that wish to promote missions activity around the world currently support it through charitable contributions. However, individual Christians and foundations often have a much larger amount of funds devoted to investments than they do to annual giving. These portfolios are invested in companies and funds that have no relevance to Kingdom objectives. With a positive return on investment, Kingdom business funds would become an attractive prospect for investment, and the investment portfolios of Kingdom-minded individuals and foundations could be used to advance the Church as well. Kingdom business provides an avenue for the people of God to put a new and much larger asset to work for the Kingdom.

Managing OPE Kingdom Businesses

God is calling business people like Richard Chang in China to start, manage and work for Kingdom businesses. In an earlier chapter, we met Ken Crowell, to whom God gave a vision for blessing the nation of Israel through business. Galtronics became the largest employer in the city of Tiberias, was recognized with Israel's highest industrial award, and founded a growing local church.

There are many more stories of western entrepreneurs and managers with a vision for furthering the kingdom of God and blessing developing nations through business. For example, a Western businessman secured clothing contracts that resulted in employment of more than 700 people in a large, extremely poor Central Asian city. The vast majority of the clothing manufacturers that work for him are Muslim women, a large number of whom are widows who must now provide for their families. Many have children and cannot leave their homes to work. Thanks to this Western Kingdom-focused businessman, these women can operate from their homes, assembling clothing with sewing machines. Others gather in one of the company's manufacturing facilities. The businessman is now pursuing additional contracts with Western clothing brands that could employ even more locals. In a nation that presents significant challenges to the gospel, his company represents a shining expression of Christian love. It has opened the door to teaching hundreds of women about the love and sacrifice of Jesus for each person. The business is blessing many women in hardship and yielding opportunities for the gospel.

OPE Example: AMI. Clem Schultz, an American MBA who was divisional manager in China for a large multinational company, is now using his considerable entrepreneurial talents to build Kingdom businesses. Located in China, Clem's company has developed a strong understanding of local business culture and practices and has started technology factories ranging in size from $850,000 to $10 million.[6]

At age 11, Clem first sensed God's call to become a missionary. In college, he worked alongside Chinese Christians, and the call assumed more clarity. After a business education and experience in the corporate world, including a term in China with a multinational company, Clem turned his focus on Kingdom business. "I wanted to do world-class business while facilitating church planting work in the 10/40 Window," he noted. His business experience in China would be invaluable.

In 1989, Clem acquired controlling interest in a small consulting and manufacturing firm, AMI. Specializing in the technology sector, AMI first served as consultant to a larger Kingdom business that had two offices in East Asia. This allowed AMI to grow, but the first major break came the following year when the company signed a $3 million lighting equipment deal. AMI established factories for lighting equipment in China, leading to several additional offices in East and Central Asia. Over the course of the next three years, AMI averaged sales of over $10 million annually from the manufacture of lighting and other technology.

Soon AMI started to take equity stakes in the Chinese manufacturing plants it built and managed. The portfolio now includes interests in about 10 operations that produce telecommunication components, medical devices, energy-efficient lamps and more. In addition, AMI has provided management services for large American companies that do not have the expertise or desire to operate a factory in China. For example, a U.S. telecommunications venture contracted AMI to manage its production facility and showed a profit of $10 million in its first year of manufacturing. In another case, Clem managed the construction and staffing of a production subsidiary of a multinational corporation based in the United States. As the general manager starting with no employees and no order contracts, Clem built the operation from the ground up. One year later, the factory had 500 employees, $6 million in sales, and an Arthur Andersen award for "overall best manufacturing startup in China." Furthermore, every month, about 10 employees became believers. Four new house churches were planted within a five-month period. Clem considers these to be exceptional results, and his overall experience in Kingdom business is very encouraging. AMI has helped establish more than 20 factories (not all managed by Kingdom business professionals) representing more than 2,000 employees and $200 million in annual sales. The company has six offices in East Asia, the Middle East and North Africa.[7]

Clem Schultz and his staff deploy their business expertise and China experience on new manufacturing plants that typically cost $1 to $10 million. Usually, the project is a joint partnership with a technology company, and AMI's interest in a venture can be anywhere from 15 to 100 percent. This has afforded Clem and his fellow Kingdom business professionals, both at AMI and in plant management, with a major opportunity to promote the gospel. "Our large-dollar and high-technology amounts of investment provide us with strong political leverage with governments," explained Clem. "East Asian governments generally welcome foreign manufacturers, especially those with fairly large capitalization. As long as a company makes money and provides jobs for the local people, the governments will not interfere—unless it is rather openly breaking the law."

Leveraging its political favor in the regions in which it has manufacturing presences, AMI has established strategic alliances with more than 15 nonprofit organizations. AMI does not receive any direct financial benefit from these agencies, which seek to bless the local Chinese and Muslim communities through education, development and church planting. Clem's Kingdom business work has enabled Kingdom-focused Christians to flourish at AMI, in factory management and in nonprofit organizations. (Some lessons from Clem's experience are captured in the list of best practices for OPE Kingdom businesses presented later in this chapter.) His vision to facilitate church-planting work through world-class business is being fulfilled.[8]

Evaluation of OPE

OPE's Profitability and Sustainability

The OPE approach to Kingdom business is largely untested, and while there is evidence of individual successes, no aggregate observations about profitability and sustainability to date can be made.

Secular OPE funds have had very mixed results. The IFC has experienced real returns in the single digits. But the entire emerging markets stock market has underperformed in recent years, and many funds are young and have not yet completed a full cycle (approximately 7 to 10 years). Therefore, interim evaluations are difficult to make. Venture capital and private equity investments in the industrialized world have traditionally yielded very good returns, and there remains a real hope for OPE in the developing world. Lessons have been learned, and many approach the next round of OPE investing with guarded optimism. OPE is clearly the frontier of the future. If it can be developed, the money available for Kingdom business will be significant.

OPE's Impact on Local Job and Wealth Creation

Successful microenterprises might create one or two jobs. Profitable SMEs might add several dozen employees. Promising OPE ventures that are poised for significant growth have the potential to create jobs by the hundreds, if not thousands. OPE jobs typically represent a higher skill and pay level. They are also more likely to involve the use of technology, and there is greater potential for advancement. ET's Indian employees are educated, trained, well paid and upwardly mobile—so much so that they are highly desirable to competitors. (Interestingly, the raiding of some of ET's quality employees has resulted in Christians being sent out into the rest of the industry!) The amount of capital required for OPE Kingdom businesses is much greater, but so is the potential impact on employment, the local economy, the business culture and the society.

Though perhaps more risky by nature, OPE Kingdom businesses also have a higher potential for wealth creation, both to local founders and owners and to foreign investors. Kingdom business professionals whose OPE ventures succeed can take the profits and fund additional ventures. Ken Crowell's success with cell phone antennas at Galtronics led to expansion into a number of other businesses. And as local business people and employees reap the rewards of profitable commerce, they too are able to invest in the local economy, impact the standard of living, and fund local churches and ministries.

OPE's Impact on Advancement of the Local Church

An OPE Kingdom business operating on biblical principles can transform the business climate and culture in an industry or a city into one in which spiritual capital is built. Often operating in environments in which corruption and bribery prevail, OPE Kingdom business shines a light of integrity on the local business climate. The platform of success allows OPE Kingdom business leaders to speak of God, their faith and biblical business principles. They can proclaim the One who is the motivation for blessing the nation.

OPE efforts can also impact the spiritual condition of employees, partners and customers. There is a tremendous opportunity to bring the gospel to those encountered in the everyday course of work. Furthermore, specific Christian education and Bible-based training can be offered. Since some OPE Kingdom business professionals are part of a church-planting or ministry team, they are conscious of and active in meeting the spiritual objectives within their region. For example, Clem Schultz's Kingdom-focused employees are all accountable to a missions organization for specific spiritual objectives. The employees of SMIC in China and Galtronics in Israel founded thriving churches that were connected to their Kingdom businesses.

As Christian employees and local owners are enriched through profitable business activities, they are able to support the mission of the local church financially. Churches in developing nations are too often dependent on Western funding. OPE Kingdom businesses represent a significant opportunity for local wealth creation and, thus, for local support of the church.

Issues and Opportunities in OPE

OPE Investment: Lessons Learned

Secular private equity funds have only ventured into the emerging markets within the past 10 years, with most activity in the past five years. Buoyed by returns seen in similar funds in the United States and Europe, there was tremendous initial success in attracting investors to OPE funds. However, some of the conditions that resulted in profitable venture capital and private equity investments in the industrialized world were lacking in developing nations, and early results have been disappointing. Still, valuable lessons have been learned and mistakes have been identified—mistakes that OPE Kingdom business efforts can avoid. The following is a list of missteps gleaned from the IFC's significant OPE experience:

Fund Management Mistakes:
- Taking minority stakes in family-run businesses; these too often present serious corporate governance issues
- Expecting local capital markets to provide acceptable exit opportunities
- Putting too much faith in fund managers' financial engineering skill rather than in their level of operational expertise
- Participating too often in privatizations; asset values are driven up by competitive auctions and strategic investors
- Failing to hedge exchange-rate risk

Investor Mistakes:
- Failure to insist on experienced, high-quality fund management
- Lack of attention to the existence of clear and realistic fund objectives and operating strategies
- Ignoring poor fund structures
- Need more rigorous cash management by funds
- Fee structures must be more closely aligned with performance
- Lax supervision of funds
- Unrealistic optimism about the enabling environment in many emerging markets for private equity[9]

This last point is particularly noteworthy. I believe that the critical "enabling environment" the IFC has found missing in many developing nations is a sufficiently high level of spiritual capital. Underestimating the importance of spiritual capital leads to the "unrealistic optimism" experienced by the IFC. Thus, a further lesson from the first round of

OPE investing is the need for emerging markets to grow spiritual capital and the need for economic development efforts to help them transform.

Recognizing past mistakes, OPE investors are looking increasingly to experienced fund managers who give heavier consideration to taking control positions in companies they finance, are more effective at leveraging their equity stakes with well-structured debt, are determined to hold portfolio companies more strictly accountable to meet defined objectives, and give earlier and more rigorous attention to exit strategies.

OPE Kingdom Businesses: Lessons Learned

It is also important to internalize the lessons learned from Kingdom business professionals who have started and managed OPE Kingdom businesses. Clem Schultz, who has years of firsthand experience in a number of Kingdom businesses, has outlined several best practices. The following list captures some of his insight and experience. It may not apply to every situation, but it should serve as a helpful guideline for OPE Kingdom business.

- The Kingdom business has a strategy coordinator on its board of directors (ideally) or on its board of advisors (next best) who helps ensure that there are annual Great Commission plans that are ambitious yet culturally achievable. Similar to a business plan, the Great Commission plan outlines the goals for evangelism and discipleship.
- The Kingdom business professionals are part of a church-planting or ministry team that is focused on a city or people group. The leader of this team should focus primarily on spiritual objectives and not be the general manager of the business.
- Western Kingdom business professionals in the company are spiritually accountable to a church or mission agency in their home country. Ideally, there is a written contract between the Kingdom business and a spiritual accountability group that concerns the Kingdom business professional's situation.

- There is a careful screening process for the Kingdom business leadership team prior to starting or expanding the company.
- The Kingdom business management team is multinational or multiethnic, ideally representing three or more countries. Not all managers have to be Christian, but a majority should be Kingdom business professionals, and no key managers should be antagonistic to the Kingdom objectives of the company. In other words, every key manager understands that the Kingdom objectives are aligned with and supportive of the world-class business goals of the company.
- Compensation is primarily performance-based rather than flat or donor-supported.
- The Kingdom business is able to serve a significant export market. The inflow of foreign currency provides leverage and serves as a barrier to corruption.
- The Kingdom business has a formal employee training program on business ethics. Employees must internalize business principles that are based on biblical values.[10]

To these I might add the following ingredients that help larger Kingdom businesses from losing their focus in challenging times:

- The company has an excellent board of directors with a clear faith vision for the enterprise.
- Unanimity of purpose exists among the founding team and all senior management.
- A mission statement crafted by the founders guides the spiritual and business objectives of the venture and supports the creation of a company culture based on spiritual capital. The Great Commission plan should speak to this mission statement. It can be different from the company's mission statement, which may need to deal more strictly with business and company culture objectives.
- The company's Kingdom business professionals conduct annual "spiritual impact" audits that assess the progress

toward meeting spiritual objectives.
- The company partners with other Kingdom businesses to increase total impact and to hold each other accountable.

Business opportunities and relationships can take on many forms, and God can open doors to advance the Kingdom even at companies without a large Christian presence in senior management. The model used at ET is a case in point. Though not explicitly committed to advancing the Church through his business, the Indian founder was open to my suggestion that he recruit qualified Christians. As a result, hundreds of Christians are now employed, and the company has been educated in biblical principles that grow spiritual capital. There are several lessons related to this model to be learned as well:

- There must exist one or more individuals with Kingdom objectives who are in positions of influence.
- Business leadership need not be committed to missions goals itself, but it must be open to taking steps that both benefit its business objectives and advance the Kingdom.
- Spiritual capital must be grown. This is best achieved through education and training in biblical principles by a Kingdom business organization from outside the company.
- The Kingdom-building initiative must be conducted in conjunction with the local church. Pastors and Christians in the area must become instrumental in the evangelism, discipleship and fellowship effort.

Conclusion

Christians with gifting and experience in business are involved in the formation and management of OPE Kingdom business efforts in various locations. In fact, a call center business in India similar to ET is managed by a group of Kingdom-focused Christians. "The company's purpose is to minister to both spiritual and practical needs," the founding Kingdom business professionals stated. "It is a founding principle of the company that 'the earth is the Lord's and everything in it' and that all of life is to come under the glorious freedom of the kingdom rule of God." That is the vision for OPE Kingdom business—to create a sustainable model that both blesses the nations by addressing spiritual and practical needs and advances the kingdom of God. In the process, OPE Kingdom business has the potential to build spiritual capital in nations by influencing industries and regions.

I believe Kingdom business ventures like Richard Chang's billion-dollar technology company in China only represent the beginning of what God will do. Have you caught the vision yet? What could God do through Kingdom business? One thing is for sure: God is in the business of doing the outrageous. Let me tell you of one particular experience in my life that made this unmistakably clear.

CHAPTER 13

CURRENT TRENDS AND OUTRAGEOUS VISIONS

More than a decade of building the company and months of preparation culminated in this event. Inmac was ready to go public. We had gone through all the steps required to complete an IPO. The morning of the public offering, the market was scheduled to open at 9:00 A.M. Eastern Standard Time as usual, and we expected the offering to go out with the opening of the market.

Just before 9:00 A.M., I got a call from our lawyer indicating that the Securities and Exchange Commission (SEC) lawyers were not satisfied with one point relating to our public offering. The issuance and sale of new stock to the public would net Inmac $10 million in cash, but the SEC lawyers had looked at our very healthy balance sheet and couldn't

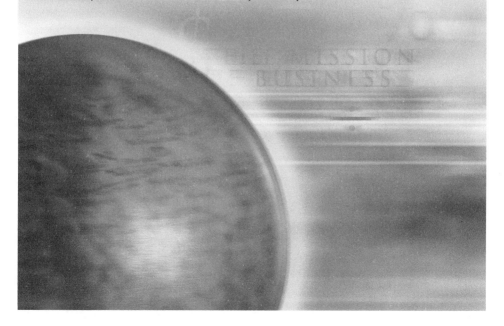

determine why we would need these funds. A one-page letter explaining our plans for the money was needed. It was 6:00 A.M. in California, and the SEC lawyers wanted the answer on our lawyers' letterhead. However, they did agree to accept a fax. By the time we faxed the letter to the SEC, it was 8:45 A.M. in California, 11:45 A.M. in Washington, D.C.

It was the fall of 1986, October 20, a Friday. In 1986, the United States federal government was experiencing funding problems, and in order to save money, the government had decided to shut down at noon on that particular Friday. We reached the appropriate SEC lawyer by phone and explained that the fax had been sent and was waiting for him at the SEC's fax center. His response was firm: "I cannot approve this offering today because the office closes at noon. There simply is not enough time to get the fax and issue a formal response."

That was devastating news. The stock market was weak. It was described to us as "choppy," and the feeling of our investment bankers was that if the stock did not go public that day, the environment would be too soft the next few weeks to accomplish the stock sale. We would then have to reapply for our public offering and essentially start over. It would set back the IPO date, cost us a lot of money, and potentially make the company less attractive to investors. Devastating news, indeed.

Something had to change. Only God could solve this problem. My wife, Roberta, and I began to pray for a miracle. At 11:50 A.M., 10 minutes before the government was scheduled to close, God gave us the vision to pray for the outrageous. Though it seemed impossible, we prayed that He would get our company on the public market that day. But how could He possibly do that? I didn't even want to speculate.

Suddenly, we heard over the loudspeaker on the trading floor at Solomon Brothers that the government was going to remain open for another hour! It would now officially close at 1:00 P.M. Having the government stay open an extra hour for us seemed like God stopping the sun from moving across the sky for Joshua! We called the SEC lawyer back, the SEC soon issued a favorable response, and Inmac's IPO happened at 12:03 P.M. We could only give our outrageous God the glory.

An Outrageous God at Work

In my years in business, there have been other instances in which God's hand was unmistakably at work. So outrageous were the results that there was no doubt to whom the credit was due.

Of course, Scripture is filled with examples of God doing outrageous things. Competing against 450 prophets of Baal to see whose god would answer by sending fire, Elijah ordered the offering and wood on his altar drenched with water three times. Then he called upon God to ignite the offering. Not only did the fire of the Lord fall upon the sodden sacrifice, it even burned up the altar itself (see 1 Kings 18:16-38). Or consider God's outrageous fulfillment of His promise to make childless Abraham the father of many nations. Abraham was 100 years old and his wife, Sarah, was 90 years old when God gave them Isaac (see Gen. 17:17-21). Most outrageous of all—Jesus, God himself, died for the sins of the world. Yes, God is in the business of doing the outrageous.

How can God do the outrageous through Kingdom business? Jesus told us that if we have faith the size of a mustard seed, we can move mountains. We must have faith that *God is capable of doing the outrageous.* Jesus also compared the kingdom of God to a mustard seed. Though originally the smallest of seeds, it grows to become a tree larger than all other herbs, such that birds can rest in it. God's Kingdom will grow beyond our expectations. *God will do the outrageous* (see Matt. 13:31-32; Mark 4:30). We can achieve the ordinary; only God can do the extraordinary. Not even the sky is the limit. But first we must identify the current trends to recognize where seeds are sprouting and conceive of outrageous visions to picture the enormous trees that will exist.

Current Trends

I believe that God is poised to do the outrageous through Kingdom business. Harnessing the power of business represents a massive sea change for the worldwide missions movement. Change comes as a result of trends that close doors to existing methods of doing things. But these same trends create openings for new approaches that may hold even more potential. In order to take advantage of any change, first we must recognize it.

Trends Shaping Our Future

The world is becoming a smaller place. Worldwide communication and transportation have been greatly enhanced and the era of globalization is upon us. Internet and cell phone access is growing rapidly, even in developing nations. Technology is becoming cheaper and connectivity is more affordable. A new Japanese-designed cell phone system is being installed in China and India. This village-based system has a total installation cost per phone of approximately $1,250, and in five years, even the smallest Indian village will have Internet connections. The world's shantytowns reveal television antennas everywhere. International travel has become more accessible as the cost and time required have come down remarkably. The world is becoming more connected and reachable.

Socialism has run its course. Developing countries are rejecting socialism and embracing capitalism as the economic system that holds the greatest promise for solving the problem of pervasive poverty. They are looking to the West for assistance in developing successful capitalism. There is a danger that many of these countries will adopt a capitalism that is void of spiritual values. Where the economic system is instituted without biblical principles and the development of spiritual capital, a dysfunctional economy like the Russian model results.

Some nations are beginning to see the importance of Christian faith for successful capitalism. As mentioned previously, former Chinese president Jiang Zemin made the connection, even stating he would make China a Christian nation. I have met national leaders in Fiji who also recognize the critical role faith must play in their country's economic development. As the U.S. helps Africa conquer the AIDS epidemic, African governments are looking ahead to the issue of business growth that will be possible with a longer life expectancy. They are seeking ways to institute the (biblical) business principles that have resulted in thriving economies in the West.

Some countries are restricting access for traditional missionaries. China, Pakistan and Vietnam are some of the 69 closed (or restricted-access) countries that include 265 megacities.[1] While these countries are completely off limits to evangelizing Christian missionaries, in others the pinch of increased religious worker visa restrictions is being felt. As a result, missionaries are resorting to covert or illegal means of gaining access to restricted nations. Those missionaries operating in those countries then face significant barriers to natural interaction with locals. Even when contact is made, missionaries working under false pretenses can arouse suspicion of hidden illegal activity. As long as they are considered to bring no value (and possibly even harm) to a country, there will continue to be restrictions on traditional missionaries.

Many countries are now opening to business. While closed to missionaries, governments in developing nations are recognizing foreign investment and foreign business expertise as important to their economy's growth. For centuries, believers have been welcomed due to the badly needed expertise or skill they bring. Christians in business are working in every nation today, even in those most closed to the gospel. From Afghanistan to North Korea, Kingdom-focused believers are blessing nations through business. Doors open to successful Western business professionals who bring experience and capital.

The cost of foreign missions is increasing. Bearing the financial burden of full-support Western salaries, the Church is pouring billions of dollars annually into traditional missionary efforts. Yet on a macro level, we are at a point of diminishing returns. Though programs have expanded and more regions have been reached, the Christian faith has made no recent overall gains. One-third of the world population calls itself Christian, a figure that has not changed in the last century. In an environment in which production costs are dropping in virtually every industry, alternatives to the costly 200-year-old model of sending fully funded Western missionaries need to be developed.

Foreign missions have seen no increase in funding in the last decade. For whatever reason, giving to foreign missions efforts by Christians in sending nations has stagnated (in constant dollars). According to the Barna Research Group, the share of born-again adults in the United States who give more than 10 percent to the church declined from 12 percent in 2000 to 6 percent in 2002.[2] Furthermore, churches are committing more resources to their internal programs. Support for foreign missions simply has not been growing.

Private investment to developing nations has increased four-fold in the last decade. Capital follows the growing business opportunities in the Third World, and investment is seen as the best way of assisting emerging economies. Moving capital in and out of developing nations is often still a problem. More and more countries are concerned with stabilizing their currencies. Wage differences between the West and the Third World have forced more business to locate in developing regions. Private investors have followed this opportunity with more investment dollars flowing into these countries.

International trade is increasing. There is an increased recognition that foreign trade is a key step on the path to economic development. The most prosperous economic advancement results from the production of goods and services in areas that have a comparative advantage. For example, that advantage might be lower production cost or greater technical expertise. Once these goods and services have been produced, they must be traded among people and countries. More manufacturing is relocating to lower-cost emerging nations, and more countries are recognizing that open trade benefits all. Therefore, barriers to trade are coming down, and international trade is increasing. The United States is currently running a $500 billion annual trade deficit, but what many perceive as a potential problem presents an opportunity to build international business relationships and take the gospel to the nations.

Economic development efforts have proven financially sustainable. Now even programs serving the poor through microloans can be profitable and economically viable. As previously noted, Bank Rakyat Indonesia, the country's largest microloan issuer, has realized a considerable profit from its microfinance business. Profitability also means that a return to investors is now available from a number of economic development funds. These funds invest in profitable institutions that support micro, small, medium and large enterprises in the developing world. A profitable economic development program is sustainable without any donor support; a number of them have reached that point.

Secular economists and writers are recognizing the significant role played by Judeo-Christian faith in developing successful capitalism. At least at a superficial level, the connection between the economic institutions that result from Judeo-Christian values and prosperous business has been identified. Economist Douglass North demonstrated that both the formal rules of the legal system and the informal rules of the moral-spiritual system play important roles in economic outcomes. Organized by the John Templeton Foundation, a group of secular scholars recently convened to discuss the launching of a new social science field that explores the contributions of religion to economic and social developments. "Now seems an ideal time to understand and assess the public effects of spiritual and religious action," the organizers observed, "because there seems to be a growing openness in the social sciences towards nonmaterial factors. It is no longer unusual to consider that trust, behavioral norms, and religion profoundly shape economic, political, and social developments."[3]

The movement to achieve integration between faith and work is spreading in the Church. A July 2001 *Fortune* magazine article reported on the "mostly unorganized mass of believers—a counterculture bubbling up all over corporate America—who want to bridge the traditional divide between spirituality and work."[4] Mike McLoughlin, Founder and Director of Youth With a Mission's Marketplace Mission, observes that "ten years ago, we could identify only twenty-five national or international nonprofit workplace ministries. Today we can identify several hundred."[5] The *International Faith and Work Directory* currently lists more than 1,200 organizations and ministries that focus on the integration of faith and work. Many Christians are coming to realize that their Sunday does relate to their Monday. "There is truly no division between sacred and secular except what we have created," concludes Dallas Willard.[6]

The marketplace is being recognized as the emerging ministry venue for believers. In 2001, George Barna predicted that "workplace ministry will be one of the core future innovations in church ministry."[7] Today, many others are sensing the same move of the Spirit. "God has begun an evangelism movement in the workplace that has the potential to transform our society as we know it," said Franklin Graham.[8] Former Fuller Theological

Seminary professor and recognized church growth expert Peter Wagner agrees: "I believe the workplace movement has the potential to impact society as much as the reformation did."[9]

More than ever, businessmen and women are being called by God to take the gospel to the world through business. Believers involved in charity, missions, evangelism and business are coming at this from different angles, yet they are arriving at the same conclusion: God is calling them to use business to further His Church in the developing world. The Holy Spirit has been speaking to people everywhere about business as a missions vehicle. A remarkable number of people have raised this issue with me recently. Unsolicited, they have shared a vision for commerce and economic development in the worldwide missions effort. Hundreds of people gathered at recent Kingdom business conferences around the world (e.g., Virginia Beach, U.S.A.; Kuala Lumpur, Malaysia; Atlanta, U.S.A.). Eight books on the subject have been written in the United States alone in the past couple of years.

Christians are assisting more and more businesses in developing nations. The Kingdom business field is so relatively new that no definitive records on growth have been compiled. However, we can certainly discern that significant growth in the movement has taken place. Ten years ago there was a limited Christian microenterprise development effort and few to none that supported any larger businesses. Now the number and size of Christian microfinance programs has grown substantially. Several organizations with Kingdom objectives are assisting the growth of small and medium businesses. And there are missions-minded efforts to build larger companies that have created hundreds of jobs and impacted industries and cultures.

What These Trends Imply

These trends imply that business and the marketplace are becoming the primary means for ministry, providing both hands-on spiritual development and economic blessing. Change is coming not only in the way we bring the gospel to our neighbors but also in the way we carry the gospel to the world. While the thought of considerable change will elicit anxiety in some, it is important to recognize that change is sometimes the less risky option, and it often represents the greatest opportunity to save souls. The only way to deal with change effectively is to embrace it and ask God what He is showing us through these events. Change is easier to embrace if we can conceive of the outrageous results God might have in store.

Outrageous Visions

There is a reason weight-loss programs tout those before-and-after photos. They paint a stark contrast between two very different states of existence, one in which the person is unhappily obese and another in which he or she appears normal and healthy. Of course, the person himself did not notice any significant difference from week to week as two pounds are lost here and a half-pound is gained there. It is only later that the enormity of the transformation is apparent.

The objective of a vision statement is to paint an "after" picture. A vision statement does not focus on the present, but rather, it envisions a future state. It aligns the efforts of everyone involved toward the common goal of that which the organization aspires to become.

Average institutions include superlatives in their vision statements. The proclaimed goal is to become the largest, best, most respected, leading or most effective organization. Often these aspirations fail the "snicker test" (How could *that* company become the leading firm in its field?). But the vision statement serves the purpose of aligning the efforts of the organization toward an objective that will be out of reach for some time. If we don't look toward the end, we won't know where start.

The purpose here is to propose some Kingdom business visions, to posit a number of Kingdom business "after" pictures. As previously noted, Kingdom business can be the key to world missions in this century. Business people, especially entrepreneurs, are generally people of action. No doubt there are many who are chomping at the bit, already envisioning what they can do to further the Kingdom through their business skills and experience.

But these are not illustrations of what *we* might accomplish. They are visions of what *God* can do, and here we need to think in terms of the outrageous. Only God can do the outrageous. Humans are ready to take credit for accomplishments of all kinds, but when we see the outrageous, we are forced to give glory to God.

What would be outrageous for God to accomplish through Kingdom business in the next decade? In other words, what would be a result so significant that the glory will go to the Holy Spirit even though human tendency will seek to capture some of the credit? God can increase significantly the size of His Church, He can transform the prevailing business ethic, and He can reduce dramatically the level of poverty in the world. Let's dream big.

The "after" pictures offered here will be categorized into four realms of potential outcomes: (1) reaching enormous scale, (2) transforming societies, (3) strengthening the Church, and (4) impacting Western institutions.

1. Reaching Enormous Scale

God has shown that He is in the business of "going big" through the power of the Holy Spirit. Kingdom work of enormous magnitude and outrageous scale is His hallmark. What started out after the crucifixion as a small band of frightened and scattered Jewish followers has now become the body with the single largest religious affiliation on the planet. More than two billion people now identify with the Christian faith. The work of the Holy Spirit was documented from the beginning of that amazing growth, and it continues today. What might going big through Kingdom business look like?

All 6,500 unreached people groups have Kingdom business teams operating on the ground. There is no people group that does not wish to improve its prospect for economic survival and standard of living. God can plant a Kingdom business team in every one of them, even in closed nations and societies. As mentioned earlier, Kingdom business is already at work in some of the most unreached regions.

Every developing nation has short-term Kingdom business missions efforts in place. Many believers who have business expertise will be called to serve in full-time business capacities in the developed world, yet vast numbers of other experienced business people comprise a force that God can also use to bless the nations through short-term efforts to every developing nation. Short-term Kingdom business trips are already being conducted in emerging economies like China and South Africa.

There are more than 10,000 Kingdom businesses of all sizes throughout Southeast Asia. From large manufacturing organizations to small enterprises, over one million employees can be exposed to biblical principles and the Word of God in their daily work lives. Many others are the partners, suppliers and customers of those Kingdom businesses. An individual who is engaged in starting Kingdom businesses in China estimates that there are already more than 200 companies with Kingdom objectives in that nation alone.

Ten Kingdom businesses are the largest companies in their countries. Major corporations are afforded a significant platform, one that God can use to transform a society. What would happen if firms as large as Microsoft, Daimler-Chrysler, or British Petroleum were actively working to build local churches, promote biblical business principles, create meaningful jobs, and transform their nations? Several substantial companies are already the product of Kingdom business efforts. Though not the largest in the country, the Kingdom business Galtronics grew to become the biggest employer in the city of Tiberias, Israel. SMIC is leading the way in China's semiconductor chip industry. Founded by several committed Christians in 1980, E-Land Group has grown to become South Korea's leading fashion retailer with approximately 2,000 employees and annual sales approaching $1 billion. The company is also committed to Kingdom business and has sent Kingdom-focused professionals to operate its factories in Vietnam, Sri Lanka and China. "We call them 'Businaries,' which means businessmen with missionary vision," explained E-Land's chaplain Sun Ki Bang.[10]

2. Transforming Societies

From the initial covenant with Abraham, God has poured out special blessings on nations as His Spirit moves to transform their societies. The Holy Spirit's work in bringing revival to a people usually accompanies a reduction in the social ills of hunger, oppression, poverty, corruption, disease, unemployment and violence.

A modern-day example is South Korea, where a dynamic Christian body comprises more than one-third of the population. After the devastation of the Korean War, the nation had the lowest GDP per capita in the world, yet reached First-World status just a few decades later. Previously plagued by poverty and underdevelopment, South Korea now boasts an impressive high-technology export market. Rather than being a nation to which missionaries are sent, South Korea now sends more than 10,000 missionaries as lights to the world.

As Dr. David Yonggi Cho mentioned in the Foreword, in 1958 he started his church in the poorest part of Seoul, Korea, using an old army tent given to him after the Korean War as his church building. His congregation had only five members, yet when he preached, he preached as if to an audience of several thousand. Soon the church was 3,000 members strong. God kept expanding his vision. Today, Yoido Full Gospel Church is the largest church in the world with an official count reaching 700,000 members. Dr. Cho now has a vision to plant 1,000 churches throughout Korea, and his body of believers sends out almost that number of missionaries to the rest of the world. What might God's societal transformation through Kingdom business look like?

Five former Third-World nations are attributing to Christian influences their rise out of that class. True transformation involves addressing spiritual, economic and social needs, and only a comprehensive approach will lift nations out of poverty's cycle of despair. The story of South Korea's emergence from Third-World status is a good example of this.

Kingdom business efforts are credited with reducing the unemployment rate by over 10 percent in several countries. MED, SME and OPE efforts can have significant job-creation results. In a world in which a number of nations are experiencing unemployment levels well over 50 percent, God can use Kingdom business to provide meaningful work that employs individual talents. Through its CMED activities, Opportunity International alone is creating approximately 250,000 jobs per year.

Eastern Bloc nations have eliminated widespread corruption and are attributing it to Christian influences. By the witness and example of His people, God can solve what is today a significant problem hindering the economic development of Eastern Europe. The infusion of biblical principles into the marketplace, the demonstration of honest business practices and the Holy Spirit's power to sanctify lives have the potential to transform that business climate in a radical way. Companies funded and mentored by Kingdom business professionals at Integra Ventures in Eastern Europe are already impacting business practices in their region by taking a stand against corruption.

Developing nations point to Christian influence as the source of a system of fair trade with honest salaries. The power of the Holy Spirit can transform unfair business practices and cultures lacking ethical norms. The gospel can empower a nation to increase its spiritual capital. When people internalize the concept of loving their neighbor as themselves, fairness and honesty will mark their business dealings. Not only will they grow their own spiritual capital, but the satisfaction and success from treating people right can be contagious. Just as Christian influence transformed dishonest business practices through the London Livery Companies, it is impacting business practices in many areas of the world today.

3. Strengthening the Church

Beginning with Paul, missionaries have taken the good news of Jesus to every part of the globe. The Holy Spirit has touched people's hearts everywhere, and there is we now a global body of believers. However, followers of Jesus are unequally distributed, and some regions have precious little representation within the Body of Christ. Some countries are virtually closed to the gospel. Even areas that are seeing appreciable spiritual growth quite often rely on Western funds to sustain their churches. Some indigenous bodies of believers have cut the financial ties to the West, but there is plenty of opportunity for God to effect change in the Church. How might God strengthen His Church through Kingdom business?

Muslim and otherwise closed countries are welcoming Kingdom businesses. Governments are fascinated by the prospects of economic development, job creation and local wealth building. If a company is providing meaningful employment, good wages and useful products or services, it will be welcome. God can open the doors for Kingdom business even in

Muslim and otherwise closed nations. The Holy Spirit must transform hearts, but Christians must make compelling business cases. Then Kingdom businesses can take the gospel to some of the most hostile regions of the world. Kingdom business is already happening in overwhelmingly Muslim countries like Afghanistan. Completely closed to traditional missionaries, the government of North Korea has recently partnered with a CMED organization to start a business development program for its people.

Kingdom business is credited with starting 10,000 new churches around the world. As people come to Jesus, churches will spring up. As the Holy Spirit continues to move, the Body of Christ grows in number, strength and influence. Church-planting efforts have already sprung out of business ventures in places such as India, China and Israel.

Business development efforts create sufficient local wealth such that indigenous churches no longer need Western funding. By providing employment and enabling local Christians to improve their economic condition, Kingdom business efforts can help break the dependence on foreign assistance. Christians in developing countries can learn the principles of giving; in some nations, this is a much-needed lesson. Instead of relying on Western funding, local churches can become economically self-sufficient and sustainable through their own members. The Church in developing nations will benefit from the financial resources of more business people like Ivan, the Croatian who funded a new church building from his share of business earnings.

Kingdom businesses create enough financial resources to fully fund missions. We have noted that there will still be a need for church planters, evangelists and translators—traditional missionaries who have no inherent source of income. Beyond supporting the local church, Christians in developing nations can start to give to these missions efforts. Indeed, some Kingdom business owners themselves will choose to fund traditional missionaries from their operating profits. Evangelistic Commerce has started several Kingdom businesses in India and China that are now profitable enough to fund other missions initiatives.

Kingdom business is breaking down the barriers between denominations and cultures in the Church and is promoting greater partnership and cooperation among believers. Business is about establishing the necessary relationships and partnerships to accomplish the economic objective. It is about finding win-win situations that benefit both parties. Business, like politics, sometimes makes for strange bedfellows, as a common objective can unite dissimilar characters. Kingdom business can serve to unite the Church toward a common goal—to see sustainable economic and spiritual transformation in people and nations. Several conferences have brought together people from almost every denomination and tradition who desire to see God's Kingdom work promoted through business.

4. Impacting Western Institutions

Those who return from short-term missions trips often report that the experience had a greater impact on them than it did on those to whom they ministered. To be sure, Kingdom business touches developing nations with a comprehensive gospel, but there is no doubt God will also transform the sending institutions. In fact, as we will explore in the next chapter, many of the changes in developed nations are essential for any large-scale Kingdom business movement. The power of the Holy Spirit can bring significant change to a number of our institutions: business communities, churches, universities, financial markets and governments. How might God impact major Western institutions through Kingdom business?

The secular press offers recognition of the significant contribution Kingdom business plays in addressing poverty issues. Driven by deep Christian convictions, William Wilberforce devoted his parliamentary career to abolishing slavery. Three days before his death in 1833, a bill ending slavery throughout the British Empire was passed. Just as Wilberforce is honored for his heroics in combating a social ill of his day, our secular press can take notice and credit Kingdom business with effectively addressing a significant social problem of our day. Just as the national newspapers in Israel carried headlines announcing that Galtronics was given the nation's highest industrial award for "blessing the Nation of Israel," God can open the eyes of those in the secular press to recognize the impact of Kingdom business.

A recognized triple-bottom-line metric is in place, and Kingdom businesses are evaluated by that standard. You get what you measure, the saying goes.

Kingdom businesses can reflect their commitment to profitability, economic improvement and spiritual transformation by reporting their progress towards those objectives. There is already an initiative to quantify and evaluate some Kingdom businesses in terms of spiritual results. God can use this to shine His light upon a business culture that typically concerns itself with a single bottom line—profitability.

The Kingdom Business Index (KBI) is published by the secular media, and there is a significant mutual fund that invests in Kingdom businesses. Financial markets have created a number of specialized indexes including the Calvert Social Index, a broad-based benchmark for measuring the performance of United States-based, socially responsible companies. A similar index for Kingdom businesses combined with an investment vehicle that would allow participation in those business missions efforts can raise the profile of Kingdom business beyond the Christian community.

There are several large and successful funds that finance Kingdom business start-up and business development efforts. Venture capital or private equity funds can pool resources of investors and deploy them in promising businesses around the world. The fund keeps working, as profitable investments yield additional funds that can be channeled to additional attractive ventures. Currency weaknesses and money-transfer limitations often prevent interested investors from financing businesses in many countries. Funds that invest in Kingdom business ventures can also facilitate the movement of money around the world. Secular funds that invest in profitable MED organizations, such as ProFund International (Costa Rica) and BlueOrchard Finance (Switzerland), are already providing a return to investors, and there is an opportunity for Kingdom business funds that do likewise. The Business Professional Network U.S. has recently started a small fund and is investing in promising Kingdom business ventures.

All major Christian relief and development agencies and traditional missions agencies are partnering with Kingdom business efforts. The Association of Evangelical Relief and Development Organizations (AERDO) has over 40 members, and the Evangelical Fellowship of Mission Agencies (EFMA) has over 100 members. AERDO has already started an initiative to raise the profile of Kingdom business with its members. The Western missions landscape can be changed forever if all member organizations have a partnership with Kingdom business to work together to transform the nations.

Every Christian university business program is offering Kingdom business courses, and Kingdom business is the most popular concentration in Christian business education. The key to raising up successful participants in the Kingdom business movement is the education of those who are to become proficient in matters of commerce and faith. Tomorrow's leaders are learning today. They need a modified business curriculum that offers the tools required to navigate the difficult terrain of combining economic and spiritual goals in developing countries. EC Institute, an initiative of Evangelistic Commerce, is already developing Kingdom business curriculum resources. Several Christian university business programs, such as Biola University and Spring Arbor University, are already offering courses in Kingdom business.

Five Kingdom businesses are positive subjects of Stanford or Harvard Business School case studies that are presented in secular business school courses. The success of Kingdom businesses in financial and transformational terms should not go unnoticed by secular students of business. As such, case studies that document these successes can be a positive witness to biblical principles and the virtue of following a higher standard. A Harvard Business School case study has already documented the positive impact Christian leadership at the major U.S. company ServiceMaster has had on the treatment of its employees. Specific Kingdom businesses are profiled in books such as *Great Commission Companies* by Steve Rundle and Tom Steffen, but God can acknowledge their positive impact in secular business schools as well.

Ten governments of developed nations recognize the transformation achieved through Kingdom business and decide to fund these efforts—no strings attached. Western governments are throwing economic development funds at the problems of developing nations, but the realized level of permanent change often falls short. Efforts ignited by the Holy Spirit can achieve both true transformation and the recognition of governments. Already, the Swiss government has acknowledged the impact of a Kingdom business effort and has provided funding for the majority of the program administration and SME training it provides.

Watch and Wonder

This chapter has noted a number of current trends and painted a whole gallery of "after" pictures. Of course, it is impossible to know exactly what God has in mind, and it would be imprudent to focus on any single one of these visions as the definition of ultimate overall success. The purpose here is to illustrate what the power of the Holy Spirit working through the Church can accomplish. Whatever it is, if it is God at work, we can expect it to be outrageous!

Different organizations might make it their mission to see one of these visions become a reality. One might have a vision for thousands of Kingdom businesses in East Asia and therefore will seek to facilitate their establishment and promote their success. Another might have a vision for business schools and therefore will seek to advance Kingdom business coursework in Christian education. And yet another might have a vision for promoting Kingdom businesses to the Christian and secular investment communities and therefore will provide the necessary analytical research to evaluate these companies.

What we are talking about here are steps that put a vision into practice. Vision without action is useless, and it is to the specific actions within various institutions that we turn next. How are we going to accomplish this vision? In other words, how can we partner with God to help move the ball along, knowing He gives the vision? The following chapter will list some ideas.

CHAPTER 14

REALIZING GOD'S KINGDOM BUSINESS VISION

For God to do the outrageous through us, we need to be in agreement with Him and have a clear vision of where we are going. We need to identify how God is working to further His Kingdom so that we can pull in the same direction. We don't always have that vision.

Abraham did not always have a clear vision of where he was going. In the dead of the night, when all was quiet, the Lord called Abraham outside to show him a vision. "He took him outside and said, 'Look up at the heavens and count the stars—if indeed you can count them.' Then He said to him, 'So shall your offspring be.' Abraham believed the Lord,

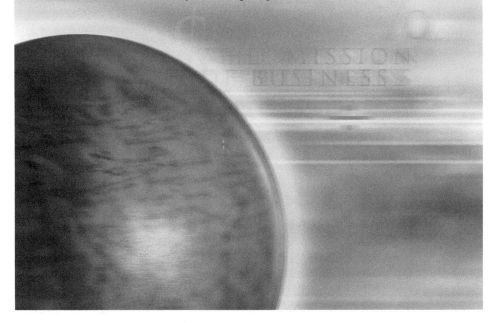

and He credited it to him as righteousness" (Gen. 15:5-6). Abraham got his vision in line with God's vision.

Getting God's vision may mean we need to change our views and rethink some paradigms. For many of us, changing our view and reaching new conclusions is easier said than done. We hold tight to beliefs and established ways of doing things. In business, as elsewhere, most change comes from the outside. Normally, it does not originate within the institution that needs to see the change. Those within the institution carry too much baggage to allow them the opportunity to pick up something new. They are entrenched in the established way and too busy with the concerns of keeping up with what they already have. They don't do enough listening in the dead of night.

It is interesting to note that most of the new ministry and evangelism efforts in the past 50 years have come from outside of the local church. Great ministries such as Young Life, Campus Crusade for Christ, Prison Fellowship Ministries, Promise Keepers and Youth With a Mission all resulted from the identification of a specific group or need that was being inadequately addressed by the local church. These parachurch efforts were initiated by people within the Church, but the Church as a whole sometimes proved slow to embrace them. God was at work, but rather than being adopted as a core thrust of the Church, these ministries remained on the periphery.

United in the Vision

Jesus prayed, "That they may be one as we are one. . . . May they be brought to complete unity to let the world know that you sent me and have loved them even as you have loved me" (John 17:22-23). Unity is a powerful thing. It can be used for good as well as for bad.

The Church must be unified in the idea that Kingdom business presents a great opportunity for the gospel, but it cannot become a replacement for all other missions efforts. Although traditional missionaries face increasing challenges, they still have a significant role to play in the overall missions strategy. Kingdom business must become an integral part of that strategy. From history, we have learned that the separation of missions from business causes both to lose their sense of direction. Separated from the marketplace, traditional missions efforts lose their relevance and fail to meet people's significant economic and physical needs. Without a Kingdom mind-set, business becomes an economic pursuit that fails to meet people's spiritual needs and produce cultural change. Only when Kingdom business and other missions approaches work in unity will we achieve the maximum impact for the gospel. As in Jesus' prayer, may we be brought to complete unity to let the world know about Him.

A Powerful Missions Strategy

Each major missionary movement in history required a new vision and a new understanding of how the Church would reach the world given new political, social and economic realities. Today's new vision includes Kingdom business, a powerful and growing missions movement for the twenty-first century.

For Kingdom business to succeed, attitudes need to change. The Church tends to have a skeptical view of the role of faith in business, and many in the Church have difficulty making the connection between the two. A subtle divide still exists between the Church and business, between business schools and seminaries, and between realms considered sacred and secular. There is an all-too-pervasive myth at work in the Church that elevates the "spiritual" pursuit of personal faith and denigrates the "secular" pursuit of business. This must be overcome.

Many in the secular world get it. Secular groups have written more on the importance of the Judeo-Christian faith for successful business than the Church has. Leading officials in a number of countries embrace the idea that Christian faith and virtues are the key to economic success. Privately, some leaders of countries have encouraged Christian business leaders to come to their nations. Of course, most of these officials want to bring Christianity for its economic and social benefits rather than for its power to transform individual lives. But once people are opened up to the gospel, lives will be changed.

Yet we in the Church have been slow to take up the challenge and the opportunity. Historically, the Church, on fire for God, led the way in business. Today, the Church is behind in the development curve. There are many MED organizations but only a few Christian MED organizations. There are a number of financially profitable MED programs but few or no financially profitable CMED programs (Christian SME and OPE efforts are newer and no more advanced). The Body of Christ must again take the initiative to promote business that thrives on biblical principles.

If the Kingdom business movement is to succeed to its fullest extent, it must have all of God's partners on board. The local church must embrace and promote Kingdom business as core to its mission, and so must our educational institutions, seminaries and Christian business schools. Missions organizations must support and partner with those who are spreading the gospel through business. Christian investors and business professionals must use their resources and talents to further the mission and growth of the worldwide Church. Exciting currents are developing in each of those areas, yet all need to experience more change.

Christian Education and Training

Christian seminaries, business schools, universities, and even high schools are preparing potential missionaries for an era that is rapidly drawing to a close—that of the fully-supported Western missionary. Christian institutions that are called to prepare their students for effective missions work in the twenty-first century must offer teaching and instruction not only on the missions paradigms of the past but also on those of the immediate future. Well beyond the opportunity to develop and support Kingdom business professionals, there is a serious need for Christian educational institutions to teach and integrate a basic understanding of business in its courses. For too long, many have focused primarily on "spiritual" training (evangelism, preaching, teaching, theology) while to some extent ignoring the "secular" pursuits of service in the marketplace. Seminaries and Bible schools must cross the divide and work with business schools to equip those who will be fluent both in business and in the Bible.

Christian universities and business schools need to begin to research and teach the philosophical, theological and practical aspects of Kingdom business. Additional research on this topic should be conducted and proven models explored. Courses on relevant subjects will open many students' minds to the power and possibilities inherent in Kingdom business as a legitimate and effective missionary pursuit. Indeed, Christian universities and business schools that take the lead in this field are likely to build a recognized expertise in an area of rapidly growing interest to potential students (and potential donors) as the twenty-first century progresses.

Unfortunately, business education, if it is offered at all at a Christian educational institution, is usually divorced from the missions education program. This separation between business education and theological training is based on the 200-year-old paradigm that fully supported Western missionaries and business students have differing needs and aspirations. Yet to prepare Kingdom business professionals for the twenty-first century, Christian educational institutions must develop management skills along with spiritual training (the model of the Basel Mission Training School, which sought to impart both business and theological training, might be instructive). This entails curriculum changes in Christian executive education programs, Christian business schools, Christian seminaries and Christian high schools.

Christian executive education programs should equip business professionals with the resources required to work in a Kingdom business environment. The challenges of entrepreneurship, management and discipleship in another culture and business climate can be significant. There is a need for institutions and programs that provide assistance, mentoring, connections and instruction to seasoned and retiring Christian businessmen and women who are called to Kingdom business.

Christian business schools are uniquely positioned to equip aspiring Kingdom business professionals and retrain missionaries with the mentality, skills and tools they need to be effective. Successful business principles mirror the attributes of God, and Christian business schools can make the connection between biblical values, spiritual capital and business success. Because good business concepts are found in the Bible, this is far more than teaching students how to draw examples from the Bible. Some schools have started down this road already.

A great deal can already be learned from the experience of pioneers in the field of Kingdom business. By instructing students in the successful models, relevant case studies, and proven business and management techniques that will help them become successful Kingdom business professionals, Christian business schools can be true catalysts for the growth of effective Kingdom-focused ventures around the world. At a recent conference, a seasoned Kingdom business professional presented some lessons he learned from his experience founding and managing profitable Kingdom businesses in East Asia. "Two businesses are to be avoided: crafts and coffee shops," he instructed the audience. Afterward, a missionary came up to him and related that they had tried to operate some commercial ventures on the mission field but finally gave up after years of anguish. "Those two businesses are exactly the ones we attempted to run," he confessed sheepishly. "People have just learned in 10 minutes what took me 9 years and thousands of dollars to understand." Lessons learned in the classroom are often much less costly than lessons learned in the field.

Experiences in Kingdom business have already yielded plenty of mistakes and successes. The saying is all too true: Those who don't learn from past mistakes are doomed to repeat them. There are lessons to be learned on three critical fronts: (1) how to work with and advance the local church, (2) how to maximize local job and wealth creation, and (3) how to build an enterprise that is both profitable and sustainable with a triple bottom line.

Truly effective Kingdom business professionals must understand that financial success is only a small part of their calling—and that successful partnership with the local church and the creation of jobs for the local community are success metrics at least as important as the income statement.

Christian seminaries need to equip students with an understanding of Kingdom business and its place in missiology. Seminaries can provide the context for in-depth research on the principles of successful Kingdom business. For example, there is certainly room for additional research into the use of business in missions movements throughout the ages, for further definition and affirmation of the role of Kingdom business in the context of present-day missions, and for further development of a comprehensive theological framework for the understanding and practice of Kingdom business.

Seminary education should include validation of Kingdom business as a legitimate calling for full-time Christian workers, not as an inferior alternative to the ministry. Seminarians should leave with a vision for mobilizing the laity—and especially business people—for the Kingdom, understanding the tremendous untapped potential of business professionals in the pews.

Christian high schools should teach the basics of free market economics and business. Instruction in the principles of commerce is one significant way that these schools could further differentiate their curriculum from the outdated educational offerings of most public schools. A high school graduate who has a basic understanding of how the world's predominant economic system works is far more likely to be a successful member of society than one who does not. Even at the high school level, a basic understanding of successful capitalism, its biblical basis and the vital role of businessmen and women in our society may well encourage young students to explore a possible calling to Kingdom business.

Example Initiatives: Christian Education and Training

- Under the leadership of Dean John Mulford, the Graduate School of Business at Regent University (Virginia, U.S.A.) in October 2002 hosted the first conference to convene a number of individuals interested and involved in Kingdom business. The event focused on the principles, power and practice of Kingdom business and led to the publication of a significant work in this field entitled *On Kingdom Business: Transforming Missions Through Entrepreneurial Strategies* (Crossway Books, 2003).
- EC Institute (Michigan, U.S.A.) is engaged in a concerted effort to raise the profile of Kingdom business with Christian business professors. It has developed a relationship with the

Christian Business Faculty Association and the Association of Christian Economists, which boast more than 500 university and college educators, in order to promote greater prominence for Kingdom business in their curricula. EC Institute also runs a summer program designed to educate and equip the next generation of Kingdom business professionals. Its Global Business Internship summer program has been a registered affiliate with the Council for Christian Colleges and Universities for several years.

- Several Christian business schools are offering courses on Kingdom business. In particular, Biola University's School of Business (California, U.S.A.) has developed the class "Business as Mission" and will be rolling out an international business degree program that integrates coursework in intercultural studies and missions. The curriculum is modeled after the top international business degree programs in the country, yet unapologetically Christian in its worldview. Spring Arbor University's School of Business and Management (Michigan, U.S.A.) has a similar course, "Business and Missions."

- Biola University (California, U.S.A.) considers the connection between business and missions so important that it is possible the school's seminary students will soon be required to take business courses. The seminary and the school of business are working together to develop a curriculum.

- In connection with University of the Nations, the Center for Entrepreneurship and Economic Development is "a global organization for persons who have a call to disciple nations through the sphere of business."[1] The Center conducts two- or three-week seminars in various regions of the world on the issues facing current and prospective Kingdom business participants.

Local Churches

Churches in sending countries are quite accustomed to providing financial, prayer and organizational support to traditional missionaries, and they could greatly assist the expansion of the Kingdom business movement by affording this same level of structural and spiritual support for business missionaries. These types of support are equally important to those who are involved in promoting Kingdom-focused business ventures overseas.

Some of the changes that missionary-sending churches will want to consider are well-structured and regular prayer support, frequent communication and scheduled visits with its Kingdom business missionaries, recognition that Kingdom business professionals are every bit as spiritual as (and at times more effective than) traditional full-support missionaries, and validation of the calling of a Kingdom business professional as equally important as that of a traditional missionary or spiritual leader.

More far-reaching changes such as the establishment of church investment funds intended for specific Kingdom businesses in chosen countries could be great catalysts for willing and ready businessmen and women. Alongside the church missions fund, members could direct contributions to Kingdom business fund. This money could be used to provide capital for one or more Kingdom businesses that promote the local church in a given location.

Here is how this might work. Let's say a congregation has a particular heart for Romania. Two missionaries from the church are located there: a traditional missionary who has planted a growing church, and a Kingdom business professional who is assisting growing SMEs. The church's Kingdom business fund is used by the Kingdom business professional in Romania to invest in SMEs owned by people in the local church. He also trains, advises and disciples these Romanian business people. As the believers' companies grow and thrive, they are financially empowered to support the local church on their own. Romanian Christians and non-Christians are given much-needed jobs in which they use their gifts and talents. The local believers can afford to pay both for the education and employment of a Romanian pastor and for outreach ministries to their region. The church-planting missionary is free to move on and use his gifting and passion for evangelism to start another church. The Kingdom business fund grows as a result of successful investment, and it is available to be redeployed in Romania or elsewhere. A return on capital could also fund a two-week Kingdom business missions trip to help growing businesses.

I encourage laypeople to ask their church to pursue the changes outlined here. You are an important agent of change. Pastors and church leaders who give Kingdom business professionals a platform to convey what God is doing through their missions efforts will be promoting successful Kingdom work today and sowing seeds for business people to enter the mission field tomorrow.

Example Initiatives: Local Churches

- Perimeter Church (Georgia, U.S.A.) has established Business Partners International (BPI), an initiative of the church's Global Outreach ministry. Located in a suburb of Atlanta, the church believes that "Christian business people serving as professionals are integral and strategic to the expansion of the church around the world." Recognizing the unique contribution of business people, BPI seeks "to assist churches in the evangelization of local business people and in the development of Christian business leaders."[2] BPI has sent out teams of business people to developing nations, has facilitated personal relationships between its business professionals and business people overseas, and has provided training and assistance in the development of commercial enterprises.
- Advancing Churches in Mission Commitment (ACMC) has partnered with EC Institute to increase the profile of Kingdom business at missions-minded churches. As a result, business is being presented as an effective missions strategy to hundreds of pastors in seminars at large regional ACMC conferences across North America. ACMC has relationships with over 1,000 missions pastors and organizations in North America and has become the go-to resource for strategic missions advice.

Missions Organizations

Traditional missionary-sending organizations will almost certainly have a key role in the missions movement until the Lord returns. But there is a potential role for mission sending organizations that are specifically designed to meet the unique requirements for supporting Kingdom business. The training and support required for Kingdom business is sufficiently different from what is currently offered to traditional missionaries that new support organizations are needed. Just as venture capitalists evolved out of traditional commercial banking organizations in Silicon Valley in the 1960s to eventually become one of the key catalysts for the worldwide high-tech revolution that followed, it is likely that a new type of business missionary-sending organization will now come to the forefront. These are just some of the key services that a twenty-first century missions organization might provide to Kingdom business professionals:

- Providing access to Kingdom-focused investors and capital
- Educating entrepreneurs and managers about exciting business opportunities in target countries
- Creating value-added business networks that Kingdom businesses can utilize
- Connecting potential Kingdom-focused employees with Kingdom businesses
- Providing key individuals with specific functional expertise for short-term projects as needed
- Arranging long-term business mentoring relationships
- Monitoring the performance of Kingdom businesses in light of their spiritual and financial objectives
- Establishing prayer support teams for Kingdom business professionals

The beauty of such Kingdom business support organizations is that the long-term support of each missionary will not require huge amounts of expense money. In fact, a return of capital is both possible and necessary. Successful Kingdom business professionals will be self-supporting through their business ventures. Like the venture capital model of Silicon Valley, the ability to recognize and meet significant economic opportunities in target countries will be important, and successful Kingdom business professionals will become apparent within five years of their arrival in the target country.

Example Initiatives: Missions Organizations

- Integra Ventures (Illinois, U.S.A.) raises investment capital and deploys and supports seasoned business professionals in Eastern Europe. Integra's Western MBAs advise, disciple and finance promising small business leaders.
- World Partners (Netherlands and Virginia, U.S.A.) is a missions organization that supports local Christian entrepreneurial initiatives in developing nations around the world. It does this by providing financial investment as well as commercial or industry-specific assistance from Western business people.
- Business Professional Network (BPN) (Oregon, U.S.A., and Switzerland), established in 1997, is an organization that connects Western Christian professionals with Christian business people in the developing world. BPN deploys the experience and resources of a group of seasoned professionals for the benefit of fellow believers operating small businesses in the Third World.
- Organizers of the large triennial missions conference at Urbana (Illinois, U.S.A.) have decided that business as missions should be one of four major tracks at its next gathering in 2006.
- The Lausanne Committee for World Evangelism has also created a track for Kingdom business. The organization's leaders recognize the strategic importance of Kingdom business, are strongly committed to it, and plan to give it increasing prominence in the future.

Kingdom Business Investment Funds

Private equity capital and venture capital have offered some of the best rates of return of all financial investment categories over the past 30 years, including the period of the recent technology-sector decline. Of course, since there is significant risk in such investments, the most successful private equity and venture capital firms spread their risks over a significant number of investments, knowing in advance that some will fail but that others will be tremendously successful. These investments are pooled and managed in the form of a fund.

The twenty-first century will see the evolution of Christian investment funds that invest specifically in Kingdom business ventures. The difference from their secular counterparts, of course, will be that the financial rate of return on investment, while important, will not be the only measure of success for such firms. Two other criteria, local impact for the gospel (support and growth of the local church) and local economic development (creation of local jobs and financial resources), will be of equal importance to investors. Meaningful metrics need to be devised to measure how well Kingdom business investment funds perform in relation to these objectives.

Profitability is the key to significant growth of the Kingdom business missions movement. Christian investment funds that are invested in MED organizations, SME lenders and promising OPE ventures should provide a competitive rate of financial return as well as significant impact for God's Kingdom in the countries they target. Unless investors can expect a return on their investment, Kingdom business funding will attract only charitable donations. It is also important that Christian MED and SME development programs break the not-for-profit cycle. These programs demand profitability from the local client entrepreneurs they train, but this mandate rings hollow if Kingdom business development organizations themselves operate without the discipline of profitability. OPE ventures will not even get off the ground without expected profitability. In short, the not-for-profit barrier must be broken at all levels of Kingdom business in order to provide legitimate investment opportunities for Christians.

A number of investment structures will be envisioned and put to the test, and there is plenty of room for creative financing structures. For example, individual investors could choose either to take their profits or to give them as tax-deductible gifts to ministries in the host country.

Sometimes, extracting investment returns in hard currency from a developing country proves difficult; in these cases, an alternative might be for investors to use profits to cover expenses for business advisory visitations to the country.

Undoubtedly, many will question the viability of such investment funds until one or two demonstrate success; just as many in what is now Silicon Valley questioned the viability of high-tech-focused venture firms in the 1960s. But once the concept has proven viable, many such Kingdom business investment organizations will be able to attract the required capital. Certainly the secular community has proven this. The Swiss financial advisor BlueOrchard Finance operates a $43 million fund that invests in nearly 40 MED organizations. It has posted a five-year average return of 4.8 percent per year.[3] Investors have committed over $120 million to the Small Enterprise Assistance Fund in the United States, a profitable fund that invests in SMEs in the developing nations around the world. Established in 1995, a Calvert Foundation investment program provides a return of 0 to 3 percent (investor's choice) for up to 10 years. Investors may direct the funds to specific organizations involved in social and economic development efforts, including the Grameen Bank and Opportunity International. Christians must study successful models in the development of Kingdom business funds.

Example Initiatives: Kingdom Business Investment Funds

- Business Professional Network has recently established a kingdom business fund.
- Don Chapman, Vice President of Indian Operations at Mission India, is developing a business and ministry matrix that is designed to evaluate Kingdom businesses. Ministry accomplishments inside the company as well as those in the surrounding community will be considered. The initial effort is an evaluation of spiritual results at businesses located in India and

China. The analysis is designed for Kingdom-focused Western executives who are considering Kingdom businesses as potential suppliers.

Business Professionals

The Western world is full of successful, seasoned business professionals and retired business executives who desire nothing more than to leverage their years of experience to help further God's Kingdom in specific, hard-to-reach countries. Rarely tapped for more than their ability to donate finances, business professionals have a wealth of experience and contacts that could be of great value to Kingdom business efforts around the world. These individuals represent an invaluable resource to Kingdom-focused entrepreneurs abroad if connected via an effective business network, perhaps as part of a Kingdom business-sending organization or a Kingdom business investment fund.

Business professionals with directly relevant industry, international or functional expertise might serve in many capacities, from informal mentors to Board of Directors members, helping Kingdom businesses successfully meet the challenges they face. Technology makes it easier for them to assist faraway companies easily and inexpensively through e-mail and video conferencing, and such mentorship will undoubtedly help Kingdom business professionals both financially and spiritually. Other professionals can use their current place in the Western business world to assist Kingdom businesses by marketing and selling the businesses' products, establishing critical markets for those goods in First-World nations. The successful business experience of hundreds of thousands of Christian business professionals in the West is one of the greatest unused assets of the worldwide Church today, and Kingdom business efforts may be the greatest beneficiaries of that asset in the twenty-first century.

Example Initiatives: Business Professionals

- Business Professional Network connects Christian business people in the West with believing nationals engaged in business. BPN has pilot projects in Eastern Europe, Central Asia and Latin America. Business Development Groups of 8 to 12 Western professionals are formed to share their knowledge, networks, capital and encouragement with specific Christian entrepreneurs in developing nations. BPN's John Warton describes Business Development Groups as essentially "a Promise Keepers small group with a purpose." Other Kingdom business groups have adopted Business Development Groups. For example, an Integra Ventures group outside of Chicago sent eight of its members to Slovakia to visit their entrepreneur and raised money for his business expansion.

· International Micro Enterprise Development, Inc. (IMED) (Georgia, U.S.A.) helps impoverished Christians launch and operate microenterprises to the glory of God through a combination of training, consulting and funding. In partnership with an in-country sponsor, usually an expatriate Christian worker, IMED brings teams of Western business professionals to the targeted people group. These teams conduct three separate one-week training programs over a 12-month period: biblical principles of why and how to start a small business that will advance the kingdom of God, writing a workable business plan, and principles and practices for actually managing a small business. Over time, teaching and administrative responsibilities are passed over to national leaders who are expected to take full control within five years. Since 1998, IMED has supported the startup of 150 businesses in Central Asia, South and Southeast Asia, Northern Africa and Southern Russia.

· The Kingdom business ministry *Equip* (California, U.S.A.), in conjunction with Silicon Valley Fellowship, has organized several short-term Kingdom business missions trips to South Africa. Silicon Valley business professionals spend two weeks learning about and consulting and fellowshipping with local Christian small-business leaders, who are taught how to develop a better vision for how their South African companies can be repurposed to succeed economically and spiritually.

· Pura Vida (Washington, U.S.A.) is a company that imports,

roasts and distributes coffee from Central America and reinvests the profits in a ministry to at-risk children in San Jose, Costa Rica. "I often wondered if there was a way to be a passionate capitalist and a passionate Christian," says Pura Vida's CEO John Sage. "I feel like I've found that intersection."[4] John is a former Microsoft executive who met Chris Dearnley at Harvard Business School. The two have been close friends and prayer partners ever since. Chris now runs the ministry to children in Costa Rica, and the two friends founded Seattle-based Pura Vida as an innovative way to fund that work. Chris helps to source the Costa Rican coffee, which Pura Vida sells to churches, businesses and individuals throughout the United States.

- Individuals in business can assist Kingdom business efforts simply by doing their everyday jobs. A Christian friend of mine is an executive at a major United States credit card company. When I told him about the cost-effective and quality services of our call center business in India, he introduced ET to the relevant decision makers in his company. They were impressed with ET's sales presentation and value proposition. This opportunity could add 1,000 seats to the call center—a doubling of the company's size! It was all started by a Kingdom-minded business professional doing his job.

Governments

Many informal Kingdom business-building efforts have been conducted with the mind-set that governments are a major hindrance to business and spiritual success. While it is certainly true that local and even national governments in many developing nations are at best unhelpful to local business people of all types, more and more governments are recognizing the vital role that entrepreneurs and business people play in economic growth. They are working to curb the corruption, favoritism and trade-stifling policies of the past. It is surprising how responsive some governments can be to compelling business cases, even when the existence of both economic development and spiritual objectives of the business ventures is known.

By actively inviting local and national cooperation from the beginning, Kingdom businesses can also benefit from lucrative tax and worker-education incentives that many developing country governments are now offering to Western organizations that establish businesses in their countries. By working closely from the outset with progressive, pro-market elements in the host government, Kingdom business professionals help both to strengthen these elements and to establish allies who can be called upon when and if corrupt local officials come calling.

Western governments have also contributed to faith-based economic development initiatives in the Third World. Governments of some developed nations are not as hung up on separation of Church and state as North American governments are. Even the United States government is becoming more open to the idea of the federal funding of effective faith-based social programs. While governments may limit their funding to the business development objectives rather than the spiritual objectives of these efforts, they can be helpful resources in the process. However, it is critical that government support not come with attached strings that prevent or limit the pursuit of evangelism and discipleship goals.

Kingdom business professionals should look to actively partner with their own country's equivalent of the United States' Departments of State and Commerce. Both organizations actively assist U.S. businesses and entrepreneurs in countries where the United States has a diplomatic presence. Frequently such assistance can be of vital importance in establishing positive relationships with host governments and resolving tax or other financial issues. Most Western governments clearly understand that entrepreneurs are key to the production of well-paying jobs and local wealth creation—and that these elements are critical to the promotion of free market democracies and the rule of law in the developing world. Therefore, most Western governments will actively assist Western entrepreneurs wherever possible.

Example Initiatives: Governments

- Citing their enthusiasm for the establishment of new businesses in their country, Israeli government officials warmly welcomed

Galtronics when founder Ken Crowell approached them for assistance. Similarly, China welcomed Richard Chang and SMIC. These governments did this despite full knowledge of Richard's and Ken's Christian motivations for establishing their companies.

- In preparation for a major effort by Christian organizations to bless the nation of Fiji in 2004, John Warton and Ted Yamamori, working with Kingdom Business Forum Fiji, visited with the highest-ranking members of that country's government. The prime minister, president and several ministers of Fiji expressed great interest in the business development work planned by these Kingdom business professionals. They are supportive and appreciative of the assistance that is being offered to the people of Fiji. The government even appears willing to offer some funding support for Kingdom businesses.

- When approached by Jürg Opprecht of BPN and told about his program to assist the development of SMEs in Kyrgyzstan, the Swiss government responded. It agreed to fund 90 percent of the administrative and training costs associated with the Kyrgyzstan effort for the first four years.

Writing the Next Chapter in Kingdom Business

Kingdom business is poised to make a major impact for the Kingdom in this century, but changes are needed to bring about the outrageous visions that have been proposed in this book. The degree to which Kingdom business becomes a significant missions strategy depends on the attitudes and practices that prevail in education and training, local churches, missions organizations, investments, business professionals and governments. I trust that some of these ideas have yielded an appreciation for the types of institutional changes that will make Kingdom business thrive, that they have given a sense for some efforts already underway, and that they have inspired in you an idea of how God might use you to promote Kingdom business in your own sphere of influence. Whether you are a financier, missions pastor, business school student, active or retired business professional, seminary professor or entrepreneur, I hope you have come away with an idea or two about how God might use you to achieve His outrageous vision. Perhaps God will use you to write a chapter in the story.

I recently had the opportunity to join some gifted and like-minded individuals from various Kingdom business organizations. These founding visionaries are business people, academics, pastors and Kingdom business professionals. Within their own spheres of influence, they are seeking to grow the prominence and impact of Kingdom business as a powerful vehicle for the gospel. If you sense God calling you to play a part in this missions movement, I invite you to investigate the diverse organizations involved in Kingdom business. (The *God Is at Work* website, www.godisatwork.org, contains a resource for contacting Kingdom business organizations, many of which are listed in this book.)

Pointing Toward Explosive Growth

Successful entrepreneurs connect observations and emerging trends that seem unconnected to the casual observer. By seeing the link between those observations and trends, they identify new opportunities for business. The most successful entrepreneurs see the forces developing early, well before the fog has cleared. As those forces and trends play out, the entrepreneurs are positioned for explosive growth.

As I mentioned in chapter 1, in 1996, after closing down my time with Inmac, I started to explore two business ideas God had given me. One of these ideas centered around a major problem I had been dealing with at Inmac, and I believed many other companies faced the same issue. When large corporations purchased small repair maintenance and operations supplies, they often spent more to place the order than the purchase price. For example, it was not unusual for a Fortune 500 corporation to spend $250 to $350 to place, follow up, and pay for an item that had a total invoice of $250 or less. Furthermore, these smaller purchases added up to a pretty significant amount, ranging from 2 to 7 percent of total expenses (not including the cost of placing the order) for large corporations.

It was a significant problem, but nobody had found a solution to lower the cost. Meanwhile, the Internet was developing, being used almost exclusively at the time for email and information dissemination. The philosophy of many early Internet pioneers was that the Web should be a resource for free information and communication; however, others like me were recognizing that the Internet could also be used as a vehicle of electronic commerce. It had the potential for solving the problem of ordering and managing small purchases. There were still significant issues that needed to be resolved, but in the end, God was faithful to give us the breakthroughs we needed. As the fog lifted, the idea evolved into Ariba, a company that took off and was as one time valued as high as $40 billion! It all started with the recognition of a few forces and trends that were developing.

Though the picture for Kingdom business has not fully developed, from my experience, the forces and trends are in place for Kingdom business to see this same explosive growth. Whether starting a new business or developing a new field like Kingdom business, I have found some aspects to be very similar. In the beginning, the objective is clear, the environment is coming into focus, and getting started can be spasmodic. As we spin our wheels for a while, it is difficult to see clearly. But we cling to the objective. To use a homespun analogy, it is kind of like mud wrestling. The rules are not well defined, it is hard to grab hold of anything, and there are lots of arms, legs and mud flying everywhere. But the objective is clear, and in the end there is a winner. For Kingdom business, the objective is sustainable transformation that advances the kingdom of God. The winner clearly is a significant advancement of the Kingdom.

With many signs pointing in the same direction, I believe that Kingdom business is, like Ariba, poised to take off. At the outset of Ariba and other successful ventures with which I have been associated, the opportunity seemed like a small door opening. Trends, forces and observations pointed toward a positive result if the business plan was solid and executed properly. Even though we dreamt about the outcome, nobody could see the tremendous scope of the potential. But I knew God was in it. That early stage of promising indicators is the one in which I think Kingdom business finds itself today.

At the outset of this book, I likened the current Kingdom business environment to the initial days of the California Gold Rush when word of a tremendous discovery was just making its way back to the city. It took months before the meaning of the discovery of gold sunk in. But when it did, the rush was on. For Kingdom business, word is now making its way back to us. The gold is Kingdom business, which is already creating economic, social and spiritual transformation in nations all over the world. The gospel is being taken to the ends of the earth. But God is just beginning the work toward His vision through Kingdom business. He is calling us now to join the rush and participate in what should be one of the greatest missions endeavors of the twenty-first century. With a bit of work and time for exploration, the payoff for the Kingdom will be outrageously glorious.

BIBLICAL FOUNDATIONS

Recently, a respected pastor blessed my grandson Nathaniel. "He will become a pastor," the man prophesied over the infant, in a manner that evoked thoughts of Simeon and the baby Jesus. We were overjoyed. A pastor! Then it struck me. It was so subtle, but I had succumbed to it. Why did I consider the prospects of my grandson's future as a pastor more special than a future as a businessman whose ministry was to serve others and proclaim the gospel through business? After years of understanding that my calling was to be a minister of the gospel through business, I had nevertheless succumbed to the all-too-prevalent work hierarchy that considers full-time employment in the Church more spiritual than secular vocations.

Many Christian businessmen and women find it difficult to articulate why their work has any significance in the scheme of eternity. Business sometimes compounds the problem by failing to help people

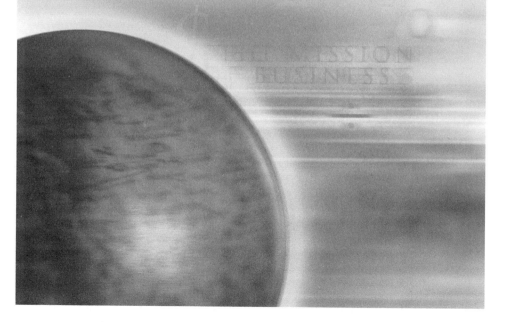

see how their work makes a difference. Churches sometimes compound the problem by failing to provide satisfactory answers to the fundamental questions facing these many lay people in their pews: Is God only interested in people getting saved? If so, how does secular work have any eternal value? What is redeeming about secular work if its ultimate goal is an increased stock price? Isn't it just taking time away from doing God's work and ministry? The goal of business is profit, but isn't profit inherently wrong since it implies somebody is being taken advantage of? And doesn't the Bible say that wealth is evil and that simplicity and poverty should be embraced?

Sadly, Christians all too commonly hold beliefs and attitudes that lead to this series of questions, and these views represent a barrier to some who are considering Kingdom business. For Kingdom business to be embraced as a laudable mission of the Church, these attitudes must be addressed. To break through some of these misconceptions, we must examine the concepts of transformation, work, business, profit and wealth. Kingdom business rests on the notions that God cares about people's spiritual, social and economic transformation, that work in the business world is both a ministry and a calling, that profit is both necessary and a sign of useful service, and that poverty is a social disease to be addressed.

Personal Transformation

Church history is replete with attempts to bring about transformation of the nations. In the fourth century, the Emperor Constantine promoted Christianity throughout the Roman Empire by changing the laws of the vast region he controlled. St. Patrick set out to transform pagan fifth-century Ireland by bringing the gospel of Jesus to the island. For most of the twentieth century, Albanian nun Mother Teresa worked to transform Calcutta, India, by meeting the physical needs of that city's poorest. In the 1950s, American missionary Jim Elliott set out to transform the Auca Indians in Ecuador by changing the spiritual conditions of the people.

Transformation is central to the mission of the Church on Earth. As we can see from these examples, Christian transformation efforts can take many different forms. Constantine changed laws; St. Patrick taught about Jesus; Mother Teresa fed the hungry and ministered to the sick and dying. But what were the concerns of Jesus in this regard? Is there a biblical model for transformation that we should follow?

The Ministry of Jesus

Various segments of the Church today emphasize different aspects of transformation. Some say, "Why should we concern ourselves with social ills when what people need is to trust Jesus? In the end, it's all about saving souls!" Others say, "Jesus met the physical needs of the sick, the poor and the outcast. Our mission should be to do likewise and address the societal needs of our day." Which of these was the concern of Jesus in His ministry? The answer is *all* of them. Jesus met people's physical, economic, social and spiritual needs. He fed the hungry, called people to personal holiness, healed the sick, taught in the synagogue, preached to thousands, and affirmed the social outcasts. His was a comprehensive ministry, not one limited to a single realm.

What Is the Kingdom of God?

The pursuit of both spiritual and physical outcomes not only reflects the concerns of Christ's own ministry, but it also fulfills His mandate to further the kingdom of God. If one had to pick a single theme in the preaching of Jesus, it is the message of the Kingdom. The Greek word for kingdom (*basileia*) can mean royal power, kingship, dominion or rule, and it appears most often in the New Testament in the phrase "the kingdom of God." So the kingdom of God is the rule or dominion of God. Jesus says, "I must preach the good news of the kingdom of God to the other towns also, because that is why I was sent" (Luke 4:43). It is interesting to note at this point how Jesus chose to convey the message of the Kingdom. Instead of offering a clear definition of the Kingdom, He imparted His vision of it indirectly through parables and stories. The choice of images He used is instructive. He used sketches from the everyday business world: farming, fishing, women baking bread, merchants buying pearls.[1]

The diverse manner in which Jesus spoke of the Kingdom has led to two specific yet decidedly different interpretations that have yielded very different approaches to transformation. Often, the kingdom of God is considered either a future end-time state, which only the saved attain, or a present earthly state in which the Church is bringing about societal advances.[2] In the Western world, satisfied with the present, we are inclined to look to the future hope. As a church, we are well off, while in Third World nations, there is need for both a present and a future hope. Let's take a look at these two interpretations of the Kingdom—future and present—to see how they influence approaches to transformation.

Future aspect of the kingdom of God. A number of Jesus' statements about the Kingdom point to a future (or even non-earthly) event. Appearing before Pilate, Jesus stated, "My kingdom is not of this world. If it were, my servants would fight to prevent my arrest by the Jews. But now my kingdom is from another place" (John 18:36). In the Lord's Prayer, Jesus instructs His followers to ask that "thy kingdom come." Many have identified this with the end-time reign of Christ on Earth described in Revelation. Only true followers of Jesus will be the ones receiving this blessing, and several parables of Jesus seem to allude to this (see the parable of the net in Matt. 13:47-50 and the parable of the 10 virgins in Matt. 25:1-13).

In the extreme, the theological perspective that points to these passages and emphasizes the future aspect of the Kingdom often forces one to keep a close eye on several "signs of the times" that must first transpire, such as natural disasters, ungodliness and depravity. "But this you MAY KNOW," prophesied Herbert Armstrong in August 1939. "This war will be ended by CHRIST'S RETURN! And MAY start within six weeks! We are just THAT NEAR Christ's coming!"[3] In 1980, Armstrong asked, "Can WE discern the signs of the times? END-TIME EVENTS are going to happen FAST from here on! The 80s well might see the END of this present world; WAKE UP!"[4] This futurist perspective sees the world, its culture and its society opposed to God, and God opposed to them. Accordingly, there is little value in the present earth, and indeed, it will be destroyed. But a better time lies ahead. The immanence of Christ's return fosters a sense of urgency. Therefore, the objective must be to save souls and transport individuals from this fallen world to the Kingdom that is to come.

The result of this purely futurist interpretation of the kingdom of God is that the focus of societal transformation efforts will be exclusively on the spiritual. Those that demonstrate great evangelistic zeal and instill fire-and-brimstone fear yet show little compassion for the needy or outcast often exemplify this view. Since a person's soul is all that will survive the fire, it is the primary target, and social and economic needs are marginalized. We can see why those who emphasize the future aspect of the kingdom of God tend to emphasize spiritual transformation and de-emphasize social and economic transformation.

Present aspect of the kingdom of God. Jesus also spoke of the Kingdom in terms that indicate it was already present during His days on Earth. Jesus stated, "The kingdom of God does not come with your careful observation, nor will people say, 'Here it is,' or 'There it is,' because the kingdom of God is within you" (Luke 17:20b-21). And again he preached, "The time has come. . . . The kingdom of God is near. Repent and believe the good news" (Mark 1:15).

Those who emphasize the present aspect of the Kingdom place it here on Earth. The kingdom of God began with the coming of Jesus and is now present in the world as the victorious Christ who is ruling His people by His Word and Spirit. The curing of physical and social problems is a primary objective of the Church as it advances the kingdom of God. In *The Kingdom of God is Within You*, Leo Tolstoy explained it this way:

[God] demands of us only what is reasonable, certain, and possible: to serve the kingdom of God, that is, to contribute to the establishment of the greatest possible union between all living beings. . . . The sole meaning of life is to serve humanity by contributing to the establishment of the kingdom of God, which can only be done by the recognition and profession of the truth by every man.[5]

According to Tolstoy, advancing the kingdom of God means serving humanity and creating unity on Earth.

Jesus instructs His disciples, "When you enter a town and are welcomed, eat what is set before you. Heal the sick who are there and tell them, 'The kingdom of God is near you'" (Luke 10:8-9). He also states that the casting out of demons is a sign that the kingdom of God has come to the people (see Luke 11:20). Note that while Jesus feeds, heals and casts out demons, faith in Him or salvation is not a requisite to these blessings. And in the Old Testament, God uses the prophets to speak out against unjust systems and practices. The prophets decry the injustices against poor and powerless people time and again.

The theological camp that takes these passages to heart and emphasizes the present aspect of the kingdom of God sees cultural and societal advances as the conditions necessary for a greater Kingdom here on Earth. Thus, the focus is on addressing the social ills of the day: poverty, hunger, homelessness, racism, injustice, war. This is what furthers the kingdom of God. Since this world will be transformed into the one that is to come, attempts to cure these social and economic problems are not only worthy but also helpful in speeding along that process. Indeed, the present aspect of the kingdom of God is more practical in developing countries where people need a hope for today as well as a hope for tomorrow.

The result of this overly present interpretation of the kingdom of God is that the focus of societal transformation efforts will be on the physical and social. Tolstoy viewed the kingdom of God as an earthly entity marked by harmony, unity and lack of social and physical ills. Some Christian relief organizations share this view. Thus, bettering society by solving economic and social problems is the key to advancing God's cause. It is easy to see why those who emphasize the present aspect of the kingdom of God tend to emphasize social and economic transformation and deemphasize spiritual transformation.

The "Already, but Not Yet" Aspect of the Kingdom of God

There is a third and middle-ground approach to reading the diverse and complex teachings of Jesus about the kingdom of God. It must be admitted that both the present and future aspects of the Kingdom are prominent in the teachings of Jesus. Philip Yancey noted that "the only possible explanation ties in Jesus' teaching that the kingdom of God comes in stages. It is 'now' and also 'not yet,' present and also future."[6] The kingdom of God was inaugurated in the ministry of Jesus, realized in part in the Church, and will be consummated with the return of Christ when He "will judge the living and the dead" (2 Tim. 4:1). It is "already" and "not yet," both present and future. With the coming of Christ, the presence of the Holy Spirit in His people, and the Church acting as His agent in the world, there is a sense in which the kingdom of God is already here. However, it is not yet present in all its glory, and the ultimate fulfillment of the kingdom of God will occur in the future when Christ returns. This "already, but not yet" emphasis acknowledges that efforts to advance both the present and future manifestations of the Kingdom are legitimate.

The ministry of Jesus and His teaching on the kingdom of God leads us to meet spiritual, economic and social needs. Jesus said, "As the Father has sent me, I am sending you" (John 20:21). Economic and social problems that plague our world must be transformed. Spiritual darkness that leads to eternal separation from God must be transformed as well. If we are to follow Jesus, we must be concerned with all of these aspects of transformation. In fact, it is by practicing this comprehensive ministry that the Church will be most effective in transforming nations. It is a comprehensive mission in which evangelism and social responsibility go hand in hand. Paraphrasing the Manila Manifesto of the Lausanne Committee for World Evangelism, Mats Tunehag stated, "the [comprehensive] mission of the kingdom is to take the whole gospel to the whole man by the whole church to the whole world. This is our mandate and our task."[7]

Transformation and Kingdom Business

The earth is the Lord's and the fullness thereof. Because the last days will be filled with evil, it does not mean that we are excused from responding to the poverty of others. There is also the danger that physical and economic improvements will result in spiritual apathy, and indeed, that was the case with Israel in the Old Testament. Though humankind is often more inclined to turn to God in times of trouble, that also does not mean that we are excused from responding to the plight of others. In the name of Jesus, we can address physical and economic needs *and* bring a hope that is now and in the future.

True transformation must be comprehensive. It must involve spiritual, economic and social transformation. The three-fold objective of Kingdom business—profitability and sustainability, local job and wealth creation, and advancement of the local church—is aligned with this comprehensive transformation. Kingdom business is aimed at developing a sustainable model for spiritual transformation, economic transformation and social transformation.

Work

In many parts of the world, certainly in the Western world, a large part of a person's identity is defined by his or her work.[8] For the believer, a person's identity is defined by his or her faith in God. Yet there is a pervasive perception among Christians and churches that work in the marketplace has very little intersection with that faith. "The problem with Christianity in America is not the content of the faith but the failure of its adherents to integrate the principles of the faith into their lifestyles," noted George Barna.[9] Most Christians experience a deep disconnect between their attempts to follow Jesus and their daily employment. At the root of this failure to integrate faith and work is an inappropriate creation of secular and sacred categories that are applied to work and church. Thus, work and faith are compartmentalized improperly, leading to a divide between church and business. This separation is often practiced and believed both individually and corporately as a church.

Integration of Faith and Work
Though many do not experience it and have difficulty articulating it, there is a connection between our relationship with God and our work. There is a way in which our work is understood, approached and practiced that relates to what God is doing in the world. Work is our calling,

and as Christians, we must operate within a biblical paradigm of work—how we are to understand it, approach it and practice it from the point of view of God's purposes.[10]

What is meant by the term "work"? In the words of John Stott, "work is the expenditure of energy (whether manual or mental or both) in the service of others, which brings fulfillment to the worker, benefit to the community, and glory to God."[11] Work is serving others. Jesus stated that by completing the work given Him to do, He brought glory to the Father (see John 17:4), and whatever work we do should be to the glory of God (see 1 Cor. 10:31). We can glorify and worship God through our work. In fact, the Hebrew root word *avodah* means "service," and derivations are translated as both "work" and "worship."

This book is concerned with the business world, and certainly the term "work" pertains to the sets of activities in that sphere. Those employed in the broader marketplace, be it a teacher, a pastor or a senator, can be said to do work as well. But a biblical view of work defines it even more broadly. At its core, work is service, and therefore it need not include any element of compensation. Homemakers, volunteers, students and those caring for the elderly—all are engaged in valuable work. "No task will be so sordid and base," said John Calvin, "provided you obey your calling in it, that it will not shine and be reckoned very precious in God's sight."[12] Paul instructs us, "Whatever you do, work at it with all your heart, as working for the Lord, not for men" (Col. 3:23). Whether financially compensated or not, work is service to others done to the glory of God.

The Sacred-Secular Divide

There exists in the Church an all-too-common tendency to classify earthly activity into two broad categories: the sacred and the secular. The sacred is that which is perceived to be spiritual or have eternal value, and the secular includes any activity that fails to meet this criterion. The sacred-secular paradigm comes from considering Jesus' life as comprising two distinct periods: "work" and "ministry." But Jesus was perfect His entire life, and His entire life's work was ministry, whether He engaged in carpentry, teaching or healing.

The sacred-secular division is a falsehood that has crept into the thinking and practice of the Church, and it is applied both to the manner in which an individual Christian organizes his or her life and to the way the Christian community thinks about the value and nobility of different occupations. Applied to one's personal life, the sacred-secular division yields a segmentation of activities in which one can engage. Those activities considered spiritual are highly endorsed while those considered non-spiritual are tolerated at best. Any serious Christian will strive towards maximizing the amount of time devoted to activities that have spiritual or eternal value while minimizing the amount of time devoted to activities that do not. The formula is simple enough: increase the sacred, decrease the secular.

Not surprisingly, this line of thinking leads to the common perception of work in the secular marketplace as a sometimes necessary obstacle that prevents us from engaging in truly valuable activities such as ministry, Bible study, fellowship, evangelism, prayer and missions. The work itself fails to contain any eternal value. For the Christian in the secular marketplace, there exists a strong tension between sacred yearnings and secular obligations. Often, the only perceived resolution to this tension is to eliminate the secular obligations, and the "truly spiritual" commonly do just that by taking on jobs that are considered inherently sacred. Missionaries, pastors and others employed in vocational Christian professions find very little tension between their work and their faith. Both are sacred. Unfortunately, this paradigm leaves those in the secular marketplace with a strong and unresolved tension.

The Work Hierarchy

Many parts of the Christian Church today operate *de facto* under a caste system. There exists an often-unstated hierarchy of labor that elevates certain occupations above others. The sacred-spiritual divide produces a ranking of occupations based on the amount of eternal value they produce. Pastors and missionaries are routinely brought before the church body to celebrate their calling and highlight the nobility of their work. But when was the last time you heard a pastor announce, "Today, we've asked Joe to share about his calling to the business world, his work of running his company on biblical principles and his service to customers by providing world-class products"? Chances are you haven't seen the spiritual value of secular work presented the way the value of ministry is presented. The absence of discussion about work in sermons further adds to the basis of this unspoken work hierarchy paradigm.

The work hierarchy is not the problem of pastors alone. Christian business people are often unable to resolve the tension between their faith and their work. Having so few models of making jobs in the marketplace effective for the Kingdom, many business people fail to see how their everyday work has spiritual value. So, they conclude it has little or none. Instead of recognizing the potential for business as ministry, they go into the business of ministry.

Paul Stevens illustrates the work hierarchy using a pyramid.[13] At the top of the pyramid are missionaries who are on the frontiers of evangelism and church planting. (Lower value is placed on missionaries who are involved in helping the poor, providing transportation or constructing buildings.) Pastors and others called to the ministry and engaged in full-time Christian work occupy the next tier. Below those occupations are ones that are considered to have social value but are not explicitly Christian. Medical professionals, teachers and social workers fall into that caste. They may not be involved in the business of saving souls, but at least their work is sometimes guided by altruistic motivations. Even further down are occupations that are seen as failing to reach this threshold. Accountants, salespeople, lawyers and factory workers are not engaged in bad work, many Christians believe, but there is nothing spiritually significant to their work either.

If the work itself is not deemed inherently noble, two byproducts of employment in the secular marketplace are considered to have spiritual value. The secular workplace is seen as a fertile venue for sharing one's faith, and the wages from secular work are seen as an important mechanism for providing financial support to those in ministry. But the work itself is typically viewed as void of eternal value, and many of the truly devoted opt to move up the hierarchy and commit their lives to "more sacred employment."[14]

The Reformers already fought the battle to eradicate this sacred-secular divide centuries ago when service in the Church was considered the highest calling and the contemplative life was deemed superior to the active life. "The man who, *par excellence*, lived a rational life in the religious sense was, and remained, alone the monk," said Max Weber of pre-Reformation attitudes. "The significance of the Reformation [was] the fact that now every Christian had to be a monk all his life."[15] Every Christian had to determine how to operate in the world and remain passionately spiritual. How was the truly spiritual life to be lived without monasteries? Martin Luther explained it this way: "Monastic vows rest on the false assumption that there is a special calling, a vocation, to which superior Christians are invited to observe the counsels of perfection while ordinary Christians fulfill only the commands; but there simply is no special religious vocation since the call of God comes to each at the common task."[16] Rather than in a monastery, the venue for Christian holiness is in everyday tasks.

"The point of the Christian religion is not to leave the world behind to live the life of faith, but to live the life of faith in the midst of the world," said Christian philosopher Lee Hardy. "The religious life is not the prerogative of a small group of spiritual specialists. Rather, it must be lived by all; and it can be lived in the context of everyday work."[17] The concept of finding spiritual fulfillment in one's daily work stands in stark contrast to the monastic concept of separation from secular work inspired by a special religious calling. It is a concept that consciously avoids the sacred-secular divide. It is a concept that the Church today would do well to reclaim.

Vocation, Calling and Ministry

Many Christians in the marketplace are frustrated by a lack of integration between faith and work. Often, a misunderstanding of the concepts of ministry, vocation, and calling prevents them from experiencing this integration.[18] There is a common belief that calling is a charge to the Church-related ministry and that vocation is synonymous with one's occupation. But those definitions fail to reflect the biblical meanings of the words and serve to relegate most to second-class citizens in the Body of Christ. *Vocatio* means calling, and ministry means service—in any capacity. Thus, everyone has a calling/vocation to ministry/service, and one's occupation is only one venue for exercising this call to serve. (Other venues include one's family, neighborhood, society and congregation.)

If calling is not reserved solely for those entering some vocational Christian profession, what does calling entail? Paul Stevens describes three levels of calling: the human calling, the Christian calling and the personal calling.[19] The human calling is a general call to man in relation to the world. It relies on two charges by God to continue the work He has done in creation and salvation. The Creation mandate (see Gen. 1:27-30) means Christians are called to be stewards of the earth, filling it, developing it and keeping it. The Great Commission (see Matt. 28:19-20) means Christians are called to witness to the ends of the earth, making disciples of all nations. Christian traditions have emphasized one or the other of these two human callings with the result that the focus of advancing God's cause is either social action or evangelism. As noted in the earlier discussion on transformation, the comprehensive ministry and message of Jesus encompass both of these charges. The Creation mandate and the Great Commission are both incorporated in the single human call to further the kingdom of God.

The Christian calling is the one most referenced in Scripture. It is a general call to man in relation to God. Before there is a call to do anything, there is a call to Someone. "Follow me," said Jesus (John 1:43, Matt. 4:19). In the New Testament, the Christian calling is used for the invitation to experience salvation ("Whoever believes in Him shall not perish but have eternal life," John 3:16), the instruction to live in corporate and personal holiness ("Go now and leave your life of sin," John 8:11), and the charge to serve ("serve one another in love," Gal. 5:13). In other words, it is a three-fold call to belong to God, to be God's people in life, and to do God's work in the Church and in the world. "All are called. All are called together. All are called for the totality of everyday life," said Stevens.[20]

The personal calling is some combination of the human and Christian callings that is unique to one's own person and life path. It is an individual call to the manner in which a person is to serve—the work he or she is to do.

The personal call is manifest through personal discipleship, personal experience, personal gifting and personal desire. Christians have different personal gifts, including abilities to manage and to help (see 1 Cor. 12:28-30), and "Each one should use whatever gift he has received to serve others, faithfully administering God's grace in its various forms" (1 Pet. 4:10). God never calls people out of their giftings; He calls people to fulfill their giftings. Those who have a passion for the arts, musical training and creative talent probably will not have a personal call to serve their fellow man by repairing automobiles, teaching accounting principles or performing bureaucratic work. "While it is extraordinary for people to have a direct, verbal 'call' (as in Acts 16:9-10)," noted Stevens, "it is entirely ordinary for God to create a desire in our hearts to do the very thing needed, whether in the church or in the world. Business people are called in this sense, as are engineers, homemakers, craftspersons, pastors, and missionaries."[21]

God calls all to continue His creation and salvation work (human calling) and to become an active member of His Body (Christian calling). However, each individual is called to a unique venue for service (personal calling). There are no insignificant or small Christian things. God asked Nehemiah to build a wall (see Neh. 1-7). He asked Rahab to show hospitality to two strangers (see Josh. 2:8-11). He asks others to market products or paint houses. "For we are God's workmanship, created in Christ Jesus to do good works, which God prepared in advance for us to do" (Eph. 2:10).

If each of us is specially crafted and endowed with different gifts to fulfill the specific mission God prepared in advance for each of us, then there is no universal highest personal calling. The highest calling for each individual is that which incorporates God's unique design, gifting and direction of the person. A limited notion of God's purpose has led many to consider evangelism and personal ministry as the only true expressions of the called life, but in reality, anyone who works by following a personal calling that is in harmony with the human and Christian callings is experiencing the called life. That includes those of us following the call to business.

Many feel called to business or other fields but allow themselves to be disconnected in their work from their equal responsibility to God. Their solution to the sacred-secular tension is to divorce their work life from their spiritual life. They experience no integration of faith and work. They allow God to be crowded out, abandoning the Christian calling in favor of some personal calling. Clearly, this falls short of God's plan. The personal calling must incorporate the human and Christian callings.

God's View of Work

Work is good. In the beginning, God created. He worked and then rested. He called it good. Then He asked man to continue His work by naming the animals, developing the land, and taking care of His creation. It was His Creation mandate to mankind. In the garden, work was good. But did the Fall change that? No, work remains good. The Fall only made work difficult and painful, but it did not change God's analysis that work is inherently good.

Jesus spent much of His life working, most of this time as a carpenter and for three years as an itinerant preacher. As Joseph's oldest child, He probably took over the family business in Nazareth, managing a number of siblings and family members. He was known as a carpenter, and like so many today, He was identified by society with His profession. "Isn't this the carpenter?" the people of Nazareth asked when they first heard Him preach (Mark 6:3). Jesus would have faced the same challenges of serving customers, producing quality goods, managing workers, paying suppliers and earning a profit that business people commonly encounter. Work is created by God, and it is good.

Work is mandated. The first man was commanded to work the Garden of Eden. Subsequent Scripture is filled with references that call people to work. Paul encouraged us to work with our hands so that we do not become a burden to others (see 1 Thess. 4:10-12), and he said enjoying the fruits of our labor is the normal way of life (see 1 Cor. 9:3-10). Several commands against idleness and instructions toward generosity with the fruits of our labor appear in Scripture as well (see 2 Thess. 3:6-15; 2 Cor. 9:11). Everything we do, including work, should be to the glory of God (see 1 Cor. 10:31). Our focus should be on working for the Lord rather than for man—He is our boss (see Eph. 6:5-9; Col. 3:22-25).[22] We are each created to do good works (see Eph. 2:10).

Work is sacred. All work that honors God and fulfills His calling is sacred, and there is no hierarchy that puts one job above another. "There are different kinds of gifts, but the same Spirit. There are different kinds of service, but the same Lord. There are different kinds of working, but the same God works all of them in all men" (1 Cor. 12:4-6). (Later in verses 27-30 of the chapter, Paul outlines the diversity of jobs in the Body of Christ, but these are not listed in any order of importance.)

Many different types of work are sacred. In the everyday activity of our work, we can advance the kingdom of God. Our work can benefit and serve our fellow man. It can provide the opportunity to preach the gospel by word and by deed. The demonstration of the gospel by example is the most important form of preaching, and those in the marketplace are given plenty of opportunity to share in this way. Work done unto God is sacred because it is living out the gospel.

Work is ministry. We have noted that work is "the expenditure of energy in the service of others." Work is a response to the calling everyone has received to serve God and man. Work is serving. Work is ministry. This is an important point at the heart of the paradigm shift many Christians need: Work *is* ministry.

Dave Evans, co-founder of video game creators Electronic Arts, described three perspectives people have regarding their work ministry. All three are valid and important perspectives, but many Christians only realize the first one.

1. Ministry *at* Work. A commonly held view of work is for Christians to consider their jobs as a place where they can do ministry by showing love and sharing their faith. The work itself is not viewed as ministry—only the byproducts of the work (such as opportunities for evangelism) are considered ministry. But a biblical view of work goes much deeper.

2. Ministry *of* Work. Our work has spiritual value for reasons well beyond any income for missions or opportunities to witness it provides. Our work *itself* is ministry to which we are called. Work is holy and ordained by God. Through it we exercise dominion and stewardship of the world. We fulfill

the Creation mandate. We serve our fellow man. Whether it involves transporting people on airplanes or creating carvings out of wood, the work itself is ministry to others done as unto God.

3. Ministry *to* Work. God has certainly put His people in positions where they can introduce others to Him, but His desires go further. We are to be salt and light to the world in order to redeem all that is in it (see Matt. 5:13-16). As redeeming agents in the workplace, we can influence its organizational structures and policies. We can influence the way business is being done. We can work to redeem the schools, governments, churches and businesses themselves.[23]

Many Christians need to adopt a new paradigm that views work itself as ministry and God's holy call on their life. By seeing the spiritual value inherent in their work, they will avoid the trappings of seeking meaning through switching to occupations that contain "a higher ministry component." I am reminded of the story of some laborers working on the same project. They were approached by a curious observer. Asked what he was doing, the first responded, "I'm making bricks." A bit later, a second worker replied to a similar inquiry, "I'm erecting a wall." A third person was asked about his activities. With joy on his face and pride in his work, he exclaimed, "We're building a cathedral!"

How many see their jobs as just making bricks? How can work become the construction of a cathedral? By viewing our work in the larger picture of God's plans, we can serve God and others through our work in the marketplace.

Business

When it comes to the nobility and practice of their work, business people rank down at the level of politicians and lawyers in the eyes of the public. In the 2003 Gallup survey of honesty and ethics of professions, only 18 percent of the public considered business executives to have "very high" or "high" standards (by contrast, 83 percent perceived nurses to exhibit superior ethical standards). Perhaps influenced by media and entertainment portrayals of money-grubbing, aggressive, heartless and crooked corporate executives, even those in business often find it difficult to see the redeeming value of their professions. But business is a very noble pursuit to which God calls many committed believers.

Two biblical concepts that apply significantly to those engaged in business are service and creation. Successful commerce is about serving one's fellow man and increasing his standard of living. It is about creating goods, services and wealth. It is about discovering people's needs and meeting them. "Legitimate business is a servant to the public in promoting the good," said theologian Stanley Grenz.[24] Business brings glory to God when it blesses man through the creation of needed products, the delivery of outstanding services, and the increase of society's living standard.

The Spiritual Value of Business

The spiritual value of business lies in its success in advancing God's own goals, in helping to serve His purpose through service and creation. Thus, the questions that should be asked in assessing the spiritual value of a business are the following: How is the business fulfilling the Creation mandate to be stewards of the earth by filling it, developing it and keeping it? In what way is the business serving mankind? How is the business redeeming its spheres of influence?

At a recent conference on Kingdom business, a participant told a moving story of a destitute Korean woman who was living with her children as foreigners in the streets of a Central Asian city. One day, this woman was able to move into an apartment, but when she arrived, she noticed it was completely infested with cockroaches. She remembered from her youth in Korea that a relative had concocted a roach repellant, but she had no idea how to make it. As it was her only hope, she prayed and grabbed ingredients from her kitchen. The resulting mixture was a miraculous roach combatant. Eventually, she obtained a small amount of funding from a Kingdom business organization and was able to start a business that produced, marketed and exported this highly effective product. She now has a very nice business serving the needs of others.

At the conclusion of the story, the response was, "Well, that's wonderful that God's hand guided her so obviously and effectively, but what's the spiritual value of her business?" A couple of people started to formulate answers to this question when one participant simply said, "No more roaches." What? How can that have spiritual significance?

The answer lies in the woman's fulfillment of God's command to serve others and continue His work of creation. She is developing the earth by creating a novel product and building a business. She is serving customers by helping them solve a significant problem, that of roaches infesting their homes. She is serving employees by treating them with respect, allowing them to use their gifts and enabling them to grow their abilities. And she is salt and light to the business network in her Central Asian country by running an honest business in a society in which corruption and duplicity are all too common. Her business is her ministry, it is her highest calling and it is inherently good. It is where her faith is played out, and it has spiritual significance. She is called to serve God and mankind in this way: No more roaches.

Service and Creation in Business

Successful companies are those that serve their customers effectively, providing a good or service for less than it would take the customers to produce it themselves or purchase it elsewhere. The role of business is to improve the provision of goods and services while ministering to others and being a witness to the community. Improved goods and services increase not only the standard of living but also total wealth. In short, there is an increase in the aggregate physical well-being of the nation. Business is all about increasing the total pie, not taking from others. A successful business means making two plus two equal five. It is about creating value.

But how can business create aggregate wealth by making two plus two equal five? The economics may be boiled down to a cogent example: Let's say a woman must walk one hour each way from her village of 50 families to get fresh water every day. Normally, she works 10 hours per day making dresses, for which she receives $0.50 per hour for her labor.

Now let's assume a Kingdom businessman sets up a pipeline from the source of the water to her town so that obtaining water is now a five-minute affair. In theory, she can now work almost two extra hours, which would result in $1.00 more income per day. What would she be willing to pay for the water?

If the Kingdom businessman were to charge her $0.10 for all the water she regularly uses, she would gladly pay it if she could make dresses with her saved time. By buying the Kingdom businessman's water and making dresses for the extra two hours, she earns $0.90 (18 percent of her income) more. Selling the water to all 50 families in the village, the Kingdom businessman earns $5.00 per day, which covers his cost, maintenance and profit in the venture. Everyone else in the village reaps the benefits of saving two hours a day as well, which totals 100 additional hours that can be put to work productively, thus increasing the total pie. Without changing the total hours of work, the village's daily income goes up $0.90 per family, or $90 total.

Business is a spiritual activity when it advances God's objectives by serving others and creating products and resources. It is a vehicle for serving God and our fellow man. It is a means through which we can act as stewards, developers and keepers of God's creation (see Gen. 1:27-30).

Profit

Several years ago, I was invited to speak at a seminar in Sweden about starting a business. It was a three-day conference for Christians, and a thousand people attended. After my presentation, several audience members confronted me with the opinion that business is "dirty." How could I as a Christian start new business ventures? Seeking to discover why they perceived business as ignoble, I asked what they thought of large established companies like Volvo and Ikea. "We have no problem with them," was their reply. "They provide our people employment and pensions." More discussion revealed that their real beef was with profit objectives. A business making a profit is benefiting at the expense of others, it seemed to them. How could a Christian start a for-profit venture?

Jesus used the parable of the talents (see Matt. 25:14-30) to show that God gives resources to be put to use and increased. A man going on a journey gave three servants five, two and one talent, respectively. On his return, the first two servants had earned a 100 percent return on their funds and were praised. Interestingly, the third servant showed no profit at all and was rebuked severely for failing to use the money wisely. A profit was expected. The talents may be money or gifts, but either way, they must be put to use and thereby benefit both the owner and the one who puts them to use.

There is a wide-standing perception that business is primarily about maximizing profits. It is not. Certainly, there are some business people who operate with the objective of squeezing the most out of employees and customers. But the redeeming value of business is as a vehicle for serving others through the efficient delivery of goods and services. When that objective is pursued, there will be an opportunity for profit.

There is also a prevailing notion that nonprofit organizations are inherently more noble than for-profit organizations. To be sure, nonprofit organizations are usually engaged in laudable activities that benefit society, but it is the service they provide rather than the absence of a profit that warrants commendation. There is no direct correlation between absence of profit and benefit to society. In fact, the greater the product or service's benefit to the recipient, the greater the potential for profit.

Where there is no profit there is no business. Profit is necessary to protect and reward employees and investors. Without profit, there can be no growth of a company. Profit is a good thing, a sign that a business is providing a beneficial product or service. In a free market economy, it is the sign that a business is serving others, not that it is taking advantage of others. The more beneficial a good or service is to a consumer relative to its production cost, the more value is created and the greater the amount of profit that can be derived. Profit, in turn, allows for an expansion of exceptional service to mankind. It is the oxygen that funds the business and keeps a healthy company growing and serving.

Business is not inherently bad simply because it is profitable, but it is also not inherently good simply because it is profitable or unprofitable. God's value of commerce is not equivalent to its profitability.

Rather, as noted earlier, the spiritual value of business lies in its alignment with God's purpose. While profit often follows from effective business, it should not be its sole sense of mission. A profit motive without a sense of God's participation and responsibility to Him can easily devolve into immoral activity, such as dishonest dealing or the selling of pornography. As business serves man, increases the standard of living and promotes the public good, it is a pursuit infused with significance. And profit is an important result.

Wealth

"But remember the Lord your God, for it is he who gives you the ability to produce wealth, and so confirms his covenant, which he swore to your forefathers, as it is today" (Deut. 8:18). Successful and profitable business can result in the creation of wealth for employees, owners and partners. The Scriptures have much to say on the topic of wealth. Many proverbs, parables and teachings concern wealth, but often the message is misunderstood. In fact, there are two misguided attitudes often encountered concerning the relationship between wealth and righteous living. Some view wealth as the evil enemy of a righteous life. Others view wealth as the essential evidence of a righteous life. But the "poverty gospel" and the "health and wealth gospel" both fall short of the rich biblical teaching about prosperity. Let's explore these two theological viewpoints before commenting on God's view of wealth.

The Poverty Gospel: Wealth as the Evil Enemy of a Righteous Life

Since the days of Francis of Assisi's teaching about the virtue of poverty, some Christians have exhibited the attitude that sees poverty as the more holy and desirable state. Poverty has a degree of romantic appeal as a conduit to righteous living, and wealth is eschewed as a danger to piety. Unencumbered by the worries and potential trappings of material possessions, those without wealth are free to focus solely on God. Money is viewed as immoral because it tends to corrupt. Some have even considered wealth and salvation to be mutually exclusive.

Those who have a romantic view of poverty often operate under the sacred-secular divide. Wealth is seen as the evidence of a misplaced focus on secular pursuits. No roads to prosperity are acceptable since all means of acquiring wealth involve undue emphasis on secular activities. Instead, poverty facilitates a focus on sacred activities and pursuits. Many who follow this line of thinking retreat from the perceived trappings of the "secular" marketplace to pursue "sacred" and nonprofit occupations.

A common text often quoted as proof by those who advocate this view of poverty is found in Matthew 19. In His encounter with the rich young ruler, Jesus said, "If you want to be perfect, go, sell your possessions and give to the poor, and you will have treasure in heaven. Then come, follow me" (v. 21). Scripture notes that the young man walked away sad, because he had great wealth. "I tell you the truth," Jesus said to His disciples, "it is hard for a rich man to enter the kingdom of heaven. Again, I tell you, it is easier for a camel to go through the eye of a needle than for a rich man to enter the kingdom of God" (vv. 16-24). Many stop there and conclude that the point Jesus is trying to make is that the righteous life requires us to renounce riches. Some may realize correctly that Jesus' instruction to the young ruler to sell his possessions was actually pointed at his heart rather than at his wealth. Clearly he had a problem of trusting in his wealth. Jesus discerned that the young man's riches were an idol his heart held above following God and thus asked the young man to give away his possessions.

The point Jesus is actually making with His audience can be seen from the exchange that follows. "When the disciples heard this, they were greatly astonished and asked, 'Who then can be saved?' Jesus looked at them and said, 'With man this is impossible, but with God all things are possible'" (vv. 25-26). In a society in which the materially prosperous were considered particularly blessed by God, Jesus' statement about the difficulty of the wealthy entering the kingdom of God was astonishing to the disciples. "Who then can be saved," they ask. Jesus is saying that *even* the wealthy—not *particularly* the wealthy—find salvation impossible without God.

There is widely held belief that since Jesus did not have significant material possessions, He denounced earthly wealth. However, while

Jesus emptied Himself of all His possessions, He did so for a reason: so that He could be every bit like *all* men, not because wealth was inherently bad. Poverty is not considered a more spiritual state.

The poverty gospel described here also suffers from a mistaken belief about the inherent nature of material resources. Prosperity is neither moral nor immoral—it is amoral. Wealth itself is not the problem, but what man does with that wealth can be. Riches may be used for noble purposes or for ignoble purposes. Scripture teaches that what man does with possessions is the issue, not the acquisition or ownership of material resources. Therefore, poverty does not imply or lead to a higher spiritual state than prosperity.[25]

A wonderful example of this can be found in the life of Job. The Bible describes him as blameless and upright man who feared God and shunned evil (see Job 1:1), and then proceeds to list the material resources he possessed, concluding with the observation that "he was the greatest man among all the people of the East" (v. 3). Satan thought Job's prosperity was the source of his allegiance to God. Surely, if Job were stripped of all his earthly possessions, he would renounce his faith. But though Job lost more than most people would ever own and was even encouraged by his wife to curse God, he stood firm. He was righteous in wealth and in poverty. It was about the attitude of his heart rather than the amount of his possessions.

God restored Job's prosperity to double of what he had before. Other righteous men of the Bible were granted wealth as well. God's covenant with Abraham (see Gen. 15) included promises of fertile land and a multitude of offspring. David and Solomon enjoyed significant prosperity. Boaz was a man of integrity and righteousness who owned much land. There is no indication that possessions were a source of division between God and these men. If anything, wealth is seen as a blessing from a God "who delights in the well-being of His servant" (Ps. 35:27).

The Health and Wealth Gospel: Wealth as the Essential Evidence of a Righteous Life

Some have taken the notion of God's blessing on the righteous to conclude that God will automatically bestow great material possessions and physical health on His people. At the extreme, this "health and wealth" theology posits that if you have enough faith, God will bless you with earthly riches and perfect health. "There will be no sickness for the saint of God," one preacher said. "God's greatest desire for the church of Jesus Christ . . . is that we be in total and perfect health." Promoters of the health and wealth gospel say that all you need is faith to claim God's bountiful material and physical blessings. But those who pick up this theology and make it their gospel will be disappointed, for their eyes are on the wrong goal.

Too often, the focus is on the blessing rather than on the Blessor and our service to Him. There is a mistaken focus on wealth rather than on righteous living. "But seek first His kingdom and His righteousness, and all these things will be given to you as well," Jesus instructed (Matt. 6:33). Wealth may follow from our pursuit of His righteousness, but it must not be our focus. When the focus is on material blessings, there is a temptation to pine after the god of wealth. As Joe Johnson, president of The Business Reform Foundation noted, "the Lord wants us to have wealth, but not wealth to have us."[26] Jesus warned that we cannot serve two masters—our focus must be on the Blessing Giver rather than on the blessing.

"I pray that you may enjoy good health and that all may go well with you, even as your soul is getting along well" (3 John 2). God does desire to bestow blessings on His people, but we should not assume that every believer will be granted health and wealth the way we might expect. God uses difficulty to teach us and perfect us (see Jas. 1:2-3), which for a time may preclude these blessings. There are plenty of examples in Scripture where God's faithful people do not experience prosperity as the world might define it. Job again serves as an example of a righteous man who experiences both riches and poverty, both sickness and health. John the Baptist and Jesus amassed little or no earthly possessions. Health and wealth is not the proof of obedience to God or sufficient faith in Him, and neither is sickness and poverty the proof of disobedience to God or lack of faith in Him.

God's Prosperity

The biblical view of prosperity is extremely complex, and many have drifted while trying to navigate it. So far, the discussion has focused on what a biblical view of wealth is *not;* the "poverty gospel" and the "health and wealth gospel" clearly both miss the mark. But are there any declarative statements that we can make about God's attitude toward wealth? Fortunately, Scripture has a lot to say about the topic, and there are some truths that may be discerned. The following six principles of wealth will be highlighted: (1) wealth is to be in all areas, (2) wealth is from God, (3) wealth is to be managed, (4) wealth is to be used for God's purpose, (5) wealth is to be enjoyed, and (6) wealth is not our source of trust.

1. Wealth is to be in all areas. Rather than material wealth, being rich toward God should be the goal (see Luke 12:21). Jesus warned against making material prosperity our objective. "Be on your guard against all kinds of greed; a man's life does not consist in the abundance of his possessions" (Luke 12:15b). The focus should not be on material wealth— God desires for us to enjoy the wealth He gives in all areas, especially spiritual wealth.

When God granted Solomon a wish, he asked for wisdom to discern between right and wrong. God responded:

> Since you have asked for this and not for long life or wealth for yourself, I will do what you have asked. I will give you a wise and discerning heart, so that there will never have been anyone like you, nor will there ever be. Moreover, I will give you what you have not asked for—both riches and honor—so that in your lifetime you will have no equal among kings. And if you walk in my ways and obey my statutes and commands as David your father did, I will give you a long life (1 Kings 3:11-14).

Solomon's focus was on spiritual wealth, and God blessed him with material and physical wealth to carry out the work God prepared for him in advance. God wants His people to enjoy prosperity in all areas.

2. Wealth is from God. The example of Solomon illustrates furthermore that God is the source of prosperity. Jesus taught that it is our Father in heaven who gives good gifts (see Matt. 7:11). God owns every animal of the forest, bird in the mountains, creature of the field, and the cattle on a thousand hills (see Ps. 50:10-11). We must never think that any honorable wealth comes from our own doing. (There is such a thing as dishonorable wealth. For example, financial gain from illegal drug dealing would be considered dishonorable.) "Remember the Lord your God, for it is he who gives you the ability to produce wealth, and so confirms his covenant which he swore to your forefathers, as it is today" (Deut. 8:18). It is God who is the Giver of all good things.

3. *Wealth is to be managed.* Another temptation lies in considering God's blessings to be our possession. They are not. "The earth is the Lord's, and everything in it" (1 Cor. 10:26). We are stewards of the material possessions entrusted to us, and that involves responsible management. The parable of the talents makes it clear that God holds us accountable for wise deployment of these resources. God commands us to grow the resources He gives. Wealth comes with huge responsibility, and proper management of it is an act of worship to God. "Possession and direction of the forces of wealth are as legitimate an expression of the redemptive rule of God in human life as is Bible teaching or a prayer meeting," said theologian Dallas Willard.[27] As God's servants, it is our duty to wisely manage the wealth He has granted in order to return more to Him.

4. *Wealth is to be used for God's purpose.* From God's perspective, there is a value to wealth. Paul wrote that those who are rich should be ready to give and willing to share (see 1 Tim. 6:17-18). The concept of returning material blessings to God predates the law given to Moses. In response to God's blessing, Abraham gave the priest Melchizedek a tenth of everything (see Gen. 14:18-20). Tithing is an important part of using prosperity for God's purpose. Scripture warns against withholding from God but promises blessings on those who give: "Bring the whole tithe into the storehouse . . . and see if I will not throw open the floodgates of heaven and pour out so much blessing that you will not have room enough for it" (Mal. 3:10). "The righteous give without sparing" (Prov. 21:26). "Give, and it will be given to you," instructed Jesus (Luke 6:38).

There is an economic giving/spiritual cycle demonstrated in Scripture. Paul said, "You will be made rich in every way so that you can be generous on every occasion, and through us your generosity will result in thanksgiving to God" (2 Cor. 9:11). Those who receive from generosity, in turn, will pray for the giver, and God will continue to bless so that more can be given. Paul is describing an economic/spiritual cycle involving giving, prayer and blessing (see 2 Cor. 9:6-15).

5. *Wealth is to be enjoyed.* While we are to realize that wealth has a Kingdom purpose, God also wants us to enjoy it. "Command those who are rich in this present world . . . to put their hope in God, who richly provides us with everything for our enjoyment" (1 Tim. 6:17). Christians often suffer from the view that wealth is immoral and that material possessions corrupt. Guilt and an embarrassment of riches prevent some from enjoying what God has bestowed. But God calls us to enjoy prosperity! We shouldn't minimize the danger of going overboard and being indulgent. For the Christian whom God has blessed with significant wealth, the defining line is between that person and God.

6. *Wealth is not our source of trust.* Paul instructed Timothy about the dangers of trusting in wealth: "Command those who are rich in this present world not to be arrogant nor to put their hope in wealth, which is so uncertain, but to put their hope in God, who richly provides us with everything for our enjoyment" (1 Tim. 6:17). Jesus also condemned trusting in wealth rather than in God. He admonished not to store up treasures on Earth, but rather to store them up in heaven (see Matt. 6:19-21). Jesus further noted that where our treasure is, there our hearts will be also (Luke 12:34). Clearly, our treasure should be serving God and His Kingdom. The blessing of wealth may follow from that, but it should not be the focus of our striving.

Prosperity seekers have a tendency to de-emphasize the real danger of forgetting God and trusting in themselves and in their wealth. In Proverbs 30:8-9, Agur made the following request: "Give me neither poverty nor riches, but give me only my daily bread. Otherwise, I may have too much and disown you and say, 'Who is the Lord?' Or I may become poor and steal, and so dishonor the name of my God." Agur knew that poverty could cause people to focus on their plight just as wealth may cause people to focus on their wealth rather than on God. Both poverty and wealth pose potential pitfalls.

The Cycles of Poverty and Success

"The wealth of the rich is their fortified city, but poverty is the ruin of the poor" (Prov. 10:15). Poverty is a disease that afflicts many millions around the world. Perhaps most damaging is the attitude that poverty often brings. Hopelessness and lack of confidence lead to depression and desperation. There are no perceptions of opportunity, no visions and dreams for the future. These attitudes often permeate a community. They are passed on to successive generations. A cycle of despair is formed, and those caught in the cycle face great challenges in extricating themselves from the generational curse of poverty. People become limited by their own view. They see themselves resigned to their plight due to fate and a lack of opportunity. When coupled with a view that creating wealth is wrong, the problem is compounded, and people are kept in poverty.

Recently, I and several others had dinner with the Honorable Asenaca Caucau, Minister for Women, Social Welfare and Poverty Alleviation in Suva, the capital of Fiji. She shared with us a presentation on the cycle of poverty that needed to be broken in Fiji. I suggested to her that she might want to concentrate instead on the cycle of success and what was necessary to bring it about. The cycle of success starts with the belief in visions and dreams and a hope for the future. It leads to a changed mind-set, which is the beginning of transformation. The minister was delighted with the idea and planned to discuss it as part of her presentation in Parliament the next day.

The cycle of success often yields an attitude of hope, anticipation and confidence. God is a God of visions and dreams. Jerusalem is even called "the Valley of Vision" (see Isa. 22:1). God speaks about the day of the Lord, saying, "I will pour out my Spirit on all people. Your sons and daughters will prophesy, your old men will dream dreams, your young men will see visions" (Joel 2:28). Joseph's first dream about his older brothers' sheaves of grain bowing down to his sheaf (see Gen. 37:5-8) was the vision that saw him through to become ruler over Egypt. He never lost his hope, even when languishing in the pit and in jail. We must be able to dream of possibilities, to see visions of the possible, to have a hope and a future. Economic success allows God to be glorified and the future to be anticipated.

Dr. David Yonggi Cho was shown by God in the 1950s that his nation of Korea needed to have a hope for the future. The people needed to see that they could dream—and dream big. Hope is one of the great antidotes to the cycle of poverty. On the back of hope and faith (today, more than one third of South Korea's 47 million people are born-again Christians, up from a few hundred thousand in 1956), Korea went from being the poorest nation to being one of the most developed nations in the world in less than 50 years.

Likewise, Silicon Valley has understood the importance of visions and dreams—and the need to encourage and foster them. Grand visions and dreams drive the entrepreneurial spirit of Silicon Valley. There is a sense of optimism. An unsuccessful venture is not seen as final failure, but it is viewed as a step toward building for the future. While Silicon Valley is not significantly Christian, it has understood this godly principle. The cycle of success begins with faith, visions and dreams, and a hope for the future.

The concepts of transformation, work, business, profit and wealth are key biblical foundations of Kingdom business. We must understand that God cares about people's spiritual, social and economic transformation, that work in the business world is both a ministry and a calling, that profit is both necessary and a sign of useful service, and that poverty is a social disease to be addressed. Kingdom business rests on these important notions.

APPENDIX B

SOCIALISM

Socialism is one of the two economic systems that have dominated the last century. Today, the number of officially communist nations can be counted on one hand—China, Cuba, Laos, North Korea and Vietnam—yet many other countries operate with varying degrees of socialist policy. Though it is no longer as popular as it was before the spectacular collapse of the Soviet empire, socialism remains the only major alternative to capitalism today. What characterizes a socialist economy?

"The theory of the Communists may be summed up," said Karl Marx, "in the single sentence: Abolition of private property."[1] Socialism is committed to the communal ownership of property, and in particular to communal ownership of the means of production, whether it be factories, farms or stores. In modern examples, the government serves as the entity that owns and controls all assets. Production decisions are

centralized, as are the allocation and use of means of production ranging from land to labor. Unfortunately, modern instances of socialism
have found the need to impose severe limitations on personal freedoms
in order to achieve this economic system.

The primary objective of socialism is the economic equality of each
community member. The sense of justice inherent in this goal has produced fertile ground for socialism in many parts of the world. Even some
followers of Christ find this equality a worthy objective and have thus
aligned themselves with socialist causes. Harvard theologian Paul Tillich
famously stated, "Any serious Christian must be a socialist."[2]

Socialism in Scripture?

Some point to the Early Church in Jerusalem as evidence of biblical
endorsement of that economic system. The account in Acts 4:32-35
notes that the believers were one in heart and mind and freely shared
their possessions with their brothers and sisters in Christ. Those with
larger assets such as land or houses sold them on occasion and brought
the proceeds to the apostles so that the needs of the less fortunate could
be met. As a result, there were no needy persons among them.

Three observations need to be made regarding the use of this passage to claim a biblical inclination toward socialism. First, it was a completely voluntary system. In no way was participation legislated the way
it is in modern socialist economies. It was a community driven by love
rather than by law. Socialism can only work when entered into freely, but
even in this case there are few if any successful examples. The utopian
Robert Owen operated a mill in Scotland on socialist principles in the
early 1800s. It failed, as did attempts at similar communities in the early
settlement of the United States. While individual socialist communities
with voluntary membership could work, nations that have instituted
socialism have not experienced economic success.

Second, the Jerusalem church did not abolish private property
rights. It did not take on the form of communal ownership. Believers
still had individual possessions—they simply offered to share them.
Some even owned major property but were not forced or even expected
to surrender it to the community. This is evident from the story of two

land-owning members of that church, Ananias and his wife Sapphira. They sold a piece of property, and claiming they were surrendering the entire proceeds, the couple put only a portion at the apostles' feet. Peter's response is instructive, for he said: "Didn't [the property] belong to you before it was sold? And after it was sold, wasn't the money at your disposal?" (Acts 5:4). Clearly, Peter was acknowledging the property rights of Ananias and Sapphira and their right to ownership and control of their property. Their sin was not failing to give up all their possessions; their sin was lying to the Holy Spirit.

Third, whatever the specific level of economic sharing, the Jerusalem church fell into poverty a short time later. The situation was so bleak that Paul made requests to the gentile churches in Macedonia, Corinth and possibly elsewhere for generous donations to support their needy brethren in Jerusalem (see 2 Cor. 8:1-15; Gal. 2:1-10). Scholars have speculated on the cause of the economic hardship that came over the Early Church in Jerusalem, and some attribute it to a drought in the area. Although its goal was not economic development but a short-term effort to develop the foundation of the Church, the practices in Jerusalem cannot be touted as an example of successful economic development.

"Everyone according to his capabilities, to everyone according to his needs" is the Marxist creed. However, in a society of fallen, selfish and greedy men and women, individuals quickly focus on what they get rather than on what they contribute. "Everyone according to his needs" takes precedence over "everyone according to his capabilities." Paul said, "If a man will not work, he shall not eat" (2 Thess. 3:10). He then noted that the weakness of human nature leads to idleness: "We hear that some among you are idle. They are not busy; they are busybodies. Such people we command and urge in the Lord Jesus Christ to settle down and earn the bread they eat" (2 Thess. 3:11-12). Jesus also sought to ensure that the gospel was not built on handouts. After feeding the five thousand, the crowd was focused on Jesus' gift of physical bread, not on spiritual bread. They were craving more. "I tell you the truth," He chastised them, "you are looking for me, not because you saw miraculous signs but because you ate the loaves and had your fill" (John 6:26). Both

Paul and Jesus denounced the idleness and dependency that can result from charity and redistribution.

Failure of Socialism

The socialist goal of achieving equal economic outcomes for all members of society is laudable, but the system ultimately fails in practice. "Socialism in general has a record of failure so blatant that only an intellectual could ignore or evade it," quipped former Marxist economist Dr. Thomas Sowell. When economic outcomes are predetermined, members of a society no longer have any incentive to innovate or even expend energy. The thought process that frequently accompanies modern socialism is limiting rather than freeing. It is what binds people to a narrow view of opportunities—and therefore to limited aspirations. It removes personal responsibility and hope. These attributes of God are thwarted. The best and the brightest lose their appetite to invent and create, and development stagnates.

Not coincidentally, socialist theory views the total economic pie as constant. Therefore, the emphasis is on wealth redistribution rather than on wealth creation. In an environment in which the pie does not increase, the only mechanism for improving the lot of those with smaller pieces is to redistribute the portion of those who have more. Taking from the rich and giving to the poor is the only solution to poverty if aggregate wealth is stagnant. However, successful commerce means the creation of useful goods and services, and aggregate wealth does increase. Socialism's aspiration of more economic equality seems good, but the system provides neither the incentive to innovate nor the recognition that innovation advances every aspect of society. It is a system that in practice has been shown to hold people back.

Neither socialism nor capitalism is a perfect system. However, there is little scriptural support for socialism, while capitalism rests on the biblical principle of personal freedom and responsibility.

KINGDOM BUSINESS FRAMEWORK

Following the framework for Kingdom business (see chapter 9), the following lists contain examples of nations with poorest, developing and industrializing regions. MED is most effective in poorest regions; SME assistance is most appropriate in developing regions; and OPE is most appealing in industrializing regions.

FIGURE 13

Poorest Regions

Afghanistan	Dominican Republic	Lebanon	Senegal
Albania	Ecuador	Lesotho	Sierra Leone
Angola	Egypt	Liberia	Somalia
Bangladesh	Eritrea	Libya	Sudan
Belize	Ethiopia	Madagascar	Suriname
Benin	Gabon	Malawi	Swaziland
Botswana	Gambia, The	Mali	Syria
Brazil	Ghana	Mongolia	Tajikistan
Burkina Faso	Guatemala	Morocco	Tanzania
Burma	Guinea	Mozambique	Togo
Burundi	Guyana	Namibia	Tunisia
Cambodia	Haiti	Nepal	Uganda
Cameroon	Indonesia	Nicaragua	Uzbekistan
Central African Republic	Iran	Niger	Vietnam
Chad	Iraq	Nigeria	Zambia
Colombia	Jordan	Pakistan	Zimbabwe
Congo	Kenya	Papua New Guinea	
Cote d'Ivoire (Ivory Coast)	Korea, North	Philippines	
Cuba	Laos	Rwanda	

FIGURE 14

Developing Regions

Algeria	Costa Rica	Latvia	Slovenia
Argentina	Croatia	Lithuania	South Africa
Armenia	Czech Republic	Macedonia	Sri Lanka
Azerbaijan	Ecuador	Malaysia	Thailand
Bahrain	El Salvador	Mexico	Trinidad and Tobago
Bangladesh	Estonia	Moldova	
Belarus	Georgia	Pakistan	Turkey
Bhutan	Ghana	Panama	Ukraine
Bolivia	Guatemala	Paraguay	United Arab Emirates
Bosnia and Herzegovina	Honduras	Peru	
	Hungary	Philippines	Uruguay
Brazil	India	Qatar	Venezuela
Brunei	Indonesia	Romania	Yemen
Bulgaria	Kazakhstan	Russia	
Chile	Kuwait	Saudi Arabia	
Colombia	Kyrgyzstan	Slovakia	

FIGURE 15

Industrializing Regions

Argentina	Czech Republic	Panama
Bahrain	Egypt	Philippines
Brazil	India	Poland
Bulgaria	Korea, South	
China	Mexico	

ENDNOTES

Author's Note

1. Sam Brannan, "Gold Discovered! The Excitement and Enthusiasm of Gold Washing Still Continues—Increases." *California Star,* June 10, 1848. Online version at http://www.sfmuseum.org/hist6/star.html.

Chapter 2: Business as the Emerging Missions Strategy

1. Patrick Lai, Prayer Letter #187, June 2004.
2. "The State of World Population 2001," chapter 3, United Nations Population Fund (UNFPA). http://www.unfpa.org/swp/2001/english/ch03.html (accessed March 2, 2005).
3. David B. Barrett and Todd M. Johnson, *World Christian Trends AD 30–AD 2000: Interpreting the Annual Christian Megacensus* (Pasadena, CA: William Carey Library, 2001).
4. David B. Barrett and Todd M. Johnson, *International Bulletin of Missionary Research,* January 2003.
5. Barrett and Johnson, *World Christian Trends, AD 30–AD 2000*; interpolations to arrive at 2003 values.
6. Ibid.
7. Ibid.
8. Billy Graham, Billy Graham Evangelistic Association conference, 2002.
9. Data from the Institute for International Finance. http://www.iif.com.
10. John Case, "The Job Factory," *Inc.,* May 2001. http://www.inc.com/magazine/20010515/22617.html (accessed March 2, 2005).
11. A nation's gross domestic product is the total market value of goods and services produced by workers and capital within that country's borders during a given period (usually one year).
12. About 336,000 bachelors and masters degrees in business were awarded in 1998. U.S. Department of Education, *The Chronicle of Higher Education,* quoted by Thomas Sudyk in Tetsunao Yamamori and Kenneth A. Eldred, eds., *On Kingdom Business: Transforming Missions Through Entrepreneurial Strategies* (Wheaton, IL: Crossway Books, 2003), p. 154.
13. Barrett and Johnson, *World Christian Trends AD 30-AD 2000,* n.p.
14. Henry T. Blackaby and Claude V. King, *Experiencing God* (Nashville, TN: Broadman and Holman, 1998), n.p.

Chapter 3: Defining Kingdom Business

1. Interview with Dan Carless, August 16, 2004; Jack Dennison, Impact Colorado Springs organization ministry update, July 22, 2004.
2. Clem Schultz with Sonia Chou, from Tetsunao Yamamori and Kenneth A. Eldred, eds., *On Kingdom Business: Transforming Missions Through Entrepreneurial Strategies* (Wheaton, IL: Crossway Books, 2003), pp. 37-44.
3. Steven L. Rundle, adapted from Yamamori and Eldred, *On Kingdom Business: Transforming Missions Through Entrepreneurial Strategies,* pp. 229-230.

4. R. Paul Stevens, "What Makes a Business Christian?" Presentation to Christian business leaders in Ndola, Zambia, August 1994.
5. Chuck Buck, Chairman, Buck Knives, product registration and warranty document.
6. Ibid.
7. Ibid.
8. Ibid.
9. Adrienne S. Gaines with Eric Tiansay, "Christians Expose Ponzi Scheme That Bilked Ministries of $160 Million," *Charisma* (February 2004), pp. 25-27.
10. Framework adapted from Sun Ki Bang, "Business and Mission." http://www.cson line.net/tie/prev1.htm (accessed December 12, 2003); and Mats Tunehag, "Business as Mission," October 2002. http://www.ywamconnect.com/c9/images/15/93/ 2/29315/37324.doc (accessed December 12, 2003).
11 Tentmakers International Exchange. http://www.tieinfo.com (accessed August 6, 2003).
12. David Aikman, *Jesus in Beijing: How Christianity Is Transforming China and Changing the Global Balance of Power* (Washington, D.C.: Regnery Publishing Inc., 2003), p. 17.

Chapter 4: Successful Capitalism and Biblical Principles

1. Harold Lindsell, *Free Enterprise: A Judeo-Christian Defense* (Wheaton, IL: Tyndale Press, 1982), p. 13.
2. Michael Novak, *The Spirit of Democratic Capitalism* (Lanham, MD: Madison Books, 1991), p. 26.
3. *CIA World Factbook.* Analysis based on GDP per capita data (2002).
4. Jaap Sleifer, "United, Divided and Reunited: Comparative Economic Performance of the East and West German Economies from 1936 to 1997," Duitsland Instituut Amsterdam, Working Document No. 5 (June 1999).
5. Douglass North, *Institutions, Institutional Change and Economic Performance* (Cambridge: Cambridge University Press, 1990).
6. Considering the issue too controversial at the time, the founders of the United States omitted the abolition of slavery from the nation's founding documents. With the understanding that slavery would be addressed later, they agreed to disagree in order to achieve a consensus Constitution.
7. Brian Griffiths, *Capitalism, Morality and Markets* (London: Institute of Economic Affairs, 2001), pp. 20-25.
8. Ibid., pp. 25-35.
9. Richard Whately, *Thoughts and Apothegms,* pt. II, ch. XVIII, Pious Frauds.
10. Michael Novak, *Business as a Calling* (New York: The Free Press, 1996), p. 22.
11. Griffiths, *Capitalism, Morality and Markets,* p. 35.
12. John Adams, Address to the Military (October 11, 1798), cited in C. F. Adams, ed., *The Works of John Adams, Second President of the United States* (New York: AMS Press, 1971), n.p. Emphasis added.
13. W. Cleon Skousen, "Religion and Government in America: Are They Complementary?" http://www.forerunner.com/mandate/X0035_Religion_and_Law_0in_.html (accessed March 2, 2005), from Skousen, *The Five Thousand Year Leap: Twenty-Eight Great Ideas That Are Changing the World* (Washington, D. C.: National Center for Constitutional Studies, 1981).

14. Alexis de Tocqueville, *Democracy in America* (New York: Signet Books, 2001), n.p. Emphasis added.

15. Ibid., n.p.

16. Andree Seu, "France's Veil," *World* (February 7, 2004), p. 51. Online version at http://www.worldmag.com/displayarticle.cfm?id=8493.

17. "Russia: President Putin Cracks Down," *BusinessWeek* (International Edition), (April 3, 2000), cover story. Online version at http://www.businessweek.com/2000/00_14/b3675013.htm (accessed March 2, 2005).

18. Attributed to Alexis de Tocqueville by several sources (e.g., U.S. President Dwight D. Eisenhower in his final campaign address in Boston, Massachusetts, November 3, 1952) but not found in his published works.

19. Max Weber, *The Protestant Ethic and the Spirit of Capitalism* (London: Routledge Classics, 2002).

20. David Bradford, quoted in Janet Zich, "Ideas: We're All in This Together," *Stanford Business* (September 1998). Online version at http://www.gsb.stanford.edu/community/bmag/sbsm9809/ideas.html (accessed March 2, 2005).

21. "W. Edwards Deming: Statistical Quality Control," *TheWorkingManager.com*. http://www.theworkingmanager.com/articles/detail.asp?ArticleNo=337 (accessed May 21, 2004).

22. Chuck Ripka, interview with author, August 12, 2004.

23. Adapted from Mark Markiewicz, Youth With a Mission, presentations at the Central Asia Business Consultation 1999 and 2000.

24. The Worshipful Company of Glass Sellers, "Our Heritage: Livery Tradition." http://www.glass-sellers.co.uk/LiveryTraditionMain.htm (accessed May 2005).

25. Website of The Worshipful Company of Builders Merchants. http://www.wcobm.co.uk/introduction.htm (accessed November 12, 2003).

26. Attributed to Alexis de Tocqueville by several sources (e.g., U.S. President Dwight D. Eisenhower in his final campaign address in Boston, Massachusetts, November 3, 1952) but not found in his published works.

27. Niall Ferguson, "Why America Outpaces Europe (Clue: The God Factor)," *New York Times* (June 8, 2003), Week in Review section. Online version at http://www.nytimes.com/2003/06/08/weekinreview/08FERG.html (accessed March 2, 2005).

28. Ibid.

Chapter 5: Spiritual Capital

1. Bill Child, quoted in Marc Gunther, "God and Business," *Fortune* (July 9, 2001), p. 66. Online version at http://www.marcgunther.com/article_godandbus01.html (accessed March 2, 2005).

2. Liberia, Panama, Ecuador and some Pacific Island nations use the United States dollar as their official currency. A number of other countries have small or unstable economies and have thus chosen to peg their currency to the dollar (e.g., Egypt, Syria, Jordan, Lebanon, Hong Kong, The Bahamas, The Netherlands Antilles, Barbados).

3. Askold Krushelnycky, "Corruption Destroys People's Faith In Democracy," *Radio Free Europe/Radio Liberty* (September 6, 2000).

4. Ajay Goyal, "The Russia Journal," Center for Defense Information Russia Weekly, no. 196 (March 8, 2002).
5. Larry Diamond and Marc F. Plattner, *Economic Reform and Democracy* (Baltimore, MD: Johns Hopkins University Press, 1995), p. xxi.
6. Dennis M. Mahoney, "A Growing Flock," *The Columbus Dispatch* (January 31, 2003).
7. Harold Caballeros, "Economic Development and the Individual Spirit," speech at Kingdom Business Forum conference, Atlanta, Georgia (April 23, 2004).
8. George W. Bush, speech at the Santa Clara Convention Center, Santa Clara, California (March 4, 2004).
9. Timur Kuran, "The Islamic Commercial Crisis: Institutional Roots of Economic Underdevelopment in the Middle East," USC Center for Law, Economics and Organization Research Paper No. C01-12, 2002.
10. Ibid.

Chapter 6: Government, Culture and Kingdom Business

1. David S. Landes, "Culture Makes Almost All the Difference" in Lawrence E. Harrison and Samuel P. Huntington, eds., *Culture Matters* (New York: Basic Books, 2000), p. 2.
2. Richard A. Shweder, "Moral Maps, 'First World' Conceits, and the New Evangelists" in Harrison and Huntington, *Culture Matters*, p. 163. Emphasis added.
3. Noah Webster, cited in David Barton, *Original Intent: The Courts, the Constitution, and Religion* (Aledo, TX: WallBuilder Press, 2000), p. 157.
4. George Washington, cited in Barton, *Original Intent: The Courts, the Constitution, and Religion*, p. 156.
5. John Adams, cited in Barton, *Original Intent: The Courts, the Constitution, and Religion*, p. 156.
6. Bruce Bueno de Mesquita and Hilton L. Root, *Governing for Prosperity* (New Haven, CT: Yale University Press, 2000), p. 9.
7. Stephen Haber, Douglass C. North and Barry R. Weingast, "If Economists Are So Smart, Why Is Africa So Poor?" *Wall Street Journal* (July 30, 2003).
8. Larry Diamond and Marc F. Plattner, *Economic Reform and Democracy* (Baltimore, MD: Johns Hopkins University Press, 1995), pp. xxviii-xxii.
9. Ronald Inglehart, "Culture and Democracy" in Harrison and Huntington, *Culture Matters*, p. 96.
10. Haber, North and Weingast, "If Economists Are So Smart, Why Is Africa So Poor?"
11. Michael E. Porter, "Attitudes, Values, Beliefs, and the Microeconomics of Prosperity" in Harrison and Huntington, *Culture Matters*, p. 14.
12. Mariano Grondona, "A Cultural Typology of Economic Development" in Harrison and Huntington, *Culture Matters*, pp. 47-53.
13. Daniel Etounga-Manguelle, "Does Africa Need a Cultural Adjustment Program?" in Harrison and Huntington, *Culture Matters*, p. 75.
14. Ibid.
15. Diamond and Plattner, *Economic Reform and Democracy*, p. 3.
16. Louis Berkhoff, *Systematic Theology* (London: Banner of Truth, 1971), p. 527.

Chapter 7: Historical Perspective of Business in Missions

1. Heinz Suter and Marco Gmür, *Business Power for God's Purpose* (Greng, Switzerland: Verlag für kulturbezogenen Gemeindebau, 1997), p. 12.
2. Ibid.
3. Norbert Brox, *Zur christlichen Mission in der Spätantike* (Basel, Switzerland: Editiones Herder, 1982), pp 224-225. Translated and quoted by Suter and Gmür, *Business Power for God's Purpose*, p. 12.
4. Suter and Gmür, *Business Power for God's Purpose*, p. 14.
5. Ibid., p. 19.
6. J. Christy Wilson, *Today's Tentmakers* (Wheaton, IL: Tyndale, 1985), pp. 26-27. Cited by Suter and Gmür, *Business Power for God's Purpose*, p. 20.
7. Suter and Gmür, *Business Power for God's Purpose*, pp. 20-21.
8. William Carey, *An Enquiry into the Obligation of Christians to Use Means for the Conversion of the Heathens* (Leicester, England: Ann Ireland, 1792).
9. Hendrik E. Neimeijer, "Dividing the Islands: The Dutch Spice Monopoly as a Catalyst of Indigenous Religious Contrasts and Resistance in the 17th-Century Maluku," Kampen Theological University, abstract of session at the 1999 Association for Asian Studies Annual Meeting.
10. Paul E. Pierson, "Moravian Missions," in *Evangelical Dictionary of World Missions*, ed. A. Scott Moreau, p. 660.
11. Jonas Clark, "Count Nicolaus Ludwig von Zinzendorf." http://www.jonasclark.com/ludwig_vonZinzendorf.htm (accessed March 2, 2005).
12. William J. Danker, *Profit for the Lord: Economic Activities in Moravian Missions and the Basel Mission Trading Company* (Grand Rapids, MI: Eerdmans, 1971), pp. 23, 27-29. Cited by Dwight P. Baker, "William Carey and the Business Model for Mission," Overseas Ministries Studies Center report (June 5, 2002), p. 7. http://www.global connections.co.uk/business.asp (accessed May 18, 2005).
13. Suter and Gmür, *Business Power for God's Purpose*, p. 24.
14. "History of C. Kersten and Co., N.V." http://www.kersten.sr (accessed August 29, 2003).
15. Suter and Gmür, *Business Power for God's Purpose*, pp. 25-27.
16. International Religious Freedom Report 2002 (United States Department of State) and CIA World Factbook 2004.
17. "Mission Statement of C. Kersten and Co., N.V." http://www.kersten.sr. (accessed August 29, 2003).
18. Carey, *An Enquiry into the Obligation of Christians to Use Means for the Conversion of the Heathens*, p. 67.
19. Ibid.
20. David Livingstone, lecture delivered at Cambridge University, December 1857.
21. Richard Borreca, "Sugar yields sweet deal for 'Big-Five' firms," *Honolulu Star-Bulletin*, July 12, 1999.
22. Suter and Gmür, *Business Power for God's Purpose*, pp. 32-33.
23. Baker, "William Carey and the Business Model for Mission," p. 8.
24. Extract from the Basel Mission Christian Association's "Festival of Christmas Music '82" brochure, Bangalore, India. Online version available at http://www.child ren-of-bangalore.com/basel.htm (accessed May 2005).

25. Suter and Gmür, pp. 32-34.
26. Ibid., p. 35.
27. Ibid., p. 38.
28. Extract from the Basel Mission Christian Association's "Festival of Christmas Music '82" brochure.
29. Ibid.
30. Suter and Gmür, *Business Power for God's Purpose,* p. 37.
31. Extract from the Basel Mission Christian Association's "Festival of Christmas Music '82" brochure.
32. Suter and Gmür, *Business Power for God's Purpose,* p. 39.
33. Swiss Embassy in Ghana, "History of Trade Development Between Switzerland and Ghana." http://www.eda.admin.ch/accra_emb/e/home/buseco/ecorel.html (accessed March 2, 2005).

Chapter 8: Kingdom Business Objectives and Approaches

1. Trim Line Bakery is a client of Integra Ventures. Details of this example are courtesy of Terry Williams, President of Integra Ventures, and from Paul Borthwick, "Business Can Heal the Community," *World Pulse* (February 21, 2003).
2. Johnson and Johnson, "Our Credo Explained." http://www.jnj.com/careers/credo.html (accessed September 25, 2003).
3. Glenn J. Schwartz, "An Introduction to the Subject of Dependency and Self-Reliance for Church and Mission Leaders in East, Central and Southern Africa," manuscript of May 1992 lectures at Rosebank Bible College, Johannesburg, South Africa. Available online at http://www.wmausa.org/art-introtodepend.htm (accessed March 2, 2005).
4. A summary of the address entitled "Missions Beyond the Economic Earthquake," given by Glenn Schwartz, WMA Executive Director, at a banquet in Mount Joy, PA (January 27, 1995). See http://www.wmausa.org/art-beyond.htm.
5. Opportunity International, "Meet Our Clients." http://www.opportunity.org/site/pp.asp?c=7oIDLROyGqF&b=212825.
6. Integra Ventures, "Portfolio" (March 2002), pp. 1-2.
7. Ken and Margie Crowell, cited in Tetsunao Yamamori and Kenneth A. Eldred, eds., *On Kingdom Business: Transforming Missions Through Entrepreneurial Strategies* (Wheaton, IL: Crossway Books, 2003), pp. 45-48.

Chapter 9: Role of Each Kingdom Business Approach

1. Franklin Graham, "The Gathering" annual conference, Carlsbad, California, September 25-28, 2003.

Chapter 10: Microenterprise Development (MED)

1. Opportunity International, 2001 Report. http://www.opportunity.org/site/pp.asp?c=7oIDLROyGqF&b=212825.
2. Stanley Fischer, quoted in Phil Roosevelt, "Tiny Loans, Big Dreams," *Barron's Online,* December 8, 2003. Online copy of the article (not from Barron's site) available at http://www.unitus.com/docs/pdf/12-08-03.pdf (accessed March 2, 2005).

3. ACCION Ventures, Annual Reports/Newsletter, Spring 2003. http://www.accion.org.
4. Opportunity International, 2001 Report.
5. Shahidur R. Khandker, *Fighting Poverty with Microcredit: Experience in Bangladesh* (Washington, DC: World Bank Publications, 1998), p. 145. Quoted in United Nations Food and Agriculture Organization (FAO), *The State of Food and Agriculture 2000*, Rome, Italy, 2000.
6. David Bussau and Russell Mask, *Christian Microenterprise Development* (Christian Transformation Resource Center, 2001), p. 20.
7. Roosevelt, "Tiny Loans, Big Dreams."
8. A typical cutoff point is a value of 250 percent of per capita GNP. Those institutions with an average loan size of less than that value are considered microlenders; those with an average loan size of more than that value are considered to be in the small and medium enterprise arena.
9. Lou Haveman, "What is Entrepreneurial Success?" Christian Reformed World Relief Committee Development Stories, July 22, 2002. http://www.crwrc.org.
10. Christian Enterprise Trust of Zambia (CETZAM). http://www.scruples.org/web/entrust/cetzam.htm. Emphasis added.
11. Data from a 2001 analysis of 40 Christian MED programs around the world.
12. David Bussau, interview with the author, April 4, 2002.
13. "Microfinance in the Pacific: Success Stories," *UNVNews*, no. 86 (December 1999). Online version at http://www.unv.org/infobase/unv_news/1999/86/99_12_86SLB_fishb.htm.
14. Rosalind Copisarow, "Micro-finance Technology and the United Kingdom: Key Commercial and Policy Issues," *Microfinance Article Library*. http://www.alternative-finance.org.uk/cgi-bin/summary.pl?id=63&sourcelang=E&view=html (accessed May 2005).
15. Transparency International, Corruption Perceptions Index 2002. http://www.transparency.org/pressreleases_archive/2002/2002.08.28.cpi.en.html (accessed May 2005).
16. Dave Larson, vice president of programming for HOPE International, World Relief. Interview with author, March 18, 2002.
17. Ibid.
18. Cris Prystay, "In Tiny Loans, a Bank's Bonanza," *Wall Street Journal* (November 6, 2003), p. A12.

Chapter 11: Small and Medium Enterprises (SME)

1. John Case, "The Job Factory," *Inc.*, May 2001. Online version at http://www.inc.com/magazine/20010515/22617.html (accessed March 2, 2005).
2. Courtesy of Integra Ventures.
3. John Warton, telephone interview with author, November 23, 2003.
4. Charles Dokmo, telephone interview with author, March 2002.
5. Roger Leeds, interview with author, March 29, 2002.
6. Terry Williams, telephone interview with author, November 20, 2003.
7. Terry Williams, unpublished document to author.
8. Adapted from *The MicroBanking Bulletin*, Issue No. 7: Focus on Transparency, November 2001. http://www.mixmbb.org/en/mbb_issues/07/mbb_7.html.
9. Case, "The Job Factory."

Chapter 12: Overseas Private Equity (OPE)

1. Evelyn Iritani, "China's Challenge: Mastering the Microchip," *Los Angeles Times*, October 22, 2002; Bruce Einhorn, "Richard Chang: Taiwan's Silicon Invasion," *BusinessWeek Online*, December 9, 2002. http://www.businessweek.com/magazine/content/02_49/b3811013.htm.

2. Richard Chang, quoted in Richard Read, "Chinese Businessman Finds Open Market for Church," *Baptist Standard* (March 31, 2003). Online version at http://www. baptiststandard.com/2003/3_31/pages/chinese.html.

3. Thompson Venture Economics/National Venture Capital Association press release (April 21, 2003).

4. Teresa Barger, former director of private equity of the International Finance Corporation, telephone interview with author, April 12, 2002.

5. Roger Leeds and Julie Sunderland, "Private Equity in the Emerging Markets: Rethinking the Approach," March 2002 draft of forthcoming article in the *Journal of Applied Corporate Finance*.

6. Clem Schultz with Sonia Chou, from Tetsunao Yamamori and Kenneth A. Eldred, eds., *On Kingdom Business: Transforming Missions Through Entrepreneurial Strategies* (Wheaton, IL: Crossway Books, 2003), pp. 37-44.

7. Steve Rundle and Tom Steffen, *Great Commission Companies* (Downers Grove, IL: InterVarsity Press, 2003), pp. 163-180.

8. Clem Schultz with Sonia Chou, from Yamamori and Eldred, *On Kingdom Business: Transforming Missions Through Entrepreneurial Strategies*, pp. 37-44.

9. Lessons from International Finance Corporation sources. http://www.ifc.org.

10. Clem Schultz with Sonia Chou, from Yamamori and Eldred, *On Kingdom Business: Transforming Missions Through Entrepreneurial Strategies*, pp. 37-44.

Chapter 13: Current Trends and Outrageous Visions

1. Barrett and Johnson, *World Christian Trends AD 30–AD 2000: Interpreting the Annual Christian Megacensus* (Pasadena, CA: William Carey Library, 2001), p. 60.

2. The Barna Group, "Tithing Down 62% in the Past Year," The Barna Update (May 19, 2003). http://www.barna.org/FlexPage.aspx?Page=BarnaUpdate&BarnaUpdateID=139.

3. From a brochure invitation to the event "Spiritual Capital: Developing a new interdisciplinary field," a strategic planning meeting and book project held October 9-10, 2003, in Cambridge, MA, organized by the Metanexus Institute on Science and Religion (http://www.metanexus.net).

4. Bill Child, quoted in Marc Gunther, "God and Business," *Fortune* (July 9, 2001), p. 66. Online version at http://www.marcgunther.com/article_godandbus01.html (accessed March 2, 2005).

5. Os Hillman, "The Faith at Work Movement: Opening 'The 9 to 5 Window'" *Regent Business Review*, Issue 9 (January/February 2004). Online version available at http://www.regent.edu/acad/schbus/maz/busreview/issue9/tableofcontents.html.

6. Mike McLoughlin, quoted in Dallas Willard, *The Spirit of the Disciplines* (San Francisco: HarperSanFrancisco, 1999), p. 214. McLoughlin has been quoted in a number of sources, for example http://www.regent.edu/acad/schbus/maz/busreview/issue9/faithatwork.html (see "The Movement in Ministries" section).

7. George Barna, *Boiling Point* (Ventura, CA: Regal Books, 2001), p. 253.
8. From a brochure promoting the "His Presence in the Workplace" conference, cohosted by the Billy Graham Evangelistic Association, The Cove, Asheville, NC, March 31-April 3, 2003.
9. C. Peter Wagner, quoted in Os Hillman, "The Faith at Work Movement: Opening 'The 9 to 5 Window'" *Regent Business Review,* Issue 9 (January/February 2004). Online version at http://www.regent.edu/acad/schbus/maz/busreview/issue9/faithat work.html.
10. Sun Ki Bang, "Business and Missions." http://www.csonline.net/tie/prev1.htm (accessed December 12, 2003).

Chapter 14: Realizing God's Kingdom Business Vision

1. Centre for Entrepreneurship and Economic Development. http://www.ceed-uofn.org.
2 Doug Hunter, Kingdom Business Forum conference, Atlanta, Georgia (April 22-24, 2004).
3. Phil Roosevelt, "Tiny Loans, Big Dreams," *Barron's Online*, December 8, 2003. Online copy of the article (not from Barron's site) is available at http://www.unitus.com/docs/pdf/ 12-08-03.pdf (accessed March 2, 2005).
4. Cydney Gillis, "Big C,—little c—John Sage finds the place where Christianity, capitalism intersect," *King County Journal* (May 21, 2000).

Appendix A: Biblical Foundations

1. Philip Yancey, "Unveiling the Kingdom of God," *Good News Magazine*, Jan/Feb 1999. Adapted from Philip Yancey, *The Jesus I Never Knew* (Grand Rapids, MI: Zondervan Publishing House, 1995). Online version of the Good News article at http://www.good newsmag.org/magazine/1JanFeb/jf99yancey.htm.
2. Anthony A. Hoekema, *The Bible and the Future* (Grand Rapids, MI: Wm. B. Eerdmans Publishing Company, 1994).
3. Herbert W. Armstrong, *Plain Truth* (August 1939). Capitalization in original. Quoted by Ambassador Watch at http://www.ambassadorwatch.co.nz/ herb2.htm.
4. Herbert W. Armstrong, *Worldwide News* (January 28, 1980). Capitalization in original. Quoted by Ambassador Watch at http://www.ambassadorwatch.co.nz/herb2.htm.
5. Leo Tolstoy, *The Kingdom of God Is Within You* (Lincoln, NE: University of Nebraska Press, 1985), chapter XII.
6. Yancey, "Unveiling the Kingdom of God."
7. Mats Tunehag, "Business as Mission" (June 2001). Online version available at http:// www.ywamconnect.com/c9/images/15/93/2/29315/73248.doc (accessed May 28, 2003).
8. R. Paul Stevens, *The Other Six Days: Vocation, Work, and Ministry in Biblical Perspective* (Grand Rapids, MI: Wm. B. Eerdmans Publishing Company, 2000), p. 106.
9. George Barna, "Igniting a Moral and Spiritual Revolution," *The Promise Keeper,* vol. 2, no. 1 (January/February 1999).
10. Adapted from Stevens, *The Other Six Days: Vocation, Work, and Ministry in Biblical Perspective.*

11. John Stott, *Issues Facing Christians Today* (Basingstoke, U.K.: Marshalls, 1984), p. 162. Quoted in Joyce Avedisian, "Spirituality of Work: An Investigation," an InterVarsity Ministry in Daily Life Reflection at http://www.ivmdl.org/reflections.cfm?study=69.

12. John Calvin, *Institutes of the Christian Religion* (Grand Rapids, MI: Wm. B. Eerdmans Publishing Company, 1990), p. III.x.6.

13. Framework adapted from Stevens, *The Other Six Days: Vocation, Work, and Ministry in Biblical Perspective.*

14. Ibid.

15. Max Weber, *The Protestant Ethic and the Spirit of Capitalism* (London: Routledge Classics, 2002), p. 74.

16. Martin Luther, quoted in R. Bainton, *Here I Stand: A Life of Martin Luther* (Nashville, TN: Abingdon, 1978), p. 156.

17. Lee Hardy, *The Fabric of This World* (Grand Rapids, MI: Wm. B. Eerdmans Publishing Company, 1990), p. 51.

18. Avedisian, "Spirituality of Work: An Investigation."

19. Stevens, *The Other Six Days: Vocation, Work, and Ministry in Biblical Perspective*, pp. 72-91.

20. Ibid., p. 88.

21. Ibid., pp. 81-82.

22. Dave Evans, "Faith and Work: A Biblical Overview" discussion notes. Online version at http://www.svfellowship.org/resources/Faith + Work Basics Outline v3.doc (accessed June 10, 2005).

23. Ibid.

24. Stanley J. Grenz, "Is It God's Business?" http://www.meda.org/calling/reflections/god_business.html.

25. Joe Johnson, "A Biblical View of Wealth," *Business Reform*, vol. 1, no. 1 (January/February 2001), p. 17.

26. Ibid, p. 18.

27. Dallas Willard, *The Spirit of the Disciplines* (San Francisco: HarperSanFrancisco, 1999), p. 213.

Appendix B: Socialism

1. Karl Marx, *Capital, The Communist Manifesto and Other Writings* (New York: Modern Library, 1932), p. 335. Quoted in Harold Lindsell, *Free Enterprise: A Judeo-Christian Defense* (Wheaton, IL: Tyndale, 1982), p. 49.

2. Paul Tillich, quoted in Richard John Neuhaus, *Doing Well and Doing Good* (New York: Random House, 1992), p. 47.